"If only a few of the 'right people' in theological education read this book, it won't change anything. But if enough church leaders and the people who care about them read it and talk about it and remember our call together, it will make a big difference."

— **David McAllister-Wilson**
Wesley Theological Seminary

"We have long underestimated the capacity of adolescents to engage and thrive in theological education run by talented teachers who believe in them enough to open the door of the theological and take them forward. This book makes us reimage the possibilities of our ministry among the young — and among ourselves as religious educators."

— **Mike Carotta**
author of *Teaching for Discipleship*

How Youth Ministry Can Change Theological Education — If We Let It

Reflections from the Lilly Endowment's High School Theology Program Seminar

Edited by

Kenda Creasy Dean and Christy Lang Hearlson

With

Elizabeth W. Corrie
Katherine M. Douglass
Fred Edie
David Horn
Andrew Brubacher Kaethler
Jeffrey Kaster
Anabel Proffitt
Judy Steers
Brent A. Strawn
Anne Streaty Wimberly
Jacquie Church Young

WILLIAM B. EERDMANS PUBLISHING COMPANY
GRAND RAPIDS, MICHIGAN / CAMBRIDGE, U.K.

Published 2016 by
Wm. B. Eerdmans Publishing Co.
2140 Oak Industrial Drive N.E., Grand Rapids, Michigan 49505 /
P.O. Box 163, Cambridge CB3 9PU U.K.
www.eerdmans.com

Printed in the United States of America

22 21 20 19 18 17 16 7 6 5 4 3 2 1

Library of Congress Cataloging-in-Publication Data

Names: Dean, Kenda Creasy, 1959- editor. | Lilly Endowment's High School Theology Program.
Title: How youth ministry can change theological education-if we let it : reflections from the Lilly Endowment's High School Theology Program Seminar / edited by Kenda Creasy Dean and Christy Lang Hearlson, with Andrew Brubacher Kaethler, Elizabeth Corrie, Katherine M. Douglass, Fred Edie, David Horn, Jeffrey Kaster, Anabel Proffitt, Judy Steers, Brent A. Strawn, Anne Streaty Wimberly, Jacquie Church Young.
Description: Grand Rapids, Michigan : Eerdmans Publishing Company, 2016.
Identifiers: LCCN 2015039466 | ISBN 9780802871930 (pbk. : alk. paper)
Subjects: LCSH: Pretheological education. | Theology — Study and teaching. | Lilly Endowment's High School Theology Program. | Church work with youth.
Classification: LCC BV4163 .H69 2016 | DDC 230.071 — dc23
LC record available at http://lccn.loc.gov/2015039466

To Craig Dykstra

Contents

Foreword

The book you are about to read tells the story of a gift — a gift given to nearly twenty thousand high school age young people from all across the United States. It is the gift of a good, strong taste of serious theological study and inquiry.

It sounds at first like an odd kind of gift. Why would anybody, much less a high school sophomore, junior, or senior, want to study theology? "Theology" sounds arcane, abstruse — the kind of thing only obscure religious intellectuals would ever take seriously. But that's a myth. For theology is the study of God — an inquiry that asks who God is and what God does, and what God's existence, presence, will, love, and call mean for each of us and for all of us, and, indeed, for all creation. It turns out that, in one way or another, most human beings, including children and youth, are deeply interested in matters such as these.

The church is a treasure-house. Contemporary Christians have inherited, both from their forbears in ancient Israel and from the church's own worldwide life and experience since its earliest days, the most incredibly profound and powerfully life-changing story about God ever told. And that story has engendered a vast storehouse of resources and reflection on all the fundamental questions human beings ask. Sadly, however, far too few Christians today have ready access to this treasure. And very few teenagers know it even exists. If they are fortunate enough to go to good schools, many American teenagers are given access to our cultural and intellectual inheritances in math and science, language and literature, history and the arts. But even our best schools teach almost nothing about religion — and theology is beyond the pale. Further, with few exceptions, our churches have failed as well to unwrap this hidden treasure.

But I was lucky. No, I was blessed. As a teenager, I was a member of a congregation that took its youth seriously, *as theologians.* We were given an early taste of what it was like to read serious and challenging theological and biblical texts, and to ask hard questions about what they meant for our own lives. Our ministers knew the treasure-house intimately, and they put it into play in their preaching and teaching and other interactions with us. They made it clear that these peculiar gifts had power to help us as we struggled to navigate the course of our daily lives during the turbulent years of the 1960s. That experience planted a seed, which many years later came to fruition when I was invited to lead the religion grant-making program of Lilly Endowment, a charitable foundation located in Indianapolis. That seed grew into the "theological programs for high school youth" that this book both describes and explores.

Since 1993, forty-seven theological seminaries have created opportunities for young people who are still in high school to come to their campuses and enter the treasure-house of theological and biblical study with seminary professors as their guides. They live in community with one another for extended periods of time. They engage together in worship and service. And they experience a larger, broader, more diverse church than most of them have ever known or imagined.

How Youth Ministry Can Change Theological Education — If We Let It tells the story of this grand experiment. Kenda Creasy Dean and Christy Lang Hearlson introduce us to the enterprise as a whole. Nearly all the following chapters are written by people who have actually designed, created, and/or led one of these programs. As you read, you will find that while all of the programs share a basic, fundamental purpose, they are quite different in their theological emphases, pedagogical dynamics, and organizational structures. Further, you will find that each chapter focuses on some particular aspect of the enterprise as a whole. The result is a rich smorgasbord of wisdom and insight gleaned both from the authors' deep engagements in their own programs and years spent in conversation with one another.

Theological programs for high school youth have been and continue to be an amazing gift to the thousands of young people who have participated in them as well as to the church and the world. As you will learn, large percentages of these young people — some now in their late twenties and thirties — have become significant Christian leaders, both as pastoral leaders in the church and as active church members whose strong sense of vocation has guided their career choices and commitments to work in service to others.

This book is a gift as well. It dispels the myth that theology is inaccessible except to a few. It displays the truth that once they have gotten a full, rich taste of it, teenagers truly do hunger for theology — and for the robust, compelling, intellectually demanding life of faith it reveals to them. Moreover, this book can help the whole church figure out how to do a lot more of this — not only in seminaries but in a wide variety of other contexts as well. It describes in considerable detail the variety of ways the church can enable its people — young and older alike — to enter the treasure-house and encounter the beautiful, powerful, life-giving resources that await them there.

When Candler School of Theology at Emory University launched the very first theological program for high school youth on July 4, 1993, its director, Don C. Richter, invited me to give the opening address to the young scholars (that's what they call them), their teachers and mentors, and the staff as they gathered for its opening convocation. Don asked me to tell the story that lay behind the idea for this new venture and to say something about my hopes for all of them as they embarked on this adventure. What follows is what I told them.

Choose Life!

Well, here you are! I've been looking forward to meeting you for about fifteen years. I am delighted to see you. I have wondered who you would be. I have wondered what your names would be . . . and where you have come from . . . and where "here" would be . . . and why you would have come . . . and what you would be feeling and thinking now, at this moment . . . and what would happen while you are here . . . and what it would all lead to — for you and for the world.

I greet you this way because your very presence here today is the beginning of the fulfillment of a dream for me. I don't want to make too much of that, but I thought you would like to know it, because it explains why I am here speaking to you tonight.

For about fifteen years, I have been hoping that a gathering like this would take place somewhere, sometime. My hopes for this have their beginnings in my own youth. When I was in high school, I received two great gifts. One of those gifts was four summers on a college campus as a participant in a music institute for youth. It was a wonderful experience, in which a whole flock of kids from across the state of Michigan came together each summer to play and sing great classical music, and to learn how to make that music from the best teachers who could be assembled. The work was hard, the discipline strenuous, the anxiety levels occasionally high, the experience of living like college students exciting, and the music . . . and the discovery of our capacities to make such beautiful music together . . . well, that was unbelievable.

That was one gift. The second gift was theology. I graduated from high school in 1965. During the four years I was there, the civil rights movement was in full sway, John F. Kennedy was assassinated, the war in Vietnam was stoking up, and the Beatles were revolutionizing rock music. In the midst of all this came a minister who thought we young people could use a strong dose of the best thought the Christian faith had to offer — at least if we were ever going to be able to make sense of what was going on all around us, much less of our own lives. The interplay between the greatest historical and contemporary Christian theology, on the one hand, and the tough questions our lives were putting to us, on the other: that was the gift he gave us.

Among the things this pastor got us high school kids to do was read theology. Not the easy stuff or the uncontroversial stuff, but some of the hardest, most challenging books of the time. Two books in particular stood out for me then. One was *Honest to God,* a book I'm sure you've never heard of. Written by John A. T. Robinson, an English bishop, this book called for a re-thinking, top to bottom, of Christian doctrine. It was the same rethinking that was going on in the theology schools, though almost nobody in the churches at the time knew it. We did. We read this book with a sense of wonder and excitement. Others simply blasted it as heretical. We loved it because it made us think through what we really believed and showed us how the questions we had anyway were precisely the questions Christianity had long been about.

The second book was *Letters and Papers from Prison.* Dietrich Bonhoeffer, its author, had been executed by the Nazis a few weeks before the end of the Second World War. They had put him in prison and then finally hung him because he was involved in the resistance movement against Hitler. A Christian deeply committed to peace, he had come to the morally tragic conclusion that Hitler had to be killed, and so he participated in a plot to assassinate him. *Letters and Papers from Prison* is a collection of letters, sermons, journal entries, and fragments of larger writings that Bonhoeffer wrote while awaiting his trial and execution. In reading this book, I met, for the first time, a person who loved life — loved not just his own life, but Life itself — so much so that he was able to die for it. And I saw, though I hardly understood, what made it possible for him to live that way.

That time was the beginning of my discovery that there exists a huge, wonderful, powerful, moving, life-changing literature called, for lack of a better name, theology. It's made up not only of essays on doctrine like *Honest to God,* but also of poems and songs and plays, of letters and journals and autobiographies, of long histories of the great adventures of whole peoples, and of brief pamphlets that provide moral advice and spiritual direction. Some of it is as contemporary as the latest movie. Some of it goes back centuries.

Do you know that all of that is there for you? Has anyone told you? Has anyone made it available to you? Don't let them hide it away! Make them give it to you! Force them, if you have to, to open it all up to you!

These were two gifts I had received: the gift of a summer youth institute and the gift of theology. They are gifts that I treasure still. They are gifts that set my own life on a course. They are gifts I have wanted others to have as well. And somewhere along the way, it hit me that these two gifts could be brought together into one — that there might sometime be a new kind of institute, one where people like you, still in high school, could go to a college or seminary campus for a month or so, be with great teachers and other kids who care about similar things, have a chance to read and study and discuss the sorts of books that had meant so much to me, and to connect all that with what was going on in the world around them and within their own lives and hearts.

That's why I'm here tonight, and why I'm so very pleased to meet you and to wish you well. But why are *you* here? And what will you do here? And what will come of your having been here?

I don't know what lured you here. Maybe you are not entirely sure yourselves. Over the next few days, you will have opportunities to say to one another a little bit about why you came. And over the next several weeks, you will discover more and more why you came as what you came for begins to happen.

You are the first. This Institute has never happened before. No one knows what it will be like, for it is not made yet. You will make it. You are the people responsible for bringing it into being. Why you came, what you will do here, and what will come of your having been here are all questions that have no answers at the moment. They are questions whose answers are to be made through the activity of creating your life together here.

And this is precisely as it should be, for the activity of creating a life together is right at the heart of what theology is. This great, wonderful literature I have been talking about is the literature that arises out of the process of creating a particular kind of life together, the kind of life together that really faces the big questions of "Why are we here?" "What will we do with our lives?" and "What will come of our having been here?"

Frederick Buechner once said that, "at its heart most theology . . . is essentially autobiography. Aquinas, Calvin, Barth, Tillich . . . are all telling us the stories of their lives, and if you press them far enough, even at their most cerebral and forbidding, you find an experience of flesh and blood, a human face smiling or frowning or weeping or covering its eyes before something that happened once."[1]

I think that's right. The written stuff, the sung stuff comes from actual life. And you don't get what it's about until you dig for the life in it and the life behind it. And the fact is, it's the life that's the important thing — the life lived, the life created. Theology is much more than what's written. Theology is ultimately the process of creating a way of living.

Furthermore, that way of living is never just individual or private. It is a way of living together, of creating life in community, of creating public life. It is the process of creating new life together in the midst of all the life that is going on within you and around you. This is what you are being called to do here at this Youth Theology Institute.

I understand that you have all been given Maya Angelou's inauguration poem, "On the Pulse of the Morning," to read and think about. That poem makes us remember the deepest, farthest part of the created world — the very earthen-ness of the Rock, the River, the Tree. Each of these is a witness in its own way to the coursing of life through the eons — and to the destruction and dying that has come along with it.

The Rock, and the River, and the Tree each plead with us — with *all* of us, whoever we are, wherever we come from — to choose something. To choose to stand up and in the open, rather than to crouch in the bruising darkness. To choose to rest beside flowing waters and to listen to their melody, rather than to thrust perpetually under siege in armed struggle. To choose to let down roots in fertile soil shared by many whose names are different from our own and whose arrivals have been by various routes. To choose to "Lift up your eyes upon/This day breaking for you." To "Give birth again/To the dream."

The poem puts choices before each of us and before all of us together, and tells us something about what is at stake in choosing. I expect you may

1. Frederick Buechner, *Alphabet of Grace* (New York: Seabury Press, 1970), p. 3.

read this poem often in the weeks to come. As you do, I hope you will listen carefully to each other to learn what each of you hears in it, sees in it, brings to it, brings to you as you read it together. Because you come from different places and have diverse insights and gifts, you can help each other to find rich treasures that none of you can discern on your own.

I also hope you will read this poem in the light of the people you meet and the things you see and do in the city of Atlanta. Let this complicated, richly various public place illuminate the poem; and let the poem focus your attention and prod you to understand features of the city and its peoples that you otherwise would miss.

Finally, I hope you will lay this poem down side by side with other poems and texts, older ones that I am sure Angelou herself remembered when she wrote her poem. As you think about the Rock in Angelou's poem, think also about "the Rock" portrayed in the Book of Deuteronomy whose "work is perfect, and all his ways are just" (Deut. 32:4). As you think about the River in Angelou's poem, remember too the rolling waters of justice and the ever-flowing streams of righteousness for which the prophet Amos yearns (Amos 5:24). When you see in your mind's eye Angelou's Tree, ask what that Tree has to do with "the tree of the knowledge of good and evil" (Gen. 2:9, 17) or that "tree" upon which hung a condemned Jew whom many called "Lord." When Angelou wrote her poem, she had these other images in mind as well. Her poem leaves all the hints we need to prove that to us.

What are you doing here? What will happen? What will it mean? A poem like this will expand your life when you read it together in this place. Included in your reading will now be the insights and experiences, the feelings and hopes of everyone here that you read it with and everyone you encounter in this city. People who are strangers to you now, whose lives are unlike your own, whose homes are quite different, whose worlds are foreign territory — all this will become part of you through your reading of this poem alongside the stories and the poems about the other rocks and rivers and trees that litter Scripture and the literature of the Christian people. Your own lives and the lives of these strangers sitting near you will mix with the lives — the passions, the fears, the adventures, the struggles, the terrible sufferings, and the huge joys — of peoples whose lives and faith have given birth to your own.

Maya Angelou's poem pleads with us to choose. Choice like this has been laid upon people before. The time came when a vagabond people weary of forty years of desert wandering climbed upon a rock, encountered a great river, saw a new vista, and prepared to enter a new land and a new future.

The man who had led them, Moses, was old and would not be able to go with them. But before his people went on without him, Moses called them together and, like Angelou, said "choose." But choose what? "Choose life," he said:

> See, I have set before you this day
> Life and good, and death and evil . . .
> therefore, choose life. (Deut. 30:15, 19, KJV)

Choose life! Choose life and good, not death and evil. What does that mean? How do we do it? A poem, a biblical text can urge us to do so. A poem and a text read in the company of strangers who more and more share their lives with one another can begin to illumine the way. A poem and a text read together while you go out into a public's life to watch how the choices of life and good and death and evil are made every day and to learn from those who have figured out, more or less, where life and good are to be found — all that can press the questions hard and enormously enrich the resources with which to answer them. But finally, a poem, a text read in this particular company of strangers striving to become community in public, while keeping in close touch with the rich and wonderful stories, prayers, poems, and ideas of generation upon generation of people who tried to know and worship and be faithful to God — well, that is, I think, itself a way of choosing . . . a way of choosing life.

Theology, I said, is ultimately a process of creating a way of life together that answers such big questions as "Why are you here?" "What will you do with your life?" and "What will come of your having been here?" That is what you are being called here to do right now and to keep doing after you leave. This theology institute for youth was once a dream not made. It had no faces, no lives to do the choosing and creating. Now it is yours to make real. "The horizon leans forward/Offering you space to place new steps of change," says Maya Angelou. "Therefore, choose life," says Moses. Both of them are saying these things to you, my friends. God bless you!

* * *

I am deeply grateful to Kenda Creasy Dean for leading the project and assembling the team that has produced this valuable resource. I have long admired the directors, staff, and faculty who have mounted and led these programs and have thoroughly enjoyed the opportunities I have had to be with many of them. I am especially grateful for those who have taken the time and employed their talents to write so eloquently about what they are doing in these programs and why. Every theological school that has mounted one of these programs has taken a big risk and made a significant investment in an endeavor that might not always have seemed in their own best institutional interest. But they have made an enormous contribution to the whole, and I am grateful for the vision and commitment to the larger good their leadership exemplifies. James L. Waits was the first to take on this experiment when he was Dean of Candler School of Theology, and Don C. Richter was the School's first director of its Youth Theology Institute. They were pioneers. Finally, I am profoundly grateful to Tom Lake, Tom Lofton, Clay Robbins, and Christopher Coble of Lilly Endowment for the support, encouragement, investment, and leadership in the grants programs that launched and have helped sustain these programs and this book project.

When I read this book and encounter these programs, I see a vision come to life. I hope that the new terrain these trailblazers have marked out will encourage and help you to create new paths of your own in the contexts where you live and work, so that for generations to come young people may receive and absorb the gift of theology as an indispensable dimension of their lives and faith.

Craig Dykstra

Acknowledgments

This book, even more than most, is a group effort. Above all, thank you to the young people whose voices punctuate these pages, and to countless other youth whose experiences have informed the High School Theology Program Seminar. To the teenage participants, program alumni, young adult staff, counselors, and peer mentors we interviewed, and to those we observed and read about: thank you. You are this book's inspiration.

This book is the culmination of a two-year research project that stretched out into almost four — which means there is a very long list of people to whom I am indebted. At the top of that list are Craig Dykstra and Christopher Coble of the Lilly Endowment, whose incomparable vision for the vocational formation of teenagers gave rise to the High School Theology Programs themselves. Craig and Chris's conviction that we can do better when it comes to adolescent faith and leadership formation has now influenced an entire generation of young leaders who are actively changing the way we think about the church and the theological education it requires. Until now, Craig Dykstra has not been thanked in print for the way High School Theology Programs — which sprang from Craig's own fertile vocational imagination — have helped change the landscape of American youth ministry. Meanwhile, it was Chris Coble who brought this particular project to life. As project director, I benefitted (with embarrassing regularity) from Chris's unflagging enthusiasm, clear vision, gentle guidance, and endless patience. Craig and Chris are the original champions of the HSTPs. Neither this book nor hundreds of young church leaders' ministries would have taken shape without them.

Projects like this one are accomplished largely through the work of unsung heroes — heroes like our intrepid project associate, Kristie Finley, who somehow viewed managing logistics as ministry, who herded cats and sent "gentle nudges" and brought chili and affirmation to our meetings. Kristie was assisted by our fearless project assistant Ashley Higgins, and later by the unflappable Brian Tanck who filled in after Ashley moved over to the research side of the project. Jennifer DiRicco, administrator for the School of Christian Education at Princeton Theological Seminary, offered technical magic, moral support, and a wry sense of humor at perfect intervals, while Chanon Ross and Abigail Rusert of Princeton's Institute for Youth Ministry — whose brilliance and hilarity dazzle me daily — created numerous vehicles for disseminating project findings throughout the youth ministry community.

Few people will appreciate the hundreds of hours logged by the research team, youth ministers, and doctoral students who met faithfully for more than twenty months to design and execute a research plan, carry out the project's primary interviews and site visits, and help interpret relevant data. Our collective gratitude to the teenagers and program directors who agreed to be interviewed for this project knows no bounds. Those gathering this data — Stephen Cady, Katie Douglass, Marcus Hong, McLane Stone, Nathan Stucky, and Wendy Mohler — gave this project insight and levity as we ploughed through hundreds of pages of transcripts and archival material. (Unless otherwise cited, all quotes from program participants come from interviews conducted for this book.)[1] Only one team member had any experience with High School Theology Programs prior to this research (Marcus Hong attended an HSTP as a teenager), but they all became ferocious advocates of the programs they visited. One team member even changed his own vocational direction as a result of being inspired by the quality of youth ministry these programs made possible.

Special thanks go to the program directors and practical theologian consultants who contributed to this research as part of the seminar itself. Christian educators Reginald Blount, Drew Dyson, Jeff Keuss, Gordon Mikoski, and Don Richter helped us contextualize the pedagogical approaches of the HSTPs in larger discussions about Christian formation underway in practical theology. In what can only be described as an act of generosity and affection, biblical scholar Brent Strawn joined the team in time to attend our writing

1. Though not formally a member of the research team, Craig Gould added significantly to our research, especially in regards to Catholic programs.

retreat, adding a chapter to this book so the perspective of an HSTP faculty member could be represented.

It was the program directors, however, who had the most to lose by being yoked to a project director who was, by design, an "outsider" to the HSTP network. These people — theological educators and passionate advocates for young people — showered me with grace (and substantial forgiveness) as they opened their programs, their writing, and their hearts to a relentless process of pedagogical scrutiny and theological reflection with peers. Andy Brubacher Kaethler, Beth Corrie, Fred Edie, David Horn, Jeff Kaster, Anabel Proffitt, Judy Steers, and Anne Streaty Wimberly — on behalf of their many colleagues who direct HSTPs — have given themselves to these ministries whole-cloth, and they held nothing back when it came to contributing to this research project. We started as colleagues and wound up as friends, and my admiration for their work on behalf of youth and the church defies words. It is no overstatement to say that these eight individuals have changed the church through the thousands of teenagers who, thanks to them and to the programs they have designed, have named and responded to God's invitation to become church leaders and change-makers.

Three more people must be mentioned, because without them this book would not exist. Ted Jordan became an accidental editorial assistant for this project, but his passion for and experience in youth ministry gave him special sympathy and insight for this work — and when we discovered his keen eye for detail and gifts as an editor, we immediately signed him up. Ted joyfully read and critiqued several versions of the "final" manuscript before it became, with his help, final.

Jon Pott, former Vice President and Editor-in-Chief of William B. Eerdmans Publishing, has taken more than one chance on a risky youth ministry manuscript, and Jon signed this book as one of his last projects before a much-deserved retirement from a celebrated publishing career. Most people consider Jon an editor, but we have discovered his secret identity. He is a theological educator who uses editing to mentor and shape young scholars and church leaders. Those of us involved in the High School Theology Program Seminar hope this book will continue Jon's legacy.

My own hero in this project is Christy Lang Hearlson, who originally signed on as associate editor but very quickly became much, much more than an associate. Her lucid, clear-eyed critique of drafts — first and final — resurrected more than one dead paragraph, including my own. An ace practical theologian and theological educator in her own right, Christy has the gift of understanding the potential of an author's ideas better than the author does, and she knows how to clear away the brush so those ideas can be fully appreciated. Above all, her vision for what this book could contribute to theological education was a continual inspiration to me and to the rest of the team. This is why she is listed as this book's co-editor.

Finally, on behalf of all the authors in this book, these most important thanks: for all of the friends and loved ones who sacrificed time with someone dear so he or she could finish a chapter, for all of the students whose papers were graded more slowly than they should have been because this manuscript was unfinished, for all of the dishes left undone and homework left unchecked because a deadline was upon us: thank you, beloved ones, for cheering and forgiving us, and for teaching us about God along the way.

Kenda Creasy Dean
Princeton, NJ

PART ONE

A More Excellent Way

Vocational Discernment as a Practice of Christian Community

Now you are the body of Christ and individually members of it. And God has appointed in the church first apostles, second prophets, third teachers; then deeds of power, then gifts of healing, forms of assistance, forms of leadership, various kinds of tongues. Are all apostles? Are all prophets? Are all teachers? Do all work miracles? Do all possess gifts of healing? Do all speak in tongues? Do all interpret? But strive for the greater gifts. And I will show you a still more excellent way.

1 CORINTHIANS 12:27-31

CHAPTER ONE

Taste Tests and Teenagers

Vocational Discernment as a Creative Social Practice

Kenda Creasy Dean and Christy Lang Hearlson

> *You did not choose me, remember. I chose you.*
>
> JESUS (JOHN 15:16, PARAPHRASE)

If you were on your way to work in Washington, DC on January 12, 2007 — and if your route happened to take you through the L'Enfant Plaza subway station at 7:51 a.m. — you might have noticed a young man in jeans and a baseball cap playing a violin. L'Enfant Plaza is the nerve center of the federal government's morning commute. The young man's violin case was open, welcoming the occasional dollar tossed inside by the various species of government workers who scuttled by. Some had children in tow on their way to day care. Everyone was in a hurry. The young man played for forty-three minutes.

During that time, several things happened. The young man played six classical pieces, netting $52.17 (one woman threw in a twenty). The videotape shows 1,097 people passing by, but only six stopped to listen for a few minutes. Children craned their necks to watch, but parents scooted them away without pausing. No one realized that the young man was playing a three-hundred-year-old, $3.5 million Stradivarius, or that he played Bach's "Chaconne," considered one of the most difficult pieces ever written for the violin. And, with the exception of the woman donating the $20 (she recognized him from a concert), no one knew that the musician was world-famous violinist Joshua Bell, who had soloed with the world's most celebrated orchestras, performed an Oscar-winning soundtrack, and appeared on *Sesame Street* and *Late Night with Conan O'Brien* — all before turning thirty-nine.

The Washington Post called the subway concert "art without a frame," an experiment to see if people would recognize a musical feast prepared by an artistic genius if it was right under their noses.[1] Turns out, they didn't.

High School Theology Programs: Feasts of Hope

This book pays attention to another experiment — "theological education without a frame," perhaps — that has continued, mostly unnoticed, for nearly two decades. The Lilly Endowment Initiative "Theological Programs for High School Youth" constitutes North American theological education's most ambitious pedagogical experiment in fifty years.[2] Distressed by congregational youth ministries' failure to seriously engage teenagers theologically, the Lilly Endowment's Religion Division enlisted teams of theological educators and youth ministers to imagine a kind of theological education for teenagers considering Christian leadership. To that end, High School Theology Programs (HSTPs) spent the better part of two decades testing various pedagogical cocktails that would "help teenagers fall in love with theology" and inspire, challenge, and shape the next generation of Christian leaders for the church and for the world.[3]

The practices these programs use to prepare young Christian leaders are striking both for the ways they echo formal theological education and for their unapologetic departures from it. Very few of these programs claim that forming future clergy is their primary aim, yet some research suggests that an astonishing one in four HSTP alumni have graduated from, are currently enrolled in, or plan to attend seminary — and another 28 percent say they "are considering" attending seminary.[4] Yet of those who "pass by" High School Theology Programs each summer (and many do this literally,

1. Gene Weingarten, "Pearls before Breakfast," *The Washington Post* (April 8, 2007), http://www.washingtonpost.com/wp-dyn/content/article/2007/04/04/AR2007040401721.html (accessed July 8, 2014).

2. North American theological education's investment in continuing education in the 1960s and 1970s was a comparable experiment in theological pedagogy. The American system of continuing education — arguably the largest pedagogical experiment in North American theological education in the twentieth century — had its roots in adult educational programs at Cooper Union in New York and San Francisco Public Schools in the 1850s, but did not become widespread until the 1960s and 1970s.

3. Lilly funded some programs as "pilots" prior to 1998.

4. Barbara Wheeler, "On Our Way: A Study of Students' Paths to Seminary," unpublished report of survey data submitted to the Lilly Endowment (August 2013), p. 46.

since most of them take place on seminary campuses), very few church leaders have taken note of how likely these students are to want theological training, how often they credit these programs with awakening their sense of calling, or how transformative practicing vocational discernment in community is for both young people and the church, as young people come to think of vocation as discerning the *church's* calling in the world, and not just their own.

We believe that approaching vocational discernment as a social practice is a distinctive theological contribution of High School Theology Programs, challenging individualized notions of vocation in ways that include, but go beyond, identifying where young people's deepest passions intersect with the world's greatest needs.[5] A different metaphor began to inform our discussion about the vocational ecologies of these programs, brought to mind by Isak Dinesen's famous short story "Babette's Feast."[6] Babette — an enigmatic maid who, as a young woman, had been a celebrated chef in Paris — makes her way to a Norwegian village where she serves two sisters, members of an austere Christian sect, for many years. Day in and day out, she prepares the plain fare they have shown her how to cook. But when Babette wins the lottery, she asks permission to make the sisters and their guests a real French meal. The food is divine; the guests warm to the wine and to each other. Old rifts are healed and old loves are confessed, and the sharp line dividing spiritual from other appetites melts in the joy of the meal. Surprised to learn that Babette will not return to France with her winnings, the sisters are aghast to learn the reason why: she has gladly spent every penny on them, offering the feast.

Like Babette's gift that awakened joy throughout the village, Lilly's decision to invest in the vocational formation of young people felt like "winning the lottery" to many scholars and practitioners interested in adolescent faith formation. Forty-seven teams of academics and youth ministers, located in seminaries across North America,[7] were given license to prepare a vocational feast for people whose joy they longed to awaken: young people, and especially teenagers who showed promise for theological leadership.

5. We are paraphrasing Frederick Buechner's famous definition of vocation in *Wishful Thinking: A Theological ABC* (New York: Harper and Row, 1973), p. 95.

6. Isak Dinesen, "Babette's Feast," *Anecdotes of Destiny* (New York: Random House, 1958), pp. 23-70. The story is available online at https://www2.bc.edu/~taylor/babette.html (accessed November 28, 2014).

7. In addition to these programs, Lilly also experimented with some HSTPs in other contexts.

Spiritually Interested Teenagers: Hungry for More

Megan LeCluyse and Emily Chudy are two young Presbyterian (USA) pastors who met at Pittsburgh Theological Seminary's Summer Youth Institute (SYI) in 2003. Megan called herself a "band kid" from Arizona; Emily was a Philadelphia athlete. Like most teenagers in High School Theology Programs, Megan and Emily did not come to faith or have a conversion experience at the Summer Youth Institute. Their faith had already been significantly formed through committed, church-going families and attentive churches, to the point that others began to notice and name their gifts for Christian leadership. Yet Emily and Megan recall being excited about being with other teenagers who also wanted to "go deeper" in their faith, and who were also trying to discern whether God was calling them to ministry. As Megan and Emily put it, "For us, [SYI] was the first time we felt 'normal.'"

For two weeks at Pittsburgh's Summer Youth Institute, Emily and Megan drank in a typical HSTP experience. They studied under seminary professors, engaged in serious Bible study, learned to preach, serve, and worship together, and — in their words — were "simply nerdy teenagers living in community." In a study of their fellow SYI alumni ten years later, they write,

> [SYI] was the first time we felt . . . that our call to ministry at a young age and a desire to academically engage our faith did not make us different from our peers. Our experience was both fun and formative. . . . As we went through seminary, we realized we were not only very close friends . . . but colleagues in ministry who care very deeply about the future of the PCUSA and its ministry to young people.[8]

Emily and Megan say their journey into ministry was decisively influenced by their participation in the Summer Youth Institute, which amounted to (in their words) "an AP course" in Christian community and theological reflection, enabling them to unapologetically profess their religious interests and articulate their desire to serve Christ.

Their words were echoed in many of the interviews our research team conducted; over and over, we heard young people say they finally felt that they had found their tribe in the program they attended, that they were being

8. Emily Chudy and Megan LeCluyse, "Promises to Keep: The Importance of Communities of Faith on the Faith Development of Adolescents and Emerging Adults," unpublished MDiv/MA thesis (Princeton, NJ: Princeton Theological Seminary, 2012), pp. iii-iv.

taken seriously for the first time as religious beings and theological thinkers, or that they wished their home churches provided similar challenge and depth in exploring faith. As it turns out, spiritually interested teenagers must confront two ironies in North American culture. The first is that — despite the fact that 40 percent of American teenagers attend religious youth groups for an extended period of time, and three out of four self-identify as Christians — most North American young people do not share Megan and Emily's depth of spiritual interest, in spite of the fact that theological and existential concerns are very much on adolescents' minds as a matter of their place in the lifecycle. Three out of five millennials say religion does not matter much to them.[9] Most young people who call themselves Christians describe their faith in terms that the 2004 National Study of Youth and Religion dubbed "moralistic therapeutic deism," a bland, superficial religiosity that helps people be nice and feel good about themselves, but otherwise keeps God in the background.[10]

In a culture where blasé spirituality is the norm, Megan and Emily's intense interest in theological questions and commitment to Christian service sound out of place. Yet Megan and Emily were not, in fact, weird in their interest in theology. Although American teenagers who say faith matters to them (even when it takes a backseat to other activities) are a minority, they are a significant minority. A full 37 percent of American teenagers describe themselves as "strong" in their faith, and 8 percent are described by the National Study of Youth and Religion as "highly devoted."[11] Ironically, these "highly devoted" young people are the very teenagers that North American youth ministry is most likely to overlook.

9. The data are based on samples from the United States. Christian Smith with Melinda Lundquist Denton, *Soul Searching: The Religious and Spiritual Lives of American Teenagers* (New York: Oxford University Press, 2005), p. 69. The vocational pedagogy most effective at countering such apathy and superficiality is the long, slow nurture of faith, through families and congregations, that models and practices discipleship as a lifelong pursuit. Families and congregations that offer this degree of intentional religious formation are increasingly rare — but they do exist, and to powerful effect.

10. Cf. Smith with Denton, *Soul Searching;* Christian Smith with Patricia Snell, *Souls in Transition: The Religious and Spiritual Lives of Emerging Adults* (New York: Oxford University Press, 2009). For consistent findings about spiritually disinclined young adults, see Pew Report, "Nones on the Rise," Pew Forum for Religion and Public Life, October 9, 2012, http://www.pewforum.org/Unaffiliated/nones-on-the-rise.aspx.

11. Alison Pond et al., "Religion among the Millennials," Religion and Public Life Project/Pew Research (February 17, 2010), http://www.pewforum.org/2010/02/17/religion-among-the-millennials/ (accessed July 10, 2014); also, Smith with Denton, *Soul Searching*, p. 110.

This, then, is the second irony facing teenagers like Megan and Emily: congregational youth ministries are not *designed* for spiritually interested youth to grow in their faith — maybe because we think the Megans and Emilies in our churches are "already won." Congregational and community youth ministries, hoping to cast a wide net, tend to cater to moralistic therapeutic deists (a case can be made that some North American churches actually help youth *become* moralistic therapeutic deists).[12] As a rule, contemporary "fellowship" models of youth ministry do not challenge young people like Megan or Emily. To be clear, church leaders appreciate these teenagers (we are not shy about employing their gifts or exploiting their reliability), but the fellowship aims of most congregational youth ministries cause youth leaders to default to programs that are designed to attract a wide array of teenagers, or that we hope will whet the spiritual appetites of the uninterested.

Meanwhile, one of the most disturbing trends facing theological education in the early twenty-first century is the fact that Christian young people who want to make a difference do not seem to think the church is the best place to do it. As one youth minister told me, explaining his decision to become an artist instead of attending seminary, "I feel like I have to choose between my creativity and the church." Spiritually interested teenagers — young people hungry for theologically substantive conversation about faith and identity — are more likely to find congregations to be places that affirm them rather than challenge them. As Chris Hughes, co-founder of the United Methodist Foundation of Faith Formation, remarked about confirmation (arguably the most common congregational vocational discernment practice): "In most churches, spiritually interested teens emerge in spite of confirmation, not because of it."[13]

Why Now?

Congregations' tendency to underinvest in spiritually interested teenagers was in fact the predicament that motivated the Lilly Endowment's Religion Division to fund High School Theology Programs. By the 1990s, the Endowment's own reports were forthright about the gifts — and limitations — of

12. I have been among those making this case; see K. C. Dean, *Almost Christian: What the Faith of Our Teenagers Is Telling the American Church* (New York: Oxford University Press), 2010.

13. Chris Hughes, Foundation for Christian Formation (Winston-Salem, NC), personal interview, August 3, 2014.

church youth fellowship programs. The reports were especially critical of these programs' effectiveness in helping youth intellectually engage Christian thought and practice:

> Many congregational and denominational youth fellowship programs nurture young people in the Christian faith and establish personal relationships with other Christians. They do not always provide adequate opportunities for youth to explore and examine critically the long and rich tradition of Christian thought and practice.[14]

Noting that the "networks and systems needed to identify and recruit talented young people into the vocation of Christian ministry are not strong enough at this time," theological educators like Craig Dykstra, then the vice president of Lilly's Religion Division, saw a clear need for helping young people see Christian leadership as a viable expression of their gifts and dreams.[15] Sensing urgency, Lilly elected to bypass incentivizing congregational reform and went straight to theological schools, gambling that if seminaries developed teenage Christian leaders, it would solve two problems at once: (1) talented youth would consider ministry as a desirable vocational option; and (2) future church leaders would be formed who — a generation hence — would reform congregations' ailing approaches to faith formation.

With these young leaders in mind, the Lilly Endowment began funding teams of theological educators and youth ministers to "(1) stimulate and nurture an excitement about theological learning and inquiry, and (2) identify and encourage a new generation of young Christians to consider vocations in Christian ministry."[16] High School Theology Program directors vigorously deny accusations that their programs cater only to the "best and the brightest" young Christians. (Overheard from one program director: "What

14. Lilly Endowment Request for Proposals (1998), cited by Carol Lytch, "Summary Report I: Strategic Advances in Theological Education: Theological Programs for High School Youth, 1999-2004," *Theological Education* 42 (2006): 3. Research on youth groups suggests that attending worship may be a stronger indicator than youth group participation of young people's connection to church, moral frameworks, and comfort with adults, though youth groups do produce positive outcomes, especially for older youth (who are more likely to say that church is a place they can think). Youth groups' contribution to faith formation seems to be indirect at best. See Patricia Snell, "What Difference Does Youth Group Make? A Longitudinal Analysis of Religious Youth Group Participation Outcomes," *Journal for the Scientific Study of Religion* 48 (2009): 572-87.

15. Lytch, "Summary Report I," p. 3.

16. Lytch, "Summary Report I," p. 4.

does that even *mean?*") Instead, they describe their participants in terms of *readiness,* referring to an openness to vocational exploration expressed by teenagers once their gifts for leadership have been recognized, named, and affirmed by others.[17]

Given free rein to develop their own recipes for adolescent vocational formation, these teams created a sumptuous array of offerings that immerse young people in communities organized around Christian practices of vocational discernment. No two curricular designs, schedules, staffing patterns, organizational partnerships, theological emphases, or signature themes and practices (liturgy, peacemaking, mentoring, hope-building, etc.) are alike. What unites all of them is a profound confidence in teenagers' capacities for theological leadership, and a commitment to giving young people concrete opportunities to practice this leadership. Each program cultivates adolescents' ability to wrestle with thorny theological problems, giving teenagers confidence in their theological agency while they encounter myriad ways in which people live their lives for God. Motivated by research in civic education that shows a predictive relationship between early leadership opportunities and adult civic engagement, each High School Theology Program provides teenagers with countless opportunities to "try on" various mantles of Christian leadership in the context of a deeply intentional, if briefly constituted, community of faith.[18] The ability to *practice* theological leadership in these communities is key. As one group of theological educators working with HSTPs pointed out,

> "Falling in love with theology" is not what motivates kids to think about ministry. . . . They respond best to a sense of agency and a sense that they can bring about greater justice. At the same time, they need help in growing theologically and developing skills for service.[19]

17. Cf. Christian Smith's influential research through the longitudinal National Study of Youth and Religion (especially *Soul Searching,* with Melinda Denton; *Souls in Transition,* with Patricia Snell). Also note the Pew Report, "Nones on the Rise," 2012.

18. The first HSTPs were explicitly patterned off the "Governors' Schools" that aimed to foster civic engagement in high school students. Peers and voluntary associations seem to have a disproportionate socializing effect on later political participation, compared to parents and schools. Cf. Ellen Quintelier, "Engaging Adolescents in Politics: The Longitudinal Effect of Political Socialization Agents," *Youth and Society* 47 (January 2015): 51-69; also James Youniss, Jeffrey A. McLellan, and Miranda Yates, "What We Know about Engendering Civic Identity," *The American Behavioral Scientist* 40 (March/April 1997): 620.

19. Lytch, "Summary Report I," p. 33.

Almost twenty years and twenty thousand alumni later, the data speak for themselves. Overwhelmingly, HSTP alumni view their professional lives as expressions of Christian discipleship. According to Barbara Wheeler's study of HSTP alumni, in addition to the one in four who are attending or finished with seminary, and the 28 percent who say they are considering formal theological education,

- Half have attended church-related or Christian colleges;
- One quarter have majored in religion or theology in college;
- Half have participated in a vocational discernment program in college;
- Eighty percent have engaged in volunteer work during college;
- More than half said they are "likely" or "very likely" to work in ministry, or are already doing so;
- Almost half (40 percent) expect to be in ministry, or some form or work that serves others in need, within ten years.[20]

These outcomes suggest that it is not only possible to challenge teenagers with rigorous theological reflection and meaningful opportunities for ministry and service, but that doing so helps teenagers imagine vocational futures that otherwise would go unnoticed.

Top Chefs and Mother Sauces

This book is the fruit of a two-year project in which HSTP directors were asked to describe the theological emphases and pedagogical practices of their programs, and — along with a team of practical theologians in Christian education and formation — discern what these programs might teach those of us concerned with educating future church leaders.[21] This book is intended to evoke more than prescribe; the chapters that follow are more invested than objective, more anecdotal than analytical. For eighteen months we convened this group, while a research team made up of PhD students combed through the archives of every seminary-based HSTP that has been

20. Wheeler, "On Our Way," p. 46.

21. At the time this project was conceived, Christopher Coble was a program director at Lilly Endowment Inc., with chief oversight of the HSTPs. He has since become the vice president for religion of the Endowment. The Lilly Endowment — funded primarily by Eli Lilly and Company (the inventors of Prozac) — has optimistically funded most of the youth ministry research conducted in the United States since the 1990s.

funded. This research team also conducted thirteen site visits to programs "in progress" in the summer of 2012, interviewed teenagers, staff, and program directors, and sifted through various theological and pedagogical analyses written about the forty-seven current programs.[22]

Stepping into the High School Theology Program universe felt a little like stepping into a Food Network show in progress. We peeked in on forty-seven "top chefs" in youth ministry who had been given access to "risk capital" and what amounts to a pedagogical carte blanche by the Lilly Endowment; what we observed was part genius and part chaos. Along with committed teams of young adult staff, seminary professors, youth ministers, community members, and high school participants themselves, these program directors created energetic test kitchens where teenagers could experiment with different aspects of spiritual and vocational formation. Through remarkably diverse settings and curricula, they helped youth unapologetically claim and articulate faith, discern how to serve Christ with their work and with their lives, and see themselves as church shapers rather than church shoppers.

The vocational pedagogies of these "top chefs" were less new than freshly interpreted in specific contexts, which gave them a boldness — and, it must be said, a hopefulness — that was as irresistible to adults as to teenagers.[23] At the heart of their pedagogical frameworks was a collection of powerful practices: practices of community building, decentering and disruption, worship, spiritual companionship, holy conversation, theological reflection, pilgrimage, and experiential learning. These pedagogies function as the "mother sauces," so to speak, of vocational discernment. Just as French cooking utilizes four or five "mother sauces" that make possible nearly every dish in the French palette, vocational pedagogies lie at the root of every effort of High School Theology Programs to help teenagers recog-

22. Seminar members included eight academic Christian educators, all of whom either serve as, or work with, HSTP directors at their schools; four practical theologians teaching in American seminaries; and a seven-member research team comprised mostly of doctoral students in discipleship formation at Princeton Theological Seminary. Seminar participants are listed in appendix B.

23. One member of the research team — an MDiv student who was hired for the project because, at the time of this study, he had completed a PhD course in empirical research methods and was actively applying to PhD programs — was so impressed by the HSTPs he visited that he pulled his PhD applications and looked for youth ministry jobs instead. (Upon his return from interviewing participants in two programs, he declared: "I want to do *that!*") He currently serves as a youth pastor in Washington, DC.

nize God's movement in their lives. The theory was simple: once teenagers learned the basic ingredients of vocational discernment, they could combine those ingredients in endlessly creative ways to cobble together a future as a Christian leader.

High School Theology Programs are not the only *de facto* laboratories for adolescents pursuing church leadership, of course. Church camps, retreat programs, volunteer service corps, denominational youth councils, and confirmation programs all can be viewed, with some accuracy, as feeder systems for future Christian leaders as well. When utilized intentionally, vocational pedagogies turn out disproportionate numbers of future pastors from many venues, partly because they cultivate experiences that are positively correlated with young people's likelihood to attend seminary: communities of faithful peers, agency in shaping those communities, primary leadership experience, "disruptive experiences" like leaving home and encountering difference, as well as access to effective Christian leaders who take youth seriously as theologians (an oft-cited virtue of HSTPs).[24] They treat youth ministry as an occasion to challenge and deepen adolescents' call to discipleship, rather than use youth ministry as a net to capture teenagers before they escape. In short, they give students opportunities to see "ministry done well, and at close range," which, as Barbara Wheeler observes, is normally a prerequisite for a young person's interest in seminary.[25]

Vocation: What It Is, What It Isn't

High School Theology Programs were formed in part to make Christian leadership an imaginable possibility for young people who might not otherwise consider it, and to prompt those already leaning in that direction to "try on" the identity of a Christian leader. Despite Lilly's stated objective for HSTPs to help teenagers "fall in love with theology," by itself this was not enough. Youth needed to make the connection between their love for theology and the church as a place where lovers of theology put their insights about Christ into action.

Thus, while it was crucial for HSTPs to help teenagers "fall in love with theology" and discern their individual gifts for leadership, a communal un-

24. Barbara Wheeler, "Pathways to Seminary," unpublished lecture reporting Auburn Seminary research on seminarians (Indianapolis, IN: Lilly Endowment), January 23, 2014.

25. Barbara Wheeler, "Pathways to Seminary," *In Trust* (Autumn 2013): 7.

derstanding of vocation gave teenagers a reason to introduce practices of vocational discernment to others. The language that Lilly most often used to describe their mission was the *cultivation of Christian leaders* through a process of *vocational discernment.* A key component of this leadership was helping the gathered community discern its collective gifts, and determine how God might use those gifts to reflect Christ in particular contexts.

Thinking about Christian vocation as God's call to *communities,* and not just to individuals, is part of the DNA of every High School Theology Program we studied and profoundly influences the way HSTP alumni understand pastoral ministry. Instead of viewing pastoral leadership as a church office or service profession, these teenagers tend to view Christian leaders as catalysts, community developers, shepherds, and bridge-builders — people who mobilize others to enact the gospel in their contexts — as well as serve as prophets, priests, and servants. While all High School Theology Programs use the language of *vocation* and *discernment* to describe their work, let us take a moment to scrutinize these terms, especially since HSTPs use them in distinctly communal ways.

The Early Church and Vocation

The early church understood vocation primarily in terms of discipleship. Every Christian's vocation is to bear the image of God, to follow Christ — a life made possible by unceasing prayer and purity (usually equated with chastity or virginity). However, since most believers could not abandon their daily toil to literally pursue a life of unceasing prayer (and most had no wish for chastity or virginity), "vocation" came to mean one's call from God to live as a religious "professional" (i.e., a monk, nun, virgin, or priest) — people who lived holy lives on behalf of others. Thus, "vocation" had a dual meaning from very early on: it referred both to Christ's call to all believers to follow him, and it referred to people whose full-time work was set apart to strive for a kind of holiness that would reflect Christ's likeness in intentional, intensified ways as representatives of the church.

By the Middle Ages, vocation had become closely identified with the work of a vowed class of religious people. After the schism in 1054, Western churches continued this trajectory with vigor. For medieval Catholics, vocation referred almost exclusively to a specific calling to holy orders; priests, monks, nuns, and various holy people were said to have a special calling, a vocation. By living simply in community, and by adopting ascetic practices aimed at eliminating all distractions from God, these "religious" could focus their attention on holiness, often viewed as an almost literal imitation of Christ's suffering and self-giving love.

In the East, vocation was less of a specialized profession. The Eastern church had religious professionals too, but "transfiguration was the central paradigm for understanding humanity's vocation."[26] Eastern Christians believed all believers were called to *theosis,* to become partakers in the divine nature. The goal of Christian life is future union with God, and — in contrast to the Roman Catholic Church — was less focused on the sin of the past. The Orthodox considered sin a serious but temporary malady that hurts us, but does not destroy God's image in us.[27] In other words, sin was less a matter of disobedience and guilt than a failure to follow the path to *theosis* — the vocation of all human beings.

Vocation in the Reformation

The sixteenth-century Protestant Reformers radically expanded the idea of calling or vocation, but maintained its association with human work.[28] Martin Luther, for example, believed that all Christians are of the "spiritual estate," though they may have different roles or belong to different classes of society. Luther believed in both an internal and an external calling. Internally, all Christians are called to the gospel faith. Externally, we are called to certain roles in particular "estates" or social classes. In other words, Luther did not think it possible for someone *not* to be called; the ordinary roles of life, he insisted, were divine callings.

While Luther's view of vocation elevated the work of ordinary life to a higher status, making the active (versus contemplative) life of ordinary Christians a part of God's plan for society, this also had the effect of identi-

26. Donald Fairbairn, *Eastern Orthodoxy through Western Eyes* (Louisville, KY: Westminster John Knox, 2002), p. 70.

27. Fairbairn, *Eastern Orthodoxy,* p. 74.

28. Paul Marshall explains that Luther broke with tradition when he translated Sirach 11:20-1 ("Stand by your agreement and attend to it, and grow old in your work") and 1 Corinthians 7:20 ("Let each of you remain in the condition in which you were called") by using *Beruf* for work or calling. There were other German words available to Luther — *Werk* and *Arbeit* — but he chose the term traditionally used to describe the calling of someone who took on a clerical position. See Paul A. Marshall, *A Kind of Life Imposed on Man: Vocation and Social Order from Tyndale to Locke* (Toronto: University of Toronto Press, 1996).

fying people's vocations with the work dictated by the social class they were born into, reinforcing common assumptions that one's social class could not be improved. Although Luther's views on social mobility are debated, his view that all work, in any station of life, should be joyfully dedicated to God failed to recognize the oppressive nature of work for the poor, and often seemed to sanction dehumanizing work imposed upon the poor by those in power.[29]

In many respects, John Calvin was in agreement with Luther. Calvin also associated calling with ordinary roles and work. Like Luther, Calvin used "calling" to refer to the fact that all people, regardless of their station in life, were called to salvation and to following Christ. And, like Luther, Calvin also used "calling" to refer to a person's work. A person of any social class could serve God and neighbor, and, as Calvin stressed, this truth elevated mundane responsibilities. For Calvin, vocation has the potential to transform how we feel about our work since, by being useful to other people, we are ultimately doing something God had asked us to do. Calvin had a more flexible view of the social order than Luther, recognizing that people sometimes had to change professions in a changing economic landscape. For Calvin, one's utility and activity within one's social class mattered more than remaining a part of that class, which made "the whole tenor of callings . . . more aggressive and busy."[30]

The gift that Luther and Calvin offer Christians today is a view of vocation that celebrates the fact that every Christian is called by God, allowing ordinary work to be consecrated as holy, something one does for the good of others and in service to God. Unfortunately, as many theologians have noted, the Reformers' identification of vocation with work also poses serious problems, leading to an array of perspectives on vocation among contemporary theologians (especially Protestants).[31]

29. Karl Barth read Luther as being against changing stations in life (*Church Dogmatics* III. 4, "The Doctrine of Creation," ed. G. W. Bromiley and T. F. Torrance, trans. A. T. Mackay et al. [Edinburgh: T & T Clark, 1961], p. 646. This is a contested point; cf. Gilbert Meilaender, *Friendship: A Study in Theological Ethics* (Notre Dame, IN: University of Notre Dame Press, 1981), pp. 86-103 and *Working: Its Meaning and Its Limits* (Notre Dame, IN: University of Notre Dame Press, 2000), pp. 1-24.

30. Marshall, *A Kind of Life Imposed on Man,* p. 26.

31. Post–Vatican II Catholicism adopted a broader view of vocation than the medieval or neoscholastic interpretation of the nineteenth and early twentieth centuries, which linked vocation to certain ecclesiastical positions, though contemporary Catholics still commonly identify the term (if not the theology) of "vocation" with religious orders. The Catholic HSTPs we studied used the word both as a term meaning discernment of a path that follows

For example, womanist theologian Joan Martin points out that the Reformers failed to take seriously the potential of economic stratification to exploit workers, or "the incipient danger of theologizing, mystifying, and romanticizing all forms of work as theologically and morally 'good.'" Martin concludes,

> By upholding an unambiguously positive notion of work as vocation without criticizing the social relations of the changing political economy, the Protestant tradition was left with no theological or moral recourse for challenging exploitative work.[32]

Like Martin, Reformed theologian Miroslav Volf also rejects the idea that "virtually every type of work can be a vocation, no matter how dehumanizing it might be (provided that in doing the work one does not transgress the commandments of God)."[33] If work and vocation are simply equated, the doctrine of vocation can be abused, functioning to "ennoble dehumanizing work." Volf agrees with Martin: this "vocational understanding of work provides no resources to foster . . . change."[34] In today's market, where people must hold down several jobs at the same time or switch jobs in order to survive, the early modern perspective of Luther is untenable.[35]

For Volf, a theology of work must be rooted in both the doctrine of *creation,* which evokes reflection on the world and social order as they already are, and also in *eschatological hope,* which evokes reflection on the world and social order in light of Christ's redemption. Fueled by hope that God's Spirit is even now changing the world and will ultimately bring about a reign of justice, peace, and love, Christians must use the gifts the Spirit has given them to cooperate with God in transforming the world.[36] Because of his concerns about equating vocation with work, Volf replaces the language

---

Christ *and* as a synonym for being a priest, nun, or monk. See Edward P. Hahnenberg, *Awakening Vocation: A Theology of Christian Call* (Collegeville, MN: Liturgical Press, 2010), pp. xi-xviii.

32. Joan M. Martin, "Between Vocation and Work," in *Feminist and Womanist Essays in Reformed Dogmatics,* ed. Amy Plantinga Pauw and Serene Jones (Lousiville, KY: Westminster John Knox, 2006), pp. 180-81.

33. Miroslav Volf, *Work in the Spirit: Toward a Theology of Work* (Eugene, OR: Wipf and Stock, 2001), p. 107.

34. Volf, *Work in the Spirit,* p. 108.

35. Volf, *Work in the Spirit,* pp. 108-9.

36. Volf, *Work in the Spirit,* pp. 98-99.

of *vocation* with *charisms* — gifts — as a way to describe what Christians are meant to be and do in the world.

Lutheran theologian Douglas J. Schuurman paints a more positive portrait of the Reformers' approach to vocation, and as a result is hesitant to separate vocation and work. Like Calvin, Schuurman believes that vocation has potential to infuse life with meaning, integrating "all spheres and relations of human life into a religious vision of love and service to God and neighbor."[37] Schuurman maintains that vocation is "neighbor-centered, theocentric, and preferential" toward those we are called to care for by virtue of our family and community relationships — and as a result "rules out triumphalism, cynicism, and moral paralysis," providing grounds to resist unjust social realities.[38] To prevent abusing the doctrine of vocation, Schuurman provides some "hedges": (1) Always keep in mind that our most encompassing "call," or "vocation," is to serve God and the common good; (2) Make love our guide; if a so-called vocation is harming people, it is not a vocation; (3) *Shalom* — divine peace and justice for all — must give form and structure to our view of vocation; (4) In a "good but fallen world," exercise discernment in searching out and fulfilling our vocations.

Combustible Communities: Vocation as a Social Practice

These views illustrate both the importance and complexity of vocation in Christian history, in contemporary society, and in High School Theology Programs. HSTPs resist equating vocation to holy orders, avoid reducing teenagers' "callings" to their employment or "day jobs," and reject identifying vocation with dehumanizing work. Even in the few programs that unapologetically identified their primary objective as forming future clergy, the HSTPs we studied were united in reminding young people that God calls all Christians to reflect Christ in the work they do in the world — and that the work God calls us to do is sometimes (but not always) work for which we are paid.

At the same time, High School Theology Programs add an additional dimension to the conversation about vocation and discernment. Historically, both Protestant and Catholic discussions of vocation focus heavily on

37. Douglas J. Schuurman, *Vocation: Discerning Our Callings in Life* (Grand Rapids: Eerdmans, 2004), p. 86.

38. Schuurman, *Vocation*, p. 90.

individuals — people's work, their jobs, their station in life. Martin, Volf, and Schuurman are all concerned about social context, but treat vocation essentially as something that happens for individuals in those contexts. Absent from these theological expositions is an explicit discussion of how the whole church is called; nor is there a recognition of vocational discernment as a social practice — an adventure, even — that the church undertakes together, as a body.

High School Theology Programs, on the other hand, explicitly approach vocational discernment as a communal, creative process. We will explore the relationship between creativity and calling in chapter 2. For now, we can simply note that doing vocational discernment with teenagers in High School Theology Programs raises a fresh set of questions around vocation. What if, in addition to focusing on vocation as an individual calling, we began to understand vocation as something Christ calls the whole church to discern *as a community?* What if vocational discernment involves more than an internal psychological process that helps individual Christians figure out how to use their gifts and time? What if discerning vocation became an ongoing practice of the whole congregation in relationship to its community? What if vocation were like fire, less a material object than a visible, tangible expression of an ongoing social process that brings many "combustible" elements together to reflect the fire of the Holy Spirit?

Teenagers in High School Theology Programs wrestle with questions like these in both explicit and implicit ways. The pedagogical practices discussed in this volume come together around this point: they are practices of communities, and not just individuals, that lead to collective as well as individual discernment and action in an attempt to participate in Christ's transformation of the world.

Combustible Theological Education

What seems clear in light of this research — and we would argue, in light of Christian tradition itself — is that, however spontaneous it may appear at the time, discerning one's call to serve Christ is the result of a combustible vocational ecology, not any single variable. Not terribly long ago, "formative ecologies" were a taken-for-granted aspect of Christian formation. Networks of social institutions like families, congregations, community organizations, campus ministries, and Christian colleges all played a part in helping young people come to know themselves as religious beings, called by God to serve

Christ in the world. Today, these formative ecologies have largely eroded, leaving young people drawn toward theological study and Christian leadership with very mixed levels of preparation and vocational awareness when they arrive at seminary (if, in fact, they arrive at seminary at all). Mounting research points to the *de facto* abandonment of religious education even in churches (and even the most intentional family or congregation struggles to convey religious identity in an hour or two a week of formal religious instruction).[39] In short, while families and congregations are the best incubators we know for mature faith, they do not always do it well, and they cannot do it alone.[40]

In this milieu, the effect of participating in something like a High School Theology Program becomes much more pronounced. Consider three of the ways in which the vocational ecologies of these programs have already contributed to the next-generation church:

1. *High School Theology Programs are yielding talented and committed young leaders for Christian communities.*

Young people who pursue religious vocations, particularly as clergy, are increasingly rare in North America. Given the superficial faith claimed by so many American teenagers, it is not surprising that many drift away from faith communities altogether by young adulthood. One-third of young Americans between eighteen and twenty-five are religiously unaffiliated. They are not atheist or agnostic; they are "nothing in particular."[41]

39. On the congregational abandonment of the religious formation of young people, see Charles R. Foster, *From Generation to Generation* (Eugene, OR: Cascade, 2012), p. 77.

40. Wheeler observes that the degree of interest in theology and church life that HSTP alumni maintain is impressive especially because most of the respondents came from mainline Protestant, Roman Catholic, or Orthodox programs — "religious sectors that have a hard time holding on to their young people these days" (Wheeler, "On Our Way," 46). Whether or not young people remain within the religious traditions of their HSTP experience is unclear. Chudy and LeCluyse's senior thesis research of alumni from Pittsburgh's Summer Youth Institute (a Presbyterian Church USA program) found that, while SYA alumni still attend worship as frequently as they did in high school, 25% have switched to other denominations, mostly conservative evangelical churches, that often reflect their involvement in parachurch campus ministries in college. See Chudy and LeCluyse, "Promises to Keep," pp. 50, 58.

41. "Religion among the Millennials," Pew Research Religion and Public Life Project (February 17, 2010), http://www.pewforum.org/2010/02/17/religion-among-the-millennials/ (accessed August 9, 2013). Sociologist Josh Packard is now augmenting this research with studies on the "rise of the dones" — religiously unaffiliated believers (*Church Refugees,* [Loveland, CO: Group, 2015]). Also see Smith with Snell, *Souls in Transition.*

Against this backdrop, the vocational trajectories of more than twenty thousand HSTP alumni are striking. Even though roughly half do *not* pursue formal theological education (at least within the first decade of completing a High School Theology Program), forming a body of committed young congregants who are accustomed to engaging their faith deeply is no small thing. And, although the HSTPs pose serious questions to the church's dominant forms of theological education, they also serve as extraordinary feeder systems for formal theological education. Not only are youth who have participated in a High School Theology Program more likely to attend seminary; they come to seminary with an excellent set of theological tools. In contrast to many of their classmates, HSTP alumni are not only deeply formed in faith; they are acquainted with basic exegetical strategies, the discipline of theological reading, an appreciation for hermeneutics and contextual analysis, and they have already experienced a range of the historic practices of Christian tradition that aim for discerning the Holy Spirit's activity in their lives and in the world. Significantly, as several chapters in this book illustrate, they have also learned how to share life with people who sit at vastly different places on the ecclesial spectrum.

Barbara Wheeler acknowledges the obvious point — students attracted to HSTPs tend to be those already anchored in church life — so perhaps they would have pursued religious vocations anyway. Yet teenagers' interest in ministry, while noticeable to others, is often vague and unarticulated in youth themselves — at least until they encounter a situation where Christian vocation is openly discussed. One program director recalled a student named James who recently contacted him for a reference to seminary, a decade after completing St. John's University's Youth, Theology, and Ministry (YTM) program. James wrote: "YTM was by far the most life-changing experience of my life. I think that it was the experience at YTM that made me first consider a career in something theology-related, then possibly the priesthood."[42] Wheeler's interviews also underscored the experience of James, Emily, and Megan: "Several interviewees described their experiences in these high school programs as the defining moment in their decision-making about ministry."[43]

Wheeler invites us to speculate about what theological school enrollment figures might look like apart from the presence of High School Theology Program alumni in seminary classrooms over the past decade. Did the unexpected dip in the average age of seminarians, which had climbed

42. Cited by Lytch, "Summary Report I," p. 34.
43. Wheeler, "On Our Way," p. 46.

steadily from 31.4 in 1989 to 34.4 in 1999 — and then unexpectedly dropped from 1999 to 2009 — in any way correspond to the presence of young HSTP alumni?[44] Clearly many cultural factors are at play here. Yet with theological schools competing for a dwindling pool of well-prepared students, the vocational interest of HSTP alumni in theological leadership is difficult to ignore.

What we *can* say with some confidence is that participating in an intentional community that values and teaches theological reflection and spiritual practices, and offers myriad opportunities for leadership goes a long way toward convincing teenagers that they have gifts for leading a faithful life, and for leading others as disciples and change-makers in the church and world. For some youth, participating in a High School Theology Program awakens a call to Christian ministry; and for others, it ignites a life of committed, often passionate discipleship in other sectors. For teenagers and staff alike, being part of a High School Theology Program seems to significantly shape expectations for what the church should look like in their lifetimes, and heightens their determination to make this kind of church a reality.

2. *High school theology programs stretch ecclesial imaginations — not just intellects and behaviors.*

One of the most refreshing contributions of High School Theology Programs is that they allow us to witness the construction of a new church, rather than the deconstruction of an old one. These programs function as creative studios that both reimagine the way churches prepare leaders and catalyze more missional ways of thinking about the church altogether. HSTP directors share the conviction that Christian leaders need "traditioned" imaginations that anchor their expectations for the church and its leaders in the church's teachings, texts, and traditions — but that also yields a nimble holy wisdom that guides discipleship in the fluid here-and-now.[45] One pro-

44. From 1999 to 2009 the average age of seminarians in the U.S. dropped from 34.4 to 32. If HSTPs had a role in these trends, it was indirect. Other possible (and related) explanations include the increase in twenty-somethings in the general population, young people's increasing interest in more "altruistic" jobs, and the increase in schools' financial resources being targeted at younger students — such as investing in youth theology programs. G. Jeffrey MacDonald, "More Young Adults Going into Ministry," *USA Today* (August 9, 2010), http://usatoday30.usatoday.com/news/religion/2010-08-09-youngseminarians09_ST_N.htm (accessed August 30, 2013).

45. I am borrowing Greg Jones' use of "traditioning" as a verb. See L. Gregory Jones, "Traditioned Innovation," *Faith and Leadership* (January 20, 2009), http://www.faithandleadership.com/content/traditioned-innovation (accessed July 25, 2014).

gram director compared this gift to the pivot foot in basketball: the player plants one foot on the court so the other foot can turn, enabling her to see what's going on elsewhere on the court as she prepares to throw the ball.[46]

A traditioned imagination starts with a deep affection for the texts and traditions of Christian faith, an explicit aim of High School Theology Programs. Aware that formal theological education often asks students to deconstruct theological traditions that they understand only at very rudimentary levels, each HSTP starts by plunging teenagers into a thicket of formative texts and practices. Quality of instruction matters; teenagers notice (and comment on) the difference it makes to be guided by an adult who, in the words of one program director, "has more than a fourth grade theological education." Challenge also matters. During a focus group conducted by the Catholic Theological Union's Peacebuilding Initiative, one teenager pleaded: "Whatever you do, please don't give us the Fisher-Price version of theology."[47] She went on to explain that what excites teenagers about spending a week at the Peacebuilding Initiative is the chance to get "undiluted theology, theology rich and complex enough to be engaged on different levels allowing a bright young person to formulate ideas about God and the church."[48]

At the same time, the HSTPs' objective of holy wisdom directly confronts "schooling" models of theological formation, where intellectual mastery, critical deconstruction, and technical proficiency are the primary goods on display. A great deal of pedagogical emphasis in HSTPs is placed on dehabituating teenagers from their accustomed vocational mindsets by inviting them to sample a feast of spiritual practices, to meet people living lives of radical discipleship, and to reflect with adult leaders who help them imagine what such discipleship might look like for them. The strategy invites comparisons to the early catechumenate, as new catechumens were apprenticed to seasoned Christians for learning the life of faith. Not only do such apprenticeships expand adolescents' view of Christian faith; they expand the number of ways young people consider taking part in it.

3. *High School Theology Programs suggest new forms of theological education.*

As Masters of Divinity programs shrink and enrollment in formal programs of theological education declines, judicatories, seminaries, and oth-

46. Andrew Brubacher Kaethler, private conversation, High School Theology Seminar Writer's Retreat (August 30, 2013).

47. Cited by Lytch, "Summary Report I," p. 26.

48. Cited by Lytch, "Summary Report I," p. 26; see footnote 44.

ers concerned with preparing future church leaders are being forced to ask whether our dominant models of theological education are the most effective ones we have.[49] We can no longer assume that students attend seminary in order to prepare for callings they have already discerned. Increasingly, students come to seminary to *discern* a call to ministry, lacking other communities to either confirm or disconfirm a call to Christian leadership. HSTPs serve a crucial "research and development" role for theological education in this context, giving seminary students, faculty, youth ministers, and scholars new ways to think about the way we help young leaders respond to God's call to Christian service — and whether our task is primarily to imbue them with knowledge or ignite them with hope.

Vocational pedagogies help create leaders and communities with ecclesial agility: the ability to bend toward God in a rapidly changing church, the ability to help communities pivot quickly in shifting cultural sands. As HSTP faculty learn to teach teenagers through High School Theology Programs' broad teaching repertoires, their approach to teaching MDiv and MA students shifts as well. Meanwhile, the young adult staff of High School Theology Programs (frequently master's and PhD students in theology) test-drive their own emerging pedagogical identities, influencing the kind of classrooms they will one day create.

Calling All Cooks: This Book Is for You

As you can see, this book is of interest to youth workers, but they are not the ones most likely to be changed by its contents. We are confident that the practices discussed here will broaden youth leaders' own vocational pedagogies, and our hunch is that they need no convincing to experiment with the practices named here. As a species, youth leaders are less risk averse than professors; nor do they have the weight of academic tradition or assessment criteria to consider when they choose curriculum. In fact, I have yet to meet a group of youth leaders who cannot reel off the list of practices described in this book, with one exception, as what *they* would do had Lilly given *them* money to expand the vocational imaginations of the teenagers they know. (The one practice youth workers often miss, by the way, is "theological re-

49. Cf. Barbara Wheeler and Anthony T. Ruger, "Sobering Figures Point to Overall Enrollment Decline," *In Trust* (Spring 2013): 5-11, http://www.intrust.org/Portals/39/docs/IT413wheeler.pdf (accessed July 29, 2014).

flection," which as we shall see is HSTPs' stock-in-trade — and is profoundly appreciated by teenagers.)

Thus, in addition to creative youth workers, we hope courageous theological educators will also take up this book, sample the pedagogical feast these programs lay out, and let the practices and concepts described here transform their own thinking and teaching. Such transformation has already happened for many who have participated in the HSTPs as designated teachers. In chapter 12, Elizabeth Corrie argues that those most dramatically affected by HSTPs' vocational pedagogies are the young adult counselors who staff them. In chapter 13, Brent Strawn describes how seminary faculty who teach in these programs learn to experiment, adapt their teaching methods, and gain practice explaining theological concepts in terms that are connected to the world of adolescents — all of which inevitably transform the way they teach seminarians as well.

Finally, we hope those who care about the formation of the next generation of Christian leaders — judicatory leaders, seminary presidents and administrators, curriculum designers, nonprofit executives, public theologians, and congregational leaders — will pay attention to the discussion in the pages that follow. High School Theology Programs till the soil, not just for next-generation church leaders, but also for the next-generation *church*. The nature of that church depends largely on what its future leaders think communities that follow Jesus should look like. In a culture where the majority of North American young people give the church very little thought, those of us who care about the church's future should listen closely to the young people who do.

Taste Tests

High School Theology Programs emerged in response to inadequate systems of vocational formation in congregations and youth ministries, but they point to a larger issue facing the church. Namely, HSTPs reveal churches' tendency to underestimate the power of "communities of discernment" in spiritually interested teenagers' vocational trajectories — just as we underestimate their capacities as theological leaders generally. The truth is that teenagers are capable of far more disciplined theological reflection, far holier lives, and far more courageous leadership than most adults assume or practice.

That, of course, is the risk: forming young people into capable theologians and Christian leaders puts those of us already wearing those mantles

— who perhaps have grown sloppy or tired or cynical over the years — on notice. As Carol Lytch observed in the first review of HSTPs in 2006, "With knowledgeable theologians and exemplary pastors in their midst, youth [immersed in the study of Scripture and liturgy] ask difficult questions about the dissonance they live with as Christ-centered people in a humanistic, consumerist, and secular world."[50] For these young people, who have neither written off the church nor ruled out the possibility of divine guidance, figuring out how to be a church that authentically follows Jesus matters, to the point that many of them are willing to forego other professional opportunities to invest their lives doing exactly that.

Here is a map of the road ahead. Part One, "A More Excellent Way: Vocational Discernment as a Practice of Christian Community," suggests some of the implications of these pedagogical practices for theological education as a whole. Our basic thesis is that vocational discernment includes but cannot be reduced to helping teenagers "name their passions" or inventory their gifts to see which ones intersect with the world's groaning needs. Instead, "a more excellent way" — to paraphrase Paul — is to challenge teenagers to a complex, creative adventure that takes place when faith communities become ecologies of discernment, as churches receive and nourish teenagers' questions of identity and purpose.

Part Two, "More Than a Job Fair: Creating Cultures of Vocational Discernment," explores some of the anchor practices that prepare congregations to become cultures of vocational discernment. These practices — community formation, spiritual mentoring, the naming and receiving of gifts — cultivate "good soil" for teenagers to discover God's hope for the world and for them, and the gifts they have been given for contributing to a divine purpose. In chapter 3, Anabel Proffitt and Jacquie Church Young testify to the power of intentional Christian community to transform young people's lives, describing Christian community's "accelerator effect" in Christian formation. In chapter 4, Anne Streaty Wimberly describes spiritual companionship as a mutual process of doing theology, as holy conversation becomes a practice through which young people lay claim to both the Christian story and to their own stories as children of God.

Katherine Douglass and Christy Lang Hearlson, in chapters 5 and 6, look closely at congregations' practices of naming and receiving young people's gifts for ministry, before and after High School Theology Programs. Douglass reminds us that vocational formation in HSTPs starts before teenagers

50. Lytch, "Summary Report I," p. 10.

arrive, since they must be nominated by their pastor or another adult leader to attend. For many youth, this nomination is their first realization that others see in them the potential for spiritual leadership. Hearlson makes an equally powerful case for the influence of homecomings. Churches handle teenagers' homecomings from HSTPs in vastly different (and sometimes indifferent) ways. Hearlson insists on the teachable moment of return, as teenagers from High School Theology Programs (or any "away from home" form of youth ministry, for that matter) are recognized as bringing something special to their home faith communities from their pilgrimages, which in turn helps youth integrate a newfound sense of divine purpose into their daily lives.

Part Three, "More Than a Summer Camp: Adventures in Vocational Pedagogies," shows how young people are spurred toward vocational discernment through pedagogies of challenge and disruption, rather than by merely being safely entertained. Safety and trust are undeniably the preconditions for vocational exploration; growth happens when teenagers experience God's call as an adventure that takes them beyond their comfort zones. In chapter 7, Andrew Brubacher Kaethler describes how decentering pedagogies help youth unmask culturally bound, self-centered interpretations of Christian faith. Likewise, Jeff Kaster describes HSTPs' shared emphasis on theological reflection in chapter 8. Calling theological reflection the "fuel" for a long-term life of discipleship, Kaster argues that it is young people's communal, intellectual engagement with Scripture and doctrine — often overlooked by congregational youth ministries — that makes faith durable over the long haul.

Underscoring the importance of immersive practices, in chapter 9 Fred Edie describes young people's need to move from ideational faith to a more bodily, affective, and experiential form of Christian witness, especially through practices of worship that engage Christian tradition bodily, reflectively, and critically. David Horn takes up the other side of the equation in chapter 10. Noting that every High School Theology Program is a spiritual pilgrimage for young people (i.e., teenagers leave home and travel toward Christ on a common road with fellow pilgrims), he introduces one program that uses the practice of pilgrimage as an experiential way to understand the internal journey of faith. Experiential pedagogies are also the focus of chapter 11, as Judy Steers presents a theological case for playfulness, the arts, leadership and service as practices of vocational formation.

Finally, in Part Four, "More Than Teenagers: Vocational Discernment of Program Staff, Faculty, and Theological Institutions," we take a look at other populations who benefit from participating in High School Theology

Programs. Chapter 12 points to Elizabeth Corrie's research from the Youth Theology Initiative (the original High School Theology Program at Candler School of Theology), which reveals how profoundly young adult counselors' own callings, leadership styles, and understandings of ministry are shaped by participating in HSTPs. Corrie suggests that young adulthood may be a kind of "critical period" for forming Christian leaders as vocational discernment converges with other life course concerns. In chapter 13, Brent Strawn — speaking from his own experience as a professor in HSTPs — argues that these programs transform the pedagogies of seminary faculty as well, since teaching teenagers emboldens them try new methods that influence their seminary teaching as well. Finally, in chapter 14 we conclude by speculating on the kind of leadership — and the kind of church — that might ensue if theological education took its pedagogical cues from a bunch of teenagers trying to figure out how to participate in the mission of God.

Coming Out of Our Shells: Learning about Leadership from Lobsters

If playing Bach in the subway will not make us notice innovative genius happening right under our noses, let's try a different metaphor — lobsters.[51] Here is the gist: lobsters never stop growing. But because they are crustaceans, in order to keep growing, they must shed their shells from time to time. This is the most vulnerable point in a lobster's life — but since a too-tight shell impedes growth, if a lobster does not shed its shell sporadically, it will die. So every so often, a lobster ingests extra water to bloat itself and loosen its outer shell. Then it turns itself inside out, even pulling its giant claws back through tiny openings at the base of the claw casing, wriggling out of the shell it has outgrown. At one point in the process, it must pop its eyes out of their sockets to get free from the shell, rendering the lobster almost blind during the transformation process.[52] When the lobster finally extracts itself from the old shell, it is utterly soft and defenseless as it waits for the new shell to harden. If it is going to get eaten by a predator, now is the time that is most likely to happen.

51. It is no coincidence that I learned about lobsters from a book on ecclesiology. See Paul Sparks et al., *The New Parish: How Neighborhood Churches Are Transforming Mission, Discipleship, and Community* (Downers Grove, IL: InterVarsity, 2014).

52. Cf. Ivan Schwab, *Evolution's Witness: How Eyes Evolved* (New York: Oxford University Press, 2012), p. 59.

You can see why this story was told in a book on ecclesiology. Churches, denominations, and theological schools are in the process of shedding our shells, too. In many cases, we have become so bloated that our structures can no longer support us, and we can feel our shells loosening. Yet we are still mid-transformation, blind to what God has in store for us, uncertain about which direction to go, and we are going to be vulnerable and awkward for a while until our new forms firm up. But if we do not go through the process of shedding our too-tight structures, we will die.

Maybe God created crustaceans who do this by instinct because no explanation could convince a self-respecting lobster that extracting itself from its shell was either possible or wise — any more than any new birth seems possible or wise. Thank heavens we do not have to persuade a baby-in-utero that the journey down the birth canal is thinkable, or convince her as a dependent newborn that this vulnerability is the route to maturity. Such irrationality is what made the incarnation a stumbling block to many. A God who assumed human form, capable of being born and capable of dying, was impossible for the ancient world to imagine, and it certainly did not seem like a wise strategy for saving Israel from its enemies. Yet God's vulnerability in Jesus Christ is precisely what saved Israel, and us, from the enemy of death — and the church's current vulnerability may be precisely what God is using to save the church from dying as well. If the North American church is currently experiencing contractions, it is because every new birth requires it.

For those of us committed to forming a new generation of Christian leaders, this scenario means that theological educators and church leaders must not only teach vocational discernment; we must practice it ourselves. Theological education is changing too, and as we grow into our calling to form people who long to participate in God's transformation of the world, many of our structures are as bloated and blind and vulnerable as any molting lobster. One thing we can be sure of: we will not find our way alone. Like all Christian communities, theological education has a vocation as well. Part of our mission, whether we form people for ministry in formal or informal ways, includes discerning the ecologies that best prepare leaders for the church — not for the church we are, but for the church we are becoming.

Of course, no one (least of all young people) knows what that church will look like or the kind of leaders it will need a generation from now. This makes the quest for Christian vocation less of a holy obligation or an individual career decision than a grand adventure undertaken by God's people, a communal exploration that tests and recombines elements of a vocational journey until it begins to take shape. Multiple ingredients for vocational formation are laid before teenagers in High School Theology Programs, and each new practice expands the palette as new forms of faithfulness come into view. As Elizabeth Corrie, director of Candler's Youth Theology Initiative, put it: "Youth [in High School Theology Programs] get a foretaste of the Kingdom — and once you taste it, then you know what you're hungry for."[53] As we visit these programs in the chapters ahead, we will see how they help young people taste their possible futures as Christian leaders, and see that the Lord is good (Psalm 34:8).

53. Elizabeth Corrie, director, Youth Theology Initiative (Candler School of Theology), HSTP seminar discussion (August 22, 2013).

CHAPTER TWO

Calling as Creative Process

Wicked Questions for Theological Education

Kenda Creasy Dean and Christy Lang Hearlson

> *Some problems are so complex that you have to be highly educated and well-informed just to be undecided about them.*
>
> LAURENCE J. PETER

In 1909, *The Blacksmith's Journal,* the "official organ of the International Brotherhood of Blacksmiths and Helpers," urged every blacksmith to "usher in a new era" by securing at least one additional recruit for the blacksmith's union.[1] In successive months, the journal reported some success in this mission. Yet within a generation, the blacksmith's trade was defunct.

You know what happened. A year before the blacksmiths' membership appeal, Henry Ford began mass-producing Model Ts. By 1910, he was manufacturing a tractor most farmers could afford. It is not that North America did not need leaders and workers in the transportation industry; it was just that the transportation industry was changing, and those changes altered the kind of skills and knowledge the industry required. In fact, many blacksmiths became the world's first auto mechanics in order to stay in business.

It would do us good to step back for a moment and honestly ask, in our earnest attempts to inspire and prepare young Christian leaders: What

1. *The Blacksmith's Journal,* vol. 10 (March 1909): 11. The call was re-issued with biblical zeal the next October: "If every blacksmith would secure one new member to the fold during the coming year, what a mighty organization this would be. And yet we have a few members who secure from one to fifty. Go thou and do likewise" (vol. 10 [October 1909]: 18).

might happen if we succeeded? After all, while we are talking about vocational pedagogy, churches are closing daily, seminary graduates struggle to find placements, and youth ministries — which for a century provided a pipeline for future church members as well as leaders — are among the first ministries cut during periods of economic duress. When the church invests in leadership development initiatives like High School Theology Programs that prepare young people for church leadership, are we preparing for the future, or recruiting more blacksmiths?

Wicked Questions

It is a "wicked question" — a question embedded in a situation so complex that every answer begets another layer of complications. Clearly Christians must form new generations of leaders if churches are to be vital and relevant in coming decades. At the same time, *even if we succeed* in recruiting more young people for church leadership through initiatives like High School Theology Programs, it is unclear whether the solution to the church's shrinking leadership pool is to do more of what we already know, with more resources and tenacity, or to look toward alternative, untested paradigms of theological formation with equally iffy outcomes. Are enrollment and graduation statistics for formal theological education our best gauge for how well we prepare future church leaders? If not, then what is? That is a wicked question.

Wicked questions stem from *wicked problems,* a term used by social planners to describe inscrutable complexity. Addressing a wicked problem is like playing with liquid mercury: it is fascinating and maddening, because if you poke at it, the situation just shifts and takes on a new form. Wicked questions don't have yes-or-no answers, only better-or-worse ones (see Figure 2.1). They tend to crop up when an organization or society faces constant change or unprecedented challenges.[2] Wicked questions emerge out of long-term, socially complex, and fluid problems that require large numbers of people with conflicting interests to change in order to resolve matters. Often, the people trying to solve the problem are the people causing it.[3] When wicked problems overlap, creating a whole system of inter-

2. John C. Camillus, "Strategy as a Wicked Problem," *Harvard Business Review Magazine* (May 2008), http://hbr.org/2008/05/strategy-as-a-wicked-problem/ar/1 (accessed August 15, 2014).

3. Tom Ritchey, "Wicked Problems: Modeling Social Messes with Morphological

acting problems, organizational theorist Russell Ackoff calls the resulting tangle "a mess."[4] (You and I would probably call it that as well.)

How Do I Know It's a Wicked Problem? (John C. Camillus, 2008)
1. The problem involves many stakeholders with different values and priorities.
2. The roots of the issue are tangled and complex.
3. The problem is difficult to come to grips with, and it changes with every attempt to address it.
4. The challenge has no precedent.
5. There's nothing to indicate the right answer to the problem.

Figure 2.1 Situations distinguishing wicked problems from hard but ordinary problems.[5]

It seems obvious that disproportionate numbers of alumni of High School Theology Programs would be interested in formal theological education, when compared to youth who do not attend HSTPs. But these programs are doing more than boosting seminary enrollment. They are unearthing a "mess" in the church, a tangle of overlapping conundrums that affect how we prepare theological leaders "for such a time as this" (Esther 4:14), and who gravitate to ecclesial forms that are, perhaps, especially suited to those raised in an era of cultural flux. If HSTPs do not offer solutions to wicked problems, they at least model practices that help churches discern what their faith community's particular witness might look like in a world of ubiquitous change.

For this reason, High School Theology Programs may contribute as much to the conversation about twenty-first century ecclesiology as Christian leadership formation. The dilemma facing church leaders and theological educators is that *we do not know what kind of churches we are shaping leaders for* — and consequently, we are unsure about the kind of theological formation these leaders need. At a loss for alternatives, we are apt to train blacksmiths, passionately and well, throwing ourselves into this holy work with fervor and faith. It is no exaggeration to say that theological education

Analysis," *Acta Morphologica Generalis* 2 (2013), http://www.swemorph.com/pdf/wp.pdf (accessed August 15, 2014).

4. See Russell Ackoff, "Systems, Messes, and Interactive Planning," *Redesigning the Future* (New York/London: John Wiley and Sons, 1974).

5. See Camillus, "Strategy as a Wicked Problem." Most descriptions of wicked problems credit Horst W. J. Rittel and Melvin M. Webber's ten heuristic devices for distinguishing "wicked" from "tame" (hard but ordinary) problems. "Dilemmas in a General Theory of Planning," *Policy Sciences* 4 (1973): 155-69.

today is more theologically nuanced, more contextually competent, and more pedagogically excellent than it has ever been; we are training the best blacksmiths the church has ever known.

Unfortunately, that century is over.

Vocational Pedagogy in an Age of Flux

The data are both sobering and tantalizing. David Roozen, who chronicled changes in American congregations between 2000 and 2010, revealed a decade of "slow, overall erosion of the strength of America's congregations" marked by a steep loss of revenue, aging memberships, and high levels of conflict. The net result? Fewer people in the pews and a decline in spiritual vitality.[6] At the same time, Roozen saw "bursts of innovation and pockets of vitality" in the data, including evidence of:

- Increased use of innovative, adaptive worship
- Rapid adoption of electronic technologies
- A dramatic increase in racial/ethnic congregations (especially in immigrant communities)
- More member-oriented *and* mission-oriented programs
- More connections across faith traditions
- More evangelical churches offering voter education/registration (the opposite is true for mainlines)[7]

Of course, no "burst of innovation" happens in a vacuum. Like all institutions, churches scramble to adapt to the unprecedented pace of cultural change of the early twenty-first century. Ubiquitous connection, the eclipse of "place" by networks, the urgency of cities, the rise of "majority minorities," the postponement of marriage, economic liquidity, the primacy of self, assumed complexity, participatory and collaborative culture, the "rise of the nones" — all represent shifts in Western society's bedrock assumptions, and point to titanic changes underlying our "whole context of understand-

6. David Roozen, "A Decade of Change in American Congregations 2000-2010," white paper, Faith Communities Today Project, Hartford Seminary (Hartford, CT), 2010; http://faithcommunitiestoday.org/sites/faithcommunitiestoday.org/files/Decade%20of%20Change%20Final_0.pdf (accessed November 29, 2014).

7. Roozen, "A Decade of Change," p. 1.

ing, in which our moral, spiritual or religious experience and search takes place."[8] Philosopher Charles Taylor calls this context an "immanent frame," a change in Western civilization's epistemological circuitry that characterizes late twentieth/early twenty-first-century thought in which the transcendent is intuited by not acknowledged.[9]

The ecclesial question, then, is how is a particular community of Christians, rooted in a particular place at this particular moment in history, to convey Christ's love? This is the question taken up by all High School Theology Programs, which rely on practices very much like those used to cultivate pastoral excellence across faith traditions:

- Participation in a structured learning community of peers
- Embodiment of a life of faith in sustained ways
- Cultivation of imagination through border-crossing[10]

High School Theology Programs demonstrate the importance of these learning experiences in influencing teenagers' ecclesial imaginations. Teenagers participating in these peer-rich, embodied, border-crossing learning experiences come to think of themselves not only as individuals who reflect Christ's love in the world, but as shapers of communities that do the same — once again relocating vocational discernment beyond the realm of individual decision-making.

Getting Beyond Buechner: Calling as a Creative Process

Spiritual writer and pastor Frederick Buechner famously described vocation by saying, "The place God calls you to is the place where your deep gladness

8. Charles Taylor, *A Secular Age* (Cambridge, MA: Belknap Press, 2007), p. 19.

9. See Taylor, *A Secular Age*. This list is adapted from several sources; cf. Henry Jenkins, *Convergence Culture: Where Old and New Media Collide* (New York: New York University Press, 2006); Amy Sullivan et al., "Ten Ideas That Are Changing Your Life," *Time* (March 12, 2012), http://content.time.com/time/magazine/article/0,9171,2108054,00.html (accessed December 1, 2014); Andy Crouch, "The Ten Most Important Cultural Trends of the Last Decade," *QIdeas*, http://qideas.org/articles/ten-most-significant-cultural-trends-of-the-last-decade/ (accessed December 1, 2014).

10. These practices were deemed "unequivocally effective" in developing pastoral leadership across faith traditions. Holly G. Miller, "Sustaining Pastoral Excellence" (Indianapolis, IN: Lilly Endowment, May 2011), p. 18; http://www.cpx.cts.edu/docs/default-source/pen-documents/sustaining-pastoral-excellence-report.pdf?sfvrsn=0 (accessed August 22, 2014).

and the world's deep hunger meet."[11] Buechner's description is beautiful, evocative, and only partly true. His point is well taken that calling is not about self-abnegation. Vocation is not a reference to our day job, and does not celebrate misery ("the more miserable we are, the more faithful we are to God"). Yet, as Buechner hints, vocation is not just a matter of doing whatever we enjoy, either, as though the outcomes of doing what we enjoy have no consequence.

At the same time, Buechner offers a subjective and individualistic definition of vocation. He neglects to say that whole communities can have a calling, just as he overlooks the role communities play in helping individuals find and follow their Christian vocation. As we have noted above, High School Theology Programs are prime examples of the complexity of vocation and vocational discernment as a practice, which is more complex, more socially situated, more layered and more multivalent than is often assumed. In short, vocational discernment for North American young people is a wicked problem.

High School Theology Programs approach vocational discernment as a more creative process than a mere mapping exercise in which we attempt to pinpoint where "the world's deep hunger" and our "deep gladness" intersect. Mihaly Csikszentmihalyi describes creativity as a "systemic rather than an individual phenomenon."[12] Noting that we usually think of creativity as "some sort of mental activity, an insight that occurs inside the heads of some special people," Csikszentmihalyi instead proposes that creativity happens "in the interaction between a person's thoughts and a sociocultural context." For Csikszentmihalyi, creativity — which he defines as "a process by which a symbolic domain in the culture is changed"[13] — is the result of three elements that interact as a system: "a *culture* that contains symbolic rules [what he also calls a domain], a *person* who brings novelty into the symbolic domain, and a *field of experts* who recognize and validate the innovation."[14]

A systems view of creativity — like a systems view of vocation — means that understanding creativity cannot be reduced to studying "the individuals who seem most responsible for a novel idea or a new thing. Their contribution, while necessary and important, is only a link in a chain, a phase in

11. Frederick Buechner, *Wishful Thinking: A Theological ABC* (New York: Harper and Row, 1973), p. 95.

12. Mihaly Csikszentmihalyi, *Creativity: Flow and the Psychology of Discovery and Invention* (San Francisco: HarperCollins, 2009), p. 23.

13. Csikszentmihalyi, *Creativity,* p. 8.

14. Csikszentmihalyi, *Creativity,* p. 6.

a process."[15] By way of illustration, Csikszentmihalyi suggests an image of combustibility: "To say that the theory of relativity was created by Einstein is like saying that it is the spark that is responsible for the fire. The spark is necessary, but without air and tinder there would be no flame."[16]

Like creativity and fire, vocation can also be seen as a series of combustible variables that help the church as a whole *hear* Christ's call to discipleship in real life and concrete situations, *consider and engage in* faithful ways of being and acting that answer that call in concrete situations, and *reflect* together on that action, as well as how the church might faithfully act in the future.[17] In this sense, vocation does not belong to or happen inside of individuals, nor is it a static object to be discovered, decided upon, and owned. Vocation and vocational practices reflect an unfolding dialogue among the Spirit of God, the Christian community, the individual, and, importantly, the cultural setting or society where individuals live. Vocational discernment participates in the process by which all of these elements combine to ignite the world's transformation through the Spirit of Christ.

Context and Vocation: Wicked Problem or Creative Necessity?

Given the ways churches struggle to address the cultural upheavals of our time, context is often seen as a vocational problem. The nature of the church, and the kind of theological formation needed to shape those who serve it, is a perpetual conundrum for church leaders who recognize the complexity of what Csikszentmihalyi calls "the cultural domain," and the importance of the church's ability to speak into it.

When vocation is a creative process, on the other hand — a process of mutual ignition between multiple domains — context becomes a creative necessity, not a wicked problem to be solved. Csikszentmihalyi views the cultural domain as a necessary element for realizing creative (or in our case, vocational) potential. Without the specific needs, social attitudes, and exigencies dictated by context, an innovation can fall flat or be ignored, like Leonardo da Vinci's flying machines that were conceived at a time when people had no imagination for (or need or desire for) flying humans. Like-

15. Csikszentmihalyi, *Creativity*, p. 7.

16. Csikszentmihalyi, *Creativity*, p. 7.

17. Practical theologians will hear in these moments echoes of the process of practical theological reflection. Cf. Richard R. Osmer, *Practical Theology: An Introduction* (Grand Rapids: Eerdmans, 2008).

wise, for vocation to be vocation, the culture in which it unfolds must both need and recognize the gifts that a certain calling offers.

This is not just a pragmatic concession. It is a deeply incarnational conviction, since God's love must always be enfleshed in the cultural settings where it is received. Each culture and each age has its own concerns, achievements, and moral failings; each culture and age hears the good news in distinct ways. This means that *vocation* is never something whose content is predetermined. The content that shapes our response to God's call are the *actual circumstances* facing the world at that time.

Understanding vocational formation as a series of overlapping, mutually activating systems reframes the way churches view our cultural context. Instead of the culture in which we live being a sticky wicket to overcome, postmodern complexity becomes a constitutive feature of vocation itself. Instead of the secular age being an evil force dissuading future leaders from ministry, it serves as the social domain that makes these leaders' innovations possible and meaningful. Unless we take seriously young people's social, political, economic, and physical contexts as places that give vocation its meaning and purpose, vocation remains an individual decision rather than the result of the Holy Spirit's presence in overlapping systems of human community. Christian vocation is not just the *fact* of being called; it is also the *content* of our response to Christ's call — content that makes sense only insofar as it addresses real life and real lives.

Christian Community and Vocation: Fields of Validation

Csikszentmihalyi describes a *field* as all the individuals who act as gatekeepers to the domain: "It is their job to decide whether a new idea or product should be included in the domain."[18] Lest we think a field could only be comprised of people with official, institutional authority, Csikszentmihalyi reminds us that fields "vary greatly in terms of how specialized versus how inclusive they are." Some fields, for example, are "as broad as society itself."[19] Take Coca-Cola:

> It took the entire population of the United States to decide whether the recipe for new Coke was an innovation worth keeping. On the other hand, it has been said that only four or five people in the world initially

18. Csikszentmihalyi, *Creativity,* p. 28.
19. Csikszentmihalyi, *Creativity,* p. 43.

> understood Einstein's theory of relativity, but their opinion had enough weight to make his name a household word. But even in Einstein's case, the broader society had a voice in deciding that his work deserved a central place in our culture.[20]

Let's assume the innovation is not new Coke, but Christian vocation: Who are the gatekeepers that allow a vocational vision to go forward; who validates it? How do we know whether young people's decisions about the church's mission align with God's? Of course, the most important validator of a vocational vision comes from the Holy Spirit, but the Spirit awakens and validates these visions in different ways. Some people experience validation of their sense of calling through inward, subjective experiences like prayer or through Scripture reading; others through works of mercy and advocacy; others through inspired human communities that notice, name, and affirm their gifts for Christian leadership and service.

The "official" church's validation of a young person's call, therefore, is only part of the story. After all, one of the primary differences between episcopal (Roman Catholic, Anglican, and Episcopal), connectional (Methodist), congregational (Baptist and Congregational), and presbyterian (Reformed and Presbyterian) polities lies in who exactly has the official power to validate vocation, especially for those called to church leadership or service. High School Theology Programs recognize that vocational validation never ends with official denominational or church leaders. As any pastor will tell you, congregations can implicitly accept or reject a leader's authority, enhancing or undermining that leader's calling in the community.[21] Furthermore, vocational validation (or invalidation) happens outside of religious settings as well. If a church's ministry regularly appears meaningless, boring, or banal to its neighbors, vocation is hardly happening since our call to love God and neighbor fully is not recognizable.

Regardless of the polity of the sponsoring theological tradition, every High School Theology Program acts as a proactive validating field for every teenager's vocation of discipleship, which has the effect of stimulating his or her ministry in more specific ways. As Csikszentmihalyi points out, fields are not neutral; they actively affect the rate of creativity by being

20. Csikszentmihalyi, *Creativity,* p. 43.

21. Pastors, for example, often recount tales of unofficial congregational authorities — choir members, ushers, big donors — who exercise maddening power in validating or invalidating a leader's ministry.

"either reactive or proactive. A reactive field does not solicit or stimulate novelty, while a proactive field does."[22] Csikszentmihalyi uses the patronage system in Florence during the Renaissance, and North American attempts to interest young people in science through science competitions, to illustrate proactive fields — but he could easily have used a High School Theology Program. As chapters 5 and 6 on the power of nominating and homecoming practices suggest, HSTPs serve as proactive fields that ignite a sense of sacred calling among teenagers and, often, in the churches that send them.

Individuals and Vocation: Cultivating Attention

By describing vocational discernment as a social practice, High School Theology Programs model ways to resist individualistic understandings of Christian vocation that reduce it to either following our bliss, or that abstract it from its social context. Still, the individual does play a part in a systemic understanding of vocation. As Csikszentmihalyi says of creativity: "While the individual is not as important as it is commonly supposed neither is it true that novelty could come about without the contribution of individuals."[23]

Csikszentmihalyi names a number of predispositions that make creativity more likely in some people than others (e.g., curiosity, wonder, early interest in the cultural domain, access to a validating field). Young people attending HSTPs often share similar characteristics: they have expressed early interest in theological thinking and Christian leadership, they are drawn to HSTPs partly out of a sense of curiosity and wonder, and they have access to both domains and fields associated with Christian leadership.[24]

This last point is critically important. Vocational discernment requires teenagers to "internalize the entire system" that makes vocation possible, which takes time, intentionality, and attention on the part of the teenager.[25] HSTPs set aside time for busy young people to focus their attention on vocation, while immersing them in practices that help them lead a community's participation in God's redemptive work in the world. Some practices

22. Csikszentmihalyi, *Creativity,* p. 43.
23. Csikszentmihalyi, *Creativity,* p. 47.
24. Csikszentmihalyi, *Creativity,* pp. 52–54.
25. Csikszentmihalyi, *Creativity,* p. 51.

introduce youth to *domains* (cultural contexts) of ministry: working with homeless people; visiting neighborhoods in crisis; learning about hunger, racism, and poverty; confronting consumerism; going on pilgrimages. Some practices introduce them to *fields* that validate Christian vocation: academic theology, church leadership, congregational life. Many HSTPs help youth strategize about how to ensure that their ideas are accepted and carried forward in the field of their home congregation. All approach vocation as a creative, constructive pursuit.

Images of Vocation as Christian Leadership in High School Theology Programs

The Lilly Endowment's unabashed emphasis on interpreting vocation in terms of Christian *leadership* gives the domains and fields of High School Theology Programs a distinctive, and somewhat counterintuitive, thrust. After all, Jesus did not cultivate leaders; he cultivated followers. Every program director is quick to point out that HSTPs understand Christian leadership to mean serving Christ in myriad forms, and many downplay the language of "Christian leadership" in favor of the more theological (and more general) term "vocation" to describe the aims of their curriculum.

Still, there is no getting around the fact that congregations, campus ministries, colleges, and seminaries find it increasingly difficult to attract, develop, and retain a large pool of talented young people for congregational ministries. The so-called "leadership vacuum" facing North American congregations is dire, and the demonstrable likelihood that High School Theology alumni will at least consider formal theological training makes it impossible to avoid viewing these programs as feeder systems for congregational leadership. Given this cultural domain, every student who attends a HSTP must grapple with the tension between Christ's call to follow him, and the church's need for people who will lead.

The term "leadership" is therefore often used and seldom defined by High School Theology Programs. Like the field of leadership studies itself, HSTPs reflect a familiar pendulum swing in the way Christian leadership is understood. At one end of the spectrum are (dominant but declining) views in which leadership is a person-centered, mostly unidirectional, sometimes heroic quality possessed by individuals.[26] This view risks making leadership

26. This perspective is represented by books like Scott Allison and George Goethals,

a utilitarian practice in which leaders inspire, influence, and sometimes control followers in order to accomplish certain ends.

In reaction to this first body of literature are studies on followership, also important to Christian discussions of leadership-as-discipleship. This perspective was memorably illustrated in Derek Sivers' three-minute 2010 TED talk, "How to Start a Movement" — aka, "Leadership Lessons from the Shirtless Dancing Guy."[27] Narrating a video taken at the 2009 Sasquatch Festival of a dancing young man who inexplicably moves hundreds of others to join in, Sivers argues that a movement cannot become a movement unless a leader — "a lone nut" — attracts a first follower. Like Sivers, followership literature emphasizes the reciprocal relationship between leaders and followers and credits followers for determining who the leaders are, making leadership less of an individual quality than a socially constructed role that responds to specific exigencies.[28]

Theologians are divided in the ways they think about leadership and about whether they think Jesus was any good at it.[29] Whether Jesus was a "lone nut" followed by others, or the Creator God's first follower who inspired others to do the same, is an open (and largely irrelevant) debate in a culture where church leaders often refine their craft by eavesdropping on business, not theology. Manuals like Laurie Beth Jones' *Jesus, Entrepreneur* and Michael Youssef's *The Leadership Style of Jesus* turn "What Would Jesus Do?" into pastoral training, and popular business books (think: "The Good to Great Pastor," "7 Habits of Highly Effective Preachers," "BlueOceanFaith .org") are quickly adapted for clergy.[30]

Heroic Leadership: An Influence Taxonomy of 100 Exceptional Individuals (New York: Routledge, 2013).

27. Derek Sivers, "How to Start a Movement," http://www.ted.com/talks/derek_sivers_how_to_start_a_movement?language=en (accessed October 2, 2014).

28. Space does not permit an extensive review of this literature here; one summary of these poles is found in Wendelin Küpers, "Integrating Leadership and Followership in Organizations," *International Journal of Leadership Studies* 2 (2007): 194-221 (Küpers argues for a view of leadership that emerges in the mutually influential interaction between leaders and followers).

29. A classic formulation of the failure of Jesus comes from Albert Schweitzer, *The Quest for the Historical Jesus* (London: Adam and Charles Black, Pub., 1911); the question of the failure of Jesus is reframed more recently by N. T. Wright, "The Historical Jesus and Christian Theology," *Sewanee Theological Review* 39 (1996), http://ntwrightpage.com/Wright_Historical_Jesus.htm (accessed October 1, 2014).

30. Interview with Jim Collins, "The Good to Great Pastor," *Leadership Journal* (Spring 2006), http://www.christianitytoday.com/le/2006/spring/7.48.html; Thom Ranier, "7

Given many large churches' corporate structures and the growing necessity to find new avenues of funding for ministry even in small congregations, there is plenty the church can learn from business literature, but High School Theology Programs take a decidedly different approach. They view leadership, above all, as a calling inspired by God's overabundant grace, especially the gift of Jesus Christ. Each program seeks to affirm young peoples' primary vocation: following Christ and participating in God's redemption of the world as Christ's witnesses. Only in light of this primary vocation does a teenager's secondary calling make sense, as she begins to recognize that God may use her particular gifts and desires to move beyond her own personal witness to further the witness of the church.[31]

As a result, three images of Christian leadership explicitly or implicitly wend their way through High School Theology Programs: *servant, witness,* and *steward.* These images are not exclusively Christian (leadership gurus Robert Greenleaf, Steven Covey, and Peter Block have all built empires around variations on these themes), but they are nonetheless deeply embedded in the texts and traditions of Christian faith. In High School Theology Programs, these images take on various hues depending on the theological tradition of the host program. Yet together they form a layered understanding of Christian leadership that defies easy categories of "leaders" and "followers." If leadership is the capacity to "get things done," we might say that High School Theology Programs form young people who place themselves at the Holy Spirit's disposal and thereby allow God to "get things done" through them, especially by mobilizing communities that bear witness to God's inbreaking grace in human culture.

Habits of Highly Effective Preachers," *ChurchLeaders,* http://www.churchleaders.com/pastors/pastor-articles/173956-thom-rainer-habits-of-highly-effective-preachers.html; www.blueoceanfaith.org (all accessed October 2, 2014).

31. Asked about his goals for the program, the program director at St. Meinrad's put it this way: "[The aim of the program] is simple and it's straightforward: that [youth] would go home and not only have the confidence to carry out liturgical tasks, but that they would consider themselves leaders in their high schools, parishes, dioceses, whatever situation they are in — they would see themselves as leaders. So, moving them beyond somewhat active participation into full conscious and active participation . . . in a way that helps others do that. I think most of our adult participants would tell you that that's why they bring their kids here. They encounter something that becomes contagious."

IMAGE OF LEADERSHIP	Theological backdrop often invoked	Formative practices often emphasized	Virtues of leadership often celebrated
Servant	Theologies of kenosis *(e.g., John Wesley, Henri Nouwen, Sarah Coakley)*	Silence Friendship Discipleship	Humility Empathy Compassion
Witness	Theologies of reconciliation *(e.g., Karl Barth, Howard Thurman, Desmond Tutu)*	Justice Confession and Forgiveness Community	Vision Courage Gratitude
Steward	Theologies of gifts *(e.g., Gregory of Nazianzus, Jean Luc Marion, Catherine Mowry LaCugna)*	Worship Relationship Eucharist	Encouragement Joy Freedom

Figure 2.2 Images of Leadership in High School Theology Programs

The Leader as Servant

The image of Jesus washing the feet of his disciples is the most iconic portrait of leadership in Christian Scripture. The life of true spiritual leadership, Henri Nouwen reminds us, is one in which "power is constantly abandoned in favor of love."[32] High School Theology Programs go to great lengths to counter power-driven visions of North American leadership by immersing teenagers in service opportunities in which students learn from, and not merely encounter, those different from them. In these contexts, service emerges from friendship and kinship — the common ground between self and other that acknowledges our status as children of God. Imitating Christ, therefore, reveals the nature of divine power as demonstrated by Jesus: the suffering servant, God's self-emptying, or *kenosis:*

> Let the same mind be in you that was in Christ Jesus,
> who though he was in the form of God,
> did not regard equality with God as something to be exploited,
> but emptied himself, taking the form of a slave,
> being born in human likeness, and being found in human form,

32. Henri Nouwen, *In the Name of Jesus* (New York: Crossroad Publishing, 1989), p. 63.

he humbled himself, and became obedient to the point of death —
even death on a cross. (Phil. 2:5-11)

This self-emptying — this divine act of friendship to human beings, this humility that makes room for the Holy Spirit to make us over in Christ's image — is the condition for leadership marked by empathy and compassion. From sharing breakfast with homeless people to talking with people from other religious traditions, High School Theology Programs cultivate kenotic opportunities that decenter young people from their accustomed notions of self and others, opening them to a notion of leadership (and a notion of God) that inverts conventional understandings of power and control.

The Leader as Witness

William Willimon describes "a young country pastor" named Karl Barth as someone who preaches "as if he has just invented fire, and week after week never fails to be shocked that this God is with us, *this* God is with us."[33] Barth himself remembered (with no trace of regret) that his hearers, the farmers and factory workers who made up his congregation at Safenwil, were mostly befuddled or bored ("If I wanted to be liked," Barth said in one sermon, "I would keep quiet").[34] For Barth, leading a congregation from the pulpit meant pointing to God — and only God — revealed in Jesus Christ, who unmasks all human pretense and reunites us with our Creator and with one another. "In Jesus Christ," wrote Barth, "there is no isolation from man to God or of God from man."[35] If others know this already, Barth believed, then it is the Christian's job to strengthen them in this knowledge. If they do not know it, "our business is to transmit this knowledge to [them]."[36]

The image of the leader as witness pervades High School Theology Programs with a similar fervor, where teenagers are encouraged to bear witness to Christ in and beyond the walls of the church, in word and in deed. HSTPs especially stress the importance of naming the discrepancies between the Reign of God as revealed in Jesus Christ and dehumanizing practices in the dominant

33. William Willimon, introduction, *The Early Preaching of Karl Barth: Fourteen Sermons with Commentary* (Louisville, KY: Westminster John Knox Press, 2009), p. xvii.

34. Willimon, *Early Preaching of Karl Barth,* pp. xvii, xiv.

35. Karl Barth, *The Humanity of God* (Louisville, KY: Westminster John Knox, 1996), p. 46.

36. Barth, *Humanity of God,* p. 53.

culture, what we might call prophetic truth telling. Truth telling is not only the task of those exercising Christian leadership, of course; Ronald Heifetz argues that "someone exercising leadership is probably generating *dis*equilibrium":

> Either [the person exercising leadership] is raising issues or asking questions that disturb people and force people to come to terms with points of view or problems that they would rather not consider; or he's protecting other people in the organization who are creating disequilibrium.[37]

High School Theology Programs do not just help youth to identify places of injustice and suffering in the world; they also help students see their own culpability in dehumanization, heightening the importance of practices like confession and forgiveness in HSTP communities themselves. These practices strengthen the community's fabric in ways that interpret individual, cultural, and theological differences as gifts rather than weaknesses. Like the church, HSTP communities *themselves* are viewed as witnesses "before the watching world," whose corporate life is intended to reflect Jesus Christ, and thereby proclaim alternative ways of relating amidst competing cultural norms.[38] This embodied witness is the common calling of all Christians, who "do not come in our own name, but in the name of the Lord Jesus who sent us."[39] The explicit horizon for human community guiding teenagers in HSTPs is the Reign of God, an eschatological vision that emboldens them to reflect God's reign with courage and gratitude.

The Leader as Steward

Perhaps the most intriguing image of leadership in High School Theology Programs is the leader who stewards gifts for the good of all — God-given gifts like forests and sleep and violin-playing, as well as human offerings of money and time.[40] Organizational consultant Peter Block distinguishes

37. Ronald Heifetz, in Tom Richman, "Leadership Expert Ron Heifetz," *Inc.* (October 1, 1988), http://www.inc.com/magazine/19881001/5990.html (accessed October 3, 2014).

38. See John Howard Yoder, *Body Politics: Five Practices of the Christian Community before the Watching World* (Harrisonburg, VA: Herald Press, 2001).

39. Nouwen, *In the Name of Jesus,* p. 41.

40. For an excellent pneumatological discussion about spiritual gifts and vocation in young people, see David White, *Dreamcare: A Theology of Youth, Spirit and Vocation* (Eugene, OR: Cascade, 2013), especially pp. 54-67.

stewardship and leadership by maintaining that leadership controls and centralizes power, whereas "stewardship can be most simply viewed as giving order to the dispersion of power" as a way to use power through the practice of partnership and empowerment.[41] High School Theology Program leaders share Block's conviction that stewardship involves giving away power — but they also reject his distinction between stewardship and leadership. In fact, as we have already noted, Christian theology maintains that relinquishing power is a *sign* of leadership that imitates Christ.

Since leaders name, develop, and deploy a community's gifts for the benefit of all, exercising stewardship is deeply connected to "a theology of gifts" — a theological theme that runs deep in the veins of every HSTP we studied. These programs are shot through with generous assumptions about teenagers' capacities for theological leadership. The importance of stewarding "gifts" reflects Paul's insistence that each gift is a "grace given to us" so the community may flourish (Rom. 12:6b). At the same time, Paul ups the ante, promising "a still more excellent way" to employ and deploy God-given gifts — out of love (1 Cor. 12:31). In this way, writes Joel White, Paul offers a definitive statement of what it means to be a leader:

> "Think of us in this way, as servants of Christ and stewards of God's mysteries" (1 Cor. 4:1). . . . Paul uses two words in this verse to elaborate what he means. The first, *hyperetes* ("servants"), denotes . . . a servant who waits on or assists someone. In this sense, a leader attends personally to the needs of the people he or she leads. The leader is not exalted, but humbled, by accepting leadership. . . . The second is *oikonomos* ("stewards"), which describes a servant or a slave who manages the affairs of a household or estate. The chief distinction in this position is that the steward is trusted. The steward is trusted to manage the affairs of the household for the benefit of the owner. Likewise, the leader is trusted to manage the group for the benefit of all its members, rather than the leader's personal benefit.[42]

White notes that the image of a steward entrusted with managing a household's resources is explicitly ascribed to Jesus, as well as to other leaders in

41. Peter Block, *Stewardship: Choosing Service Over Self-Interest,* 2nd ed. (San Francisco: Berrett-Koehler, 2013), pp. 16, 61.

42. Joel White, "1 Corinthians and Work," *Theology of Work Project* (December 16, 2011), http://www.theologyofwork.org/new-testament/1-corinthians/#leadership-as-service-1-cor-41-4 (accessed October 2, 2014).

the early church.[43] In this view of leadership, patriarchy gives way to partnership and self-interest gives way to stewardship — images that recall the patterns of discipleship ascribed to the saints of the early church, and to the example of Jesus himself.[44]

From Influence to Discernment: Experiencing Costly Leadership

What these images of leadership have in common — *servant, witness, steward* — is costliness: in each case, the leader consciously chooses to relinquish influence rather than seek it, to honor others' gifts, and to point to God's power instead of one's own. The kenotic overtones of these images depart noticeably from dominant North American images of leadership. Servants, witnesses, and stewards suggest that the task of Christian leadership has more to do with *discernment* than over *influence.* Instead of prodding communities into predetermined shapes, servants, witnesses, and stewards help faith communities discern and undertake practices that enact their missional identities. Discipleship formation becomes less something that church leaders do *to* parishioners than a mutual process in which leaders and parishioners alike help each other conform to the image of God in Jesus Christ.

Costly images of leadership call into question one of American teenagers' most cherished assumptions — namely, that the central goal of life is to be happy and feel good about ourselves.[45] Servants, witnesses, and stewards risk on behalf of others; they embody self-giving rather than self-serving values, cultivating virtues like humility, courage, and compassion that im-

43. Cf. 2 Tim. 2:3; Heb. 2:17; 1 Tim. 1:12; 2 Cor. 4:17; Eph. 6:21; Col. 4:7; and Rev. 2:13.

44. Peter Block explores these shifts explicitly in his book *Stewardship.* One congregation we learned about in Indianapolis turned a food pantry on its head when volunteers began asking clients, "What are you good at?" — and found ways for those receiving food to exercise their gifts on behalf of the congregation and the community. See Mike Mathers, "Adelita's Gift: The Value of Asking the Right Questions," *Abundant Community* http://www.abundantcommunity.com/home/stories/parms/1/story/20120314_adelitas_gift_the_value_of_asking_the_right_questions.html (accessed October 3, 2014).

45. The National Study of Youth and Religion observes Americans' tendency to see religion as useful for obtaining happiness. The dominant religious worldview described in the study (dubbed "Moralistic Therapeutic Deism") includes the belief that "the central goal of life is to be happy and feel good about myself." The specific phrase "feel happy" appeared more than two thousand times in the interview transcripts (of 3300 interviews). See Christian Smith with Melinda Lundquist Denton, *Soul Searching: The Religious and Spiritual Lives of American Teenagers* (New York: Oxford University Press, 2005), p. 168.

bue human relationships with meaning and significance. The connection between meaning and sacrifice has recurring significance for teenagers who take faith seriously. Sociologist Carol Lytch, for example, found that youth "choose church" when a faith community gives them significant experiences of competence, belonging, and meaning-making.[46] A 2013 study conducted by Stephen Cady, a member of our research team, discovered that churchgoing teenagers' (overwhelmingly) negative attitudes toward worship were significantly tied to their perception that worship

> does not carry significance; it is trivial, inconsequential, and largely meaningless. At the end of the day, it is not clear to the young people who attend the worship services, nor, it seems, to their parents, why worship matters.[47]

Cady concluded that young people failed to find worship meaningful because it lacked "magnitude," the significance that arises from anticipating an encounter with God.[48]

If, as Cady believes, churches falter when it comes to offering youth experiences of magnitude, HSTPs do not.[49] From beginning to end, teenagers in High School Theology Programs are immersed in practices that are explicitly tied to an expectation of divine encounter — and in fact, tied to a hunch that God has *already* encountered them with a call to Christian leadership. This nascent sense of call is what binds youth in HSTPs together; probing this sense of vocation is why they have come. In the context of these programs, youth frequently mentioned experiences of *liminality, competence, deep belonging,* and *holy struggle* as having special significance in this regard. Echoing the findings of Smith, Lytch, Cady, and others who argue that young people require a faith that has "weight," teenagers associated these experiences with God's encounter, and the vocational practices that contributed to these experiences as clarifying for their personal sense of call. Moreover, youth frequently contrasted these faith-intensifying experiences with "back

46. See Carol Lytch, *Choosing Church: What Makes a Difference for Teens* (Louisville, KY: Westminster John Knox, 2003).

47. Stephen Cady, "Creative Encounters: Toward a Theology of Magnitude for Worship with United Methodist Youth," unpublished dissertation (Princeton, NJ: Princeton Theological Seminary, 2014), pp. 1-2.

48. Cady, "Creative Encounters," p. 49.

49. Thanks to Duke Youth Academy alumnus Brian Tanck for making this connection for me.

home" youth ministries, where experiences of liminality, competence, deep belonging, and holy struggle were infrequent, and teenagers' anticipation of divine encounter was low.

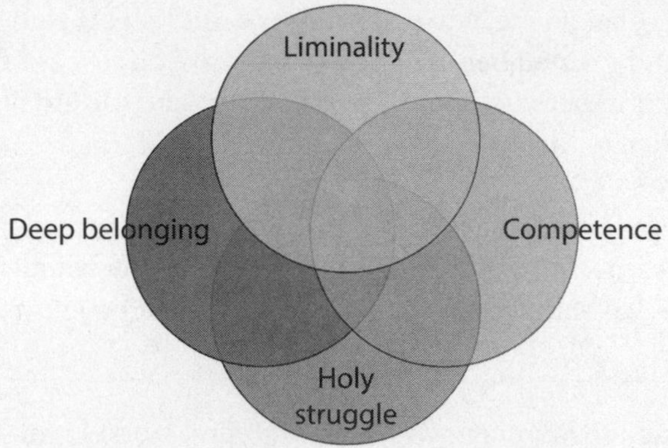

Figure 2.3 Experiences of Magnitude in High School Theology Programs

Experiences of Liminality

In some ways, every High School Theology Program functions as a pilgrimage: students leave home and head toward a holy destination, hoping to be transformed. By definition, this process of separation and reintegration becomes a liminal rite of passage, as teenagers come to think of themselves as the executors of their own spiritual estates. Dangling in between the familiar world of home and the uncertain terrain of the future, students in High School Theology Programs (as in all rites of passage) are "betwixt and between," suspended between expectations of old roles and anticipations of new commitments that await.

Liminality creates vulnerability, a risky posture for teenagers because it renders most of their accustomed defense mechanisms inoperable. Many programs intentionally intensify this defenselessness. Sixteen-year-old Jay reflected on the wilderness portion of Gordon-Conwell's Compass program:

> I definitely feel like [it was important] not being in my room at home with the different distractions. . . . Here I go outside and it's just me and God. And so I think that helps me — it makes it a more of a special time.

Even in programs where students do not literally embark on pilgrimages, liminal experiences are prominent. The arts, structured encounters with unfamiliar "others," and acts of play all place young people in existential spaces where they must, to some degree, lose themselves in the moment as they dangle "betwixt and between" their former assumptions and future selves. In music, dance, drama, film, and visual art, students find themselves in a mode of discourse that opens them to the numinous, apprehended and expressed through movement, color, sound, texture, or form. Structured encounters with "otherness" — divine or human — decenter young people from familiar assumptions as they are thrust, momentarily, into the sacred space of the "other": a conversation with homeless people, a visit to a mosque, an experience with solitude. Adrian, also from Gordon-Conwell's Compass program, reflected on the liminality of his solo day in the wilderness:

> You know, practicing solitude [lets you see] what it looks like to actually have time to listen to your own thoughts and take them to the Lord, and of course to try to listen for Him. . . . I think prayer and solitude — and just learning to be still, and to perhaps read and kind of hear God's word through reading — is kind of the practice of the wilderness.

Sometimes "holy others" had holy orders. Monks provided an endless source of fascination for students in the two programs associated with monasteries. The monks served as bridge figures, surprisingly in touch with "real life" while maintaining a sacred "set apartness" that seemed light years away from teenagers' daily lives. Sixteen-year-old Holly compared the monks at St. Meinrad's One Bread, One Body program with her "scary" youth minister at home:

> They're really interesting. When you first get here you think that they're just fat bald guys, that all they do is pray and stuff, but really they have this sense of . . . this spark in them. . . . They all have this personality that just — they're like a friend that you can always talk to. It's not scary. My youth minister is scary. He's always serious. He has God on his side as well, but he doesn't pray five times a day or do the other stuff that the monks do. The monks have a sense of peace and holiness.

Suspended between two different possibilities — the way of life of home and school, and new vocational possibilities revealed by their experience in a High School Theology Program — teenagers in High School Theology

Programs find themselves vulnerable and open to new possibilities, to others, and to God.

Experiences of Competence

Across the board, the students we interviewed were brought up short by their programs' confidence in them as leaders and "scholars."[50] Again and again teenagers told us how honored they felt to be engaged in serious reflection on theological texts and traditions, to be taught by "real" seminary professors during their classes, to be treated as capable theologians in their own right. Nicholas, an eighteen-year-old at Hellenic College/Holy Cross Greek Orthodox School of Theology's CrossRoad program, noted: "I've been to other camps and Sunday School . . . there's some theology but there's mostly community and stuff, and it's good, but [at CrossRoad] it totally focuses on theology. I feel like I'm learning a lot more here." Kate, a sixteen-year-old we met at the Lutheran School of Theology in Chicago, reflected: "I loved who I was when I was at Youth in Mission. I was honored by being taught by real professors. I wanted to be able to ask all my questions — that was taboo in my church." Catherine, a seventeen-year-old at Candler's Youth Theology Initiative, described her surprise at a professor's openness to teenagers' questions:

> The first day we walked into class and see this teeny tiny man, and he said: "You're big boys and girls now, and we expect you to be ready, and we expect you to talk about what's important to you. We're not going to poo poo you because you're seventeen. We're going to talk about serious questions, so go for it." It was the first time that I'd heard someone inside the church say, "Yeah, faithful people have questions and they're hard questions and we're going to talk about that for as long as you'd like."

Sixteen-year-old Tom explained the joy of "doing hard things" in Gordon-Conwell's Compass program:

> Everyone had four books to read. . . . Reading Christian books . . . not always my favorite thing to do. But I have never been more inspired or more

50. This is the classic formulation of Erik H. Erikson's "adult guarantor," a necessary bridge figure in the adolescent quest for identity. Cf. James Loder's discussion of this concept in Erikson in *The Logic of the Spirit* (San Francisco: Jossey-Bass, 1998), pp. 227-28.

> excited than I have been reading those books. To be able to read about God for four hours straight, I've never had that, and these books that they chose are definitely a reflection of what this program wants to teach us.

Brian, a seventeen-year-old from Calvin Theological Seminary's Facing Your Future program, concurred:

> I can honestly say, I've learned a lot more than I have ever learned. I love having conversations and discussions about Scripture. Someone else could think something completely different. You can really start to understand it better, I think. Never really done that a lot, because my youth group is more about everybody having fun. Maybe small lessons where you learn something about the Bible but you don't really have discussions. I swear I don't remember what I learned last week.

As Brian's comments demonstrate (and as we noted in chapter 1), many congregational youth ministries do not include deep intellectual engagement of theological texts as part of their programs. Yet for spiritually curious youth, the presence of challenging theological conversation in HSTPs is a clear draw. Every adult working with a High School Theology Program is of one mind on this point: teenagers are far more capable, and far better theologians, than we expect them to be. As a result, each program turns to its own teenage participants for leadership, enlisting them as community leaders, worship leaders, theologians, ministers. In theologian Howard Thurman's words, these programs "place a crown" over young people's heads that, for the rest of their lives, they "will keep trying to grow tall enough to wear."[51] This sacred coronation begins by helping teenagers discover and use their gifts for the common good of the church, starting with the High School Theology Program itself.

Experiences of Deep Belonging

As we will see in chapter 3, intentional Christian community authenticates and accelerates every other faith practice in High School Theology Programs. HSTP leaders spend a great deal of pedagogical energy developing

51. Howard Thurman, *Jesus and the Disinherited* (Boston: Beacon Press, reprint ed., 1996), p. 106.

communities of practice that shape the identities of the teenagers who belong to them. Belonging to these communities is not the same as attending them; belonging is membership's more costly cousin. Belonging implies mutual, willing vulnerability.

Of course, it seldom seems this way at first. Seventeen-year-old Deedee described her experience of the community at Candler's Youth Theological Initiative:

> Our community, it is the corniest thing ever, but once you experience it, honest to God, it's [beyond words]. You know that, "Okay, we're supposed to be one big family," but on the first day it's just all types of awkward. . . . We're all very different people, and you don't really know how it works, but [suddenly] it does. You just grow so close and you're talking and you're sharing, and now when you don't have small group time we're all like, "Wait, what? What in the world? We don't have small group time?"

Being close to one another or talking seriously about theological questions does not necessarily make a community "Christian." HSTP directors recognize the temptation to believe that, if theology is discussed, Christian community magically follows, or that if warm relationships emerge, theological discussion will ensue. Embedding theological formation in a *Christian* community, as opposed to a cozy one, is an ongoing challenge, and the teenagers we talked to struggled with what to call the "X factor" that set HSTP communities apart. Violet, Deedee's seventeen-year-old friend at YTI, attributed it to many people working for the common good:

> Volunteering at MedShare, that was just so impactful, because we come from different places, and we were helping ship supplies and medical needs to people who are from different countries. I see how small, how tiny we are, and how we're contributing in a big way, and it was just — I mean, we packaged something like 5000-something pounds, 492 boxes! It was such a big movement, and I felt like a community.

Grace, a program participant from the Lutheran Theological Seminary at Gettysburg/Philadelphia, ascribed the profound sense of community to what was missing:

> The best feeling I can think of is that this is a place that has [an absence of] shame. . . . Even if I were to say something and I didn't finish it completely,

> just by the connections that we develop, we fill in the blank. I think that is really special and I can't say that I have that connection with many other people. It is an awesome connection. It is the strongest of all of them.

But most teenagers saw an important role for faith practices that linked connecting with God to connecting with peers. At St. Meinrad's, sixteen-year-old Helen called worship the source of her community's Christian identity:

> It's amazing! So, you walk in as a community: you are one. You are one together. You share . . . like we come in we get the holy water . . . and we share it. We pick it up and we share it with the other person. So you come in as a community and you share together. The cool thing is, as you come in, you sing. You sit in the monk stalls. It's like a unique opportunity. . . . And you sit and sing together, and you pray. When the time comes, you walk down (when you're ready). You pray to the Lord to help you confess all of your sins, to confess everything you cannot share with anyone else. You can share with these monks. You're basically putting your life in their hands. . . . You get to share everything, and it's honestly one of the most amazing experiences I've ever had.

Of course, these explanations only partly account for intentionally cultivated Christian communities' distinctive power. Countless secular organizations amass large groups to alleviate hunger without becoming churches; group therapy offers safe havens that are not sanctuaries; and many worship services go through their liturgical paces without cultivating "amazing experiences" of community. Given the emphasis on theology in these programs, it was somewhat striking that few young people explicitly named God's presence in their HSTP community as a constitutive, formative variable.

Today we understand the nuances of social pedagogies, the critical importance of adult mentors in the learning process, and how to leverage what Lev Vygotsky called "zones of proximal development" that transform social modeling into internalized learning.[52] Adolescents in particular

52. Cf. Lev Vygotsky, *Mind and Society* (Cambridge, MA: Harvard University Press, 1980), pp. 85-86. Vygotsky writes of the zone of proximal development, "It is the distance between the actual developmental level as determined by independent problem solving and the level of potential development as determined through problem solving under adult guidance or in collaboration with more capable peers." He continues, "The zone of proximal development defines those functions that have not yet matured but are in the process of

follow footprints better than blueprints; discipleship, which in Christian tradition means the art of following Christ by shadowing Christ's followers — is the church's most powerful tool for communicating divine love across generations. In following Jesus, we participate in costly love; and in following those who deny themselves to follow Christ — people who surrender their lives for his sake (Mark 8:35), who lay down their lives for their friends (John 15:13) — we claim our identity in a community of costly love, where we can risk for one another only because Christ, in our midst, already has.

Experiences of Holy Struggle

Mike's journey from disorientation to transformation is a common story among HSTP participants. The seventeen-year-old from Hellenic's Cross-Road program recalled his reaction at learning he had to "unplug" to participate:

> I was terrified . . . they were like, you can't bring your cell phone; we're going to take everything from you. You can't have your iPod . . . you'll barely call your parents, you won't talk to your friends, and I was like, "That's terrible." My friends [said], "It sounds like prison camp" *(laughs)*. It just sounds horrible but when you first experience it, you experience the community and the purity of appreciating the services. I came home and I just wanted to go right back. So yeah. [Sacrificing technology] makes you feel closer and, and to feel that again you go to church more often. It's just a really cool experience.

Meaning making is forged in holy struggle. Sharon Daloz Parks maintains that the test of an adequate system of meaning — a "trustworthy truth" on which to set one's heart — is to ask, "What does your chosen god do in the face of being totally overcome — what does it do in the face of shipwreck?"[53] Is there a pattern of meaning, a faith that can survive the defeat of finite centers of power, value, and affection? An ideology devoted to a person, a

---

maturation, functions that will mature tomorrow but are currently in an embryonic state" (p. 86).

53. Sharon Daloz Parks, *Big Questions, Worthy Dreams* (San Francisco: Jossey-Bass, 2000), pp. 5, 22-24.

single cause, or an aspiration is too small to function as God. If the person dies, if the cause is defeated, if an injury forecloses on the hoped-for athletic career, do self, world, and God collapse? Can we endure hardship without collapsing beneath its weight, and at the same time reach beyond human pain toward a source of hope and redemption?[54]

Out of such struggle comes our best chance at making sense of the world. Jacob receives a new name and identity after he wrestles with the divine messenger: he is now one who has tangled with angels and prevailed (Gen. 32:22-31). Teenagers in High School Theology Programs also frequently connect their sense of identity and purpose to struggle. When teenagers navigate disruption — from bullying to divorce, from immigration to illness, from a parent's incarceration to a family member's death — they begin to ask: Do my struggles have a purpose? Is my pain meaningless? If God loves me, then why is my life so hard?

These are not only existential questions; they are *vocational* questions, as theologian James Loder points out. Loder argues that questions of meaning ("Why am I?") go hand in hand with questions of identity ("Who am I?"); the latter cannot be addressed apart from the former. Our sense of being is tied closely to our sense of purpose; young people who lack a sense of existential purpose struggle with self-understanding as well. For Loder, the primary question that haunts human beings, starting with the onset of formal operational thought during adolescence, is "What is a life, and why do I live it?"[55] Vocational identity proceeds from this point.

HSTPs all use meaningful struggles — "disorienting dilemmas," as educator Jack Mezirow calls them[56] — as learning tools that require young people to dismantle and reassemble prior conceptions of self, along with prior understandings of Christian faith and calling. Sometimes programs drew from the natural disruptions teenagers experience in the course of growing up; often programs created small decentering experiences to loosen prior assumptions and open teenagers to new possibilities; and of course, the very newness of the HSTP experience itself operates as a kind of "meta" disorienting dilemma. To the person, HSTP leaders are deeply convinced of the educational value of dehabituation when balanced by a safe community

54. For an extended discussion of Parks' notion of weaving a canopy of significance, see K. C. Dean, *Practicing Passion: Youth and the Quest for a Passionate Church* (Grand Rapids: Eerdmans, 2004), pp. 110-12.

55. Loder, *Logic of the Spirit,* pp. 3-16.

56. Cf. Jack Mezirow, *Transformative Dimensions of Adult Learning* (San Francisco: Jossey-Bass, 1991), p. 177.

of belonging. They work hard to help teenagers frame their moral questions as forms of theological inquiry, giving them a language capable of critiquing the dominant cultural scripts guiding their lives.[57]

As teenagers encounter new theological perspectives, accept challenging responsibilities, and meet people whose views and life circumstances differ vastly from their own, a reckoning must take place, with themselves and with God. Such reckonings can be deeply uncomfortable, so programs also strive to create safe zones, supportive structures, and healing rituals. Some young people said they worked out their discomfort through prayer or worship (our research team heard a lot about incense and bells); others found meaning in deep conversations about Scripture with mentors and peers. Youth like sixteen-year-old Olivia found the hunger banquet at St. John's Youth in Theology and Ministry program to be an important source of meaning:

> Everyone knows there are starving people everywhere. But it didn't really hit me until the images were just engraved in my mind. There's a point where the people hosting the hunger banquet were giving us facts about how a child dies every three or four seconds. So then, [the program director] told us just to reflect and to be silent. And for a whole minute, every three seconds he would say "death," every time a child life was lost. So that really impacted me a lot.

Without a safe community in which to experience disorientation, these experiences are simply struggles; holy struggle is made possible by "safe spaces" where teenagers can risk coming undone. Yet in a context marked by both support and challenge, young people find it possible to explore difficult subjects — and participate in difficult practices — that ask more of them than they thought they had to offer. Teenagers emerge from such experiences emboldened for ministry, more confident of their God-given agency in the church and broader culture.

57. The meaning-laden experiences cultivated by these programs reflect common theological tensions in American religious life. For example, does seeing the world differently cause people to act differently, or does behaving differently cause people to see the world differently? Does changing what we love alter our behavior, or vice versa? Is living in a community that acknowledges human value the same as living together as the body of Christ? Do practices of deconstruction make people more loving or clever? Is God a "trump card" for Christians to play when we oppose the views of the dominant culture?

Beyond the Tongs and Anvil

In some ways, the pedagogical approach utilized by High School Theology Programs echoes experiences that we associate with apprenticeship learning. Blacksmiths are still formed through communities of practice; experiences of liminality, competence, belonging, and struggle are part and parcel of receiving a tradition from a community that hands down its practices in person more than in print. If the wicked questions facing theological education force us to look beyond *how many* young people we are forming for ministry to *the ways* in which young people are formed for ministry, High School Theology Programs are instructive. If Charles Taylor is correct that the very conditions that once made faith a natural response to the human experience have changed to the point that faith becomes a nearly unthinkable way to respond to human experience,[58] then providing space for young people to grapple with alternative paradigms for thinking about the world in ways that make room for God is itself a kind of leadership formation, whether young leaders take those alternative paradigms into the pulpit, the boardroom, or the family.

Theologically, of course, the future of the church depends on Jesus Christ, not on the leaders we recruit for the twenty-first century church. The opportunities to bear witness to Christ are so varied and the need to bring life into the world's dead places is so profound that it seems obvious that we should invite as many young people into ministry as possible, no matter what happens to "church jobs" as we know them. At the same time, creating more young leaders, even young clergy, should not be viewed as a rescue operation for churches gasping for air. The truth is that many of the churches we are preparing young people to lead will not exist in a decade, making it a mistake to adopt High School Theology Programs — or any of their doppelgängers — as defensive strategies aimed at saving seminaries from economic ruin or churches from slow asphyxiation.

Vocational pedagogies do not simply form people to lead congregations; they form people who bear Christ's image in the world and who shape communities that do the same. The question is whether those of us who are theological educators and church leaders have enough eschatology in our bones to trust that, even if seminary enrollments plummet, even if available ministry positions dwindle, even if churches change in ways we cannot yet imagine, Christ will *still* be made known, because even "the very stones will cry out" (Hab. 2:11).

58. See Charles Taylor, *A Secular Age* (Cambridge, MA: Belknap Press, 2007).

High School Theology Programs routinely operate with this level of hope. Teenagers who attend HSTPs are not particularly worried about the shape the contemporary church is in. They're not terribly concerned with preserving or reforming it. They do not share adults' anxieties about the church's future. Their questions are in the moment and personal: *Does the church have room for someone like me? What would it look like for me to serve God with my life? Is there room for my gifts in the communities I know? Can I make a difference through the church, or should I work for Kiva or Tom's Shoes or start a non-profit instead? Will being a priest make me dance? Would being a youth pastor yield a meaningful life? Can I help bend the world toward God by healing the sick as a nurse or a dad or an engineer? Is it possible that the gifts that I have and the hopes that I harbor coincide with the world that God has in mind?*

HSTPs tend to foster broad, inclusive, and flexible ecclesiologies that do not solely rely on credentialed or even named leaders. Youth experiment with — and often are beneficiaries of — fluid roles demarcated more by gifts than by status, age, or ordination. In this context, leaders serve, bear witness, and steward as well as influence. As theological educators lament the murkiness of ministry in a changing church, High School Theology Programs view this ambiguity as an opportunity, allowing teenagers to reinterpret Christian witness for their moment in history. In so doing, they reinterpret the church. In the next few chapters, we will glimpse how.

PART TWO

More Than a Job Fair

Creating Cultures of Vocational Discernment

When the Lord wants to give us a mission, wants to give us a task, . . . He prepares us to do it well. . . . What is important is the whole journey by which we arrive at the mission the Lord entrusts to us. . . . [W]hen the Lord gives a mission, He always has us enter into a process, a process of purification, a process of discernment, a process of obedience, a process of prayer.

POPE FRANCIS, *Vatican Radio* (June 13, 2014)

CHAPTER THREE

Catalyzing Community

Forming the Community as Catechist

Anabel Proffitt and Jacquie Church Young

Grace arrived at a summer leadership academy not sure what to expect. Though she came to us with wounds from her past, she had gifts in abundance. She also seemed torn between the desire to fit in and be accepted by her surrounding culture — a culture that is often individualistic, materialistic, and narcissistic — and her growing recognition that she was a unique individual whose very giftedness set her apart. She quickly found that our community celebrated her gifts. Early in our time together, Grace surprised herself and the entire group by volunteering to preach a sermon. In it, she testified about what it means to feel renewed by God's grace, and she boldly addressed some of the issues and challenges facing young people today, including cutting, depression, and chronic anxiety. Listen to her honest, insightful words:

> I have spent enough hours in silence and meditation to know my relationship with God very well, and it has changed over time. Dare I say, through my hard struggles with anxiety and depression, through my past with self-harm and toxic friendships, and through each moment of pain, it has been renewed? It seems like a radical idea that all of that was part of my renewal — to me at least. Renewal is about resting and recharging, right? It is, but it's more than that. Jesus says that he will give rest to the weary and heavy-laden, but he doesn't mention what it takes to get those weary followers to him. He doesn't have to because it doesn't matter. He doesn't care what kind of burden and suffering has brought you to him, since what matters is that you're there. All the hurt that breaks you down

> and brings you to your knees leaves you in a great place to start praying. Renewal is the gentle hand that picks you up at your lowest and pours the Holy Spirit into you, filling you with God's grace and making you new in the best of ways. That is a definition I can stand by.

Grace's powerful words struck a chord with her peers. After she preached, students stood in line to talk to her about her story and to share in her pain and joy, and then to share their own stories with her. They spent the evening conversing about grace and renewal in Christ, and about the trust and courage required to share our faith and stories. Together, they wondered how they might do this back in their own churches and schools.

What kind of community opens up space for a young person to speak with this level of honesty about her own suffering and the role of faith in transforming it? What kind of community allows other youth to receive and connect to such a story? How do we nurture young people's gifts, help them interpret their experience in the context of the Christian story of God's radical grace in Jesus Christ, and encourage them to testify to that experience?

The High School Theology Programs have taught us that effective formation of young Christian leaders immerses them experientially within the story and vision of the Christian community. In our experience, it takes an "incarnational" community to nurture the gifts of young people like Grace and to help them to share their unique gifts with the world — a community that invites young people to live within and powerfully enact the vision and story of Christian faith. In many ways, community in the HSTPs operates less as a pedagogy than as a learning "accelerator," providing the nourishing matrix in which every other Christian practice becomes meaningful, and therefore formative and revelatory, as young people come to recognize these practices as means of grace that open them to one another and to Christ. In this chapter, we assert that Christian community can serve as a catalyst — perhaps even a catechist — for faith formation by incarnating the gospel in the lives of young people.

It is not enough to simply teach about Christian community, because Christian community must be lived out experientially. It must be incarnated. In order to do this, a community must: (1) root itself in the theological claim that community is a reality created by God in Christ, (2) view truth and learning in incarnational, relational terms, (3) engage in ritual practices that live out community as a gift of God, and (4) commit to collegial forms of learning and develop mechanisms for nurturing leaders who have arisen from the community, who can embody all of these practices for the next group of participants.

Be Who You Already Are in Christ: Christian Community as Created by God

One of the challenges to authentic sharing in Christian community is the consumer-capitalist view of life, an upward climb toward power and economic attainment. Our progress in this way of life is marked by ever-increasing adherence to a normative (and expensive) lifestyle. To make progress, we learn to choose the right clothes, drink the right energy drink, drive the right car, impress the right people, attract the right mate (or playmate), and create envy among our peers. Informed by a democratic spirit, this vision claims that anyone can get ahead, but at the same time it creates a society in which some get ahead, while others are left behind to serve the more successful. Even those who do get ahead are never allowed to feel that they have arrived. Nothing is ever enough. Unable to achieve the airbrushed perfection we have come to identify with the happy life, we cannot allow ourselves to admit failings, depend openly on others, or rest.

The schools our young people attend are set up on similar models of success. Students — at least those in contexts stable enough to look ahead — are encouraged to study hard, ace the tests, and get ahead in order to attend the selective college of their choice. In more affluent communities, young people's schedules are packed with activities — many of which cost a great deal of money — that will look good on their college applications, though they often miss time with families as a result. Individual young people who do not fit the desired mold because of their look, learning style, gender identity, or lack of financial and personal resources are left behind, while whole communities of youth in poor neighborhoods may despair when they realize that the touted lifestyle is forever evading their grasp.

Underlying this cultural ethos, educator William Myers wrote, is a view of community as a pyramid, one that requires a ladder of success. In his book *Theological Themes of Youth Ministry,* Myers noted that Christian community offers a more excellent way: community as a circle. The parameters of the community we create, said Myers, should be determined by the vision of the circle of *koinonia,* rather than the pyramid of success.[1] In this circle, everyone has a place at the table that Christ has set, and we discover that we are implicated in each other's lives. The circle model honors the practice of

1. William Myers, *Theological Themes of Youth Ministry* (New York: Pilgrim, 1987), pp. 5-7.

hearing one another into speech, rather than seeking to get ahead through competition and one-upmanship. It is a circle of hospitality.

Such hospitality, theologian Dietrich Bonhoeffer once wrote, does not arise out of our own efforts, but out of God's gracious action in Jesus Christ. In *Life Together,* Bonhoeffer explains that Christian community is not an *ideal* that we must work to realize. Rather, it is *a reality created by God in Christ in which we may participate.*[2] Because community is a reality already created by Christ, we do not need to be ideal people before we can be in community, nor are we permitted to demand that others fit our ideal — or that which our culture labels as ideal — before we enter into relationship with them. Rather, in Christian community, we set others free to be what they are *in Christ,* and we honor "the true image they bear as Christ's own." In Christian community, our relationships are not about gaining control or demanding achievement: "Because Christ has long since acted decisively for my brother *(sic)* before I could begin to act, I must leave him his freedom to be Christ's; I must meet him only as the person that he already is in Christ's eyes."[3]

The encounter with a Christian community that lived out this conviction set Grace free to share her deep and tender testimony with her peers. Her experience of being met as the person that she already was in Christ's eyes gave her the courage to speak her truth for the first time to others. While her home faith community had taught her the concept that Christ had acted for her, Grace experienced this truth incarnated in her youth theology program. She was then able to extend God's grace to her peers, meeting them also only as the people that they already were in Christ's eyes. This is the sort of relationship that springs from real, lived, incarnational community.

All of the High School Theology Programs testify to the power of community to transform lives. Recognizing that young people's lives "are ruled and ordered by 'law,'" in the words of one program director, many youth name their experience in these programs as their first real experience of grace and mercy, how the HSTP community lives (in community), works (in accountability), and plays (in radical inclusion and affirmation). In all learning environments characterized by relationships of forgiveness and acceptance, students thrive in both the discovery of their own deeper selves, and their relationship to God. One youth commented, "I found a place where I was heard, where I was seen, and where all my kooky weird stuff was not

2. Dietrich Bonhoeffer, *Life Together* (London: SCM, 1960), p. 20.

3. Bonhoeffer, *Life Together,* p. 92.

only accepted, but welcomed, encouraged and loved." Another young person commented, "The best feeling I can think of is that this is a place that has no shame and you don't have to be ashamed to say anything," while yet another confessed, "I feel like [the leaders] create a safe environment for us, and that we can open our minds up to anything and they are not going to laugh at something." These testimonies are clear. Christian tradition is not a set of dead doctrines, but rather the taproot of incarnational, grace-saturated communities of authenticity. Teenagers need such communities in order to bloom into who they already are in Christ, and it is urgent that we make space for such communities to grow.

Living the Truth Together: Christian Community and Relational Truth

Approaching Christian community as a circle allows room for significant, holistic pedagogies to develop. Hearkening back to the Reformation catechisms, Protestants tend to think of catechesis as a cognitive exercise, as learners are asked to understand, accept, or memorize a body of knowledge that a group of churches have labeled the *truth* about God or the world. While the High School Theology Programs — as every chapter in this book attests — encourage deep intellectual engagement of theology as a "non-negotiable" component in adolescent faith formation, identifying intellectual knowledge too closely with "truth" misses a central implication of the incarnation: namely, that the truth of God is a *person* with whom we have *relationship* (John 14:6). In *To Know as We Are Known,* educator Parker Palmer writes, "In Christian tradition, truth is not a concept that works, but an incarnation that lives."[4] This theological conviction about living truth, Palmer notes, has implications for our view of reality in general: "Truth is not a statement about reality [out there] but a living relationship between ourselves and the world."[5] Even more radically, he claims, "Truth is between us."[6] In other words, for Christians, relationality is at the heart of the search for truth. We cannot exempt ourselves from implication in one another's lives. In the words of Archbishop Desmond Tutu, we live in the reality of

4. Parker Palmer, *To Know as We Are Known: A Spirituality of Education* (San Francisco: HarperCollins, 1993), p. 14.

5. Palmer, *To Know as We Are Known,* p. 35.

6. Palmer, *To Know as We Are Known,* p. 55.

ubuntu: "My humanity is caught up, is inextricably bound up, in yours."[7] I am, because you are. To live in this reality is to live in truth.

If truth is at its core relational, then the search for truth must take place within relationships in which young people come to see the world through others' eyes, and support each other's expanding horizons. In an incarnational community, learners become accountable for one another's learning. Palmer expresses such accountability in terms of obedience. Obedience, he elaborates, "does not mean slavish, mechanical adherence to whatever one hears; it means making a personal response that acknowledges that *one is in troth* with the speaker and with the words he or she speaks." Palmer develops this image in terms of betrothal — in Old English, the act of pledging one's *troth* (faithfulness or truth) to another: "To know in truth is to become betrothed, to *engage the known with one's whole self,* an engagement one enters with attentiveness, care and goodwill."[8]

This kind of "betrothed" learning requires young people to submit to others' needs, but it also returns them to themselves with greater insight. As one male student noted, "You've got to stop thinking of self, and you've got to start thinking of others, and I feel as if now I've become more aware of others, and that's actually helped me to become more aware of myself." This young man went on to say how participating in an HSTP helped him appreciate the importance of accountability as a sign of "the beloved community."

Accountability in the Christian life can be quite demanding of youth who want to fit in and enjoy peaceful relationships. As one teenager remembered about his HSTP experience: "The hardest part was holding each other accountable. The moment someone saw one person not doing what they were supposed to do, we didn't want to go tell the mentors what they were doing." Fear of being a "snitch" made it difficult to confront behavior that was counterproductive to their community. Yet one of the important lessons many youth learn is that healthy conflict or honest confrontation can nurture life-giving community. As this young man learned, holding each other accountable to the norms they had established together strengthened individuals and the whole community.

"Betrothed" and pledged to one another in this way, teenagers in HSTPs openly aim to live incarnationally. As they do so, the programs become spaces where young people speak honestly about their suffering and their

7. Desmond Tutu, *No Future without Forgiveness: A Personal Overview of South Africa's Truth and Reconciliation Commission* (New York: Doubleday, 1999), p. 31.

8. Palmer, *To Know as We Are Known,* p. 31.

faith, and respond to one another in kind. Unlike communities in which truth is viewed only as a body of knowledge that youth must master or consume — where teenagers' understanding of themselves and their world is of secondary importance to intellectual apprehension — the embodied truth of incarnational communities offer youth a view of reality as integrated whole, demanding their participation and not merely their assent. In the absence of such mutual, accountable relationships, learners are less likely to drop their self-protective armor and share their inmost thoughts and feelings, and they are less inclined to listen attentively to the struggles of others. When learning is embedded in a relational matrix of faithful accountability to the image of Christ, the community itself becomes a catechist, opening youth to learning experiences that reveal Christ's grace and mercy and that catalyze deep searching, honest sharing, and personal transformation. Immersed in a community of betrothal, teenagers "try out" the person God has already made them to be.

Catalytic Structures: Ritual Practices that Live Out Community as a Gift of God

Christian community does not happen in the abstract. It is always made up of concrete relationships, particular contexts, and specific practices that enact grace and mercy in our life together, including worship, prayer, confession, communion, work, study, and play. In contrast to youth groups or church education programs where young people interact with peers and adults for an hour or two at a time, the HSTPs have the advantage of sustained collegial contact. Living together for a prolonged period or maintaining contact with one another throughout the year alongside mentors and congregation members creates the possibility for more three-dimensional relationships, as youth have time to become "real" with one another without defaulting to the social roles they are accustomed to playing in school or church.

High School Theology Programs take full advantage of this sustained contact. They employ a number of "catalytic structures" that pave the way for transformation by embedding these practices in significant relationships of vulnerability, challenge, and care. Among the countless ways HSTPs intentionally form such relationships among teenagers, three catalytic structures are prominent in every program: small covenant groups, collegial learning cohorts, and peer and adult mentoring.

Covenant Groups: Going Deep Together

One of the concrete practices many of these programs share is the formation of covenant groups — small groups bound by formal or informal, mutually agreed upon practices of faithfulness and care. In such groups, young people have opportunities to engage in deep conversations and to get to know a few people well.

Covenant groups are critical to the building of community. In several HSTPs, each time covenant groups gather, youth spend time talking about their experiences of the day, debriefing concerns, and telling stories of their lives. Some programs choose to focus these covenant group times around a single question per meeting — what one program refers to as "candle questions." After the initial business of the gathering, a group leader lights a candle and asks a question based on the group's experiences that day, explaining that the lighting of the candle both welcomes Christ into their midst, establishes the setting as sacred ground, and casts teenagers' perception of their conversation as sacred speech. As the program director notes, "Each voice is held as equally important in the covenant group, and we make it clear that we value their thoughts and ideas." After everyone has had a chance to answer the candle question, the group time ends with prayer.

The questions these groups discuss are intentionally wide-ranging, designed to elicit self-discovery and vocational curiosity, as well as to allow space for the basic conversations that accompany community life. Typical conversations might range from gifts that youth bring to their community, the ways Christ's presence has been discerned during the day, questions about theodicy or how youth are called to respond to the needs of others — as well as "How do I put up with my roommate?" and "How do I worship with people who believe such vastly different things?" All covenant groups work to preserve high levels of trust among participants, and a certain openness to the direction of conversation. While probe questions are often determined beforehand, the discussions they generate are not. There is no canned curriculum handed down from a denominational office or independent publisher. Instead, questions emerge from the life of the group as young people respond to the day by exploring hopes and dreams, questions about faith and God's action in the world, and vexing problems about the human condition that have surfaced through program activities.

Conversation practices that create safe space for vulnerability, and that give youth a sense of God's presence in relationships, have a "legitimizing effect" on other aspects of the program curriculum. One young person explained it this way:

> Once you feel more comfortable with yourself, you become more comfortable with others and you can interact more truly and more maturely. I've had these thoughts before, but I realize them on a much deeper and higher level than before because I'm like legit living in intentional community, and I've never really [had] this kind of experience.

Another teenager noted that her covenant group helped her to "build up relationships, develop trust, and look for Christ in each other." The trust engendered by covenant groups spills over into other forms of learning by setting a collegial tone that invites learners to risk their ideas in the educational arena. As one youth explained, building relationships in covenant group gives teenagers the confidence to "bounce ideas off each other in a bigger discussion." Smiling, she added: "We're all lame and we all just kind of [act] lame together, so it's okay to be weird."

Collegial Learning Practices: I Respect You

Christian communities that take their cues from a theology of the incarnation value how Christ is already at work in each learner. Because we are a circle and not a pyramid, and because we trust that truth emerges between us, a spirit of respect and collegiality is paramount. This spirit begins in taking young people's capacities seriously; they are not offered a "theology lite" curriculum, but are asked to wrestle with material used in college and master's level classrooms and are taught by professors and experts in their fields. Further, adults and youth are expected to show mutual respect for one another. In effect, everyone becomes a teacher and a learner, fellow travelers on the way to more faithful discipleship.

An incarnational theology of learning-in-community dovetails with what theorist Dwayne Huebner identifies as an "ethical value framework,"[9] in which education is viewed as *encounter between persons*.[10] Curriculum de-

9. Dwayne Huebner, "Curricular Language and Classroom Meanings," in *Curriculum Theorizing: The Reconceptualists*, ed. William Pinar, (San Pablo, CA: McCutcheon, 1975), p. 223.

10. Huebner, "Curricular Language," p. 227.

signed in the ethical value framework introduces students to subject matter not only as "bodies of principles, concepts, generalizations, and syntax to be learned," but as "patterned forms of response-in-the-world, which carry with them the possibilities of the emergence of novelty and newness." Such an approach helps learners "find new ways to partake of the world, and [they] become more aware of what [they] can become and what [human beings] can become."[11] This, in turn, "increases their response-ability in the world and thus aids in the creation and re-creation of the world."[12] But, Huebner notes, such an effect only occurs when educators themselves recognize that they "participate in a human situation of *mutual influence,*" and when they "accept their ability to promise and to forgive."[13]

In classrooms and facilitated learning activities, HSTPs encourage educators to self-reflectively treat their students as co-learners, a practice that teenagers soon adopt for themselves. Youth repeatedly comment with surprise and appreciation at being shown respect in these settings. Being asked their opinions, being treated with dignity, being appreciated for their intellectual and theological competence, being challenged to lead in various ways and not only to "receive" the benefits their program offers — all of this bolsters confidence, invites questions that might otherwise have been swallowed, and allows space for half-formed ideas to be articulated on the way to deeper understanding. One youth commented, "They make us feel very welcomed. We can ask any questions that we want, because they're willing to answer it in their way. And [it's] not just that they're willing to *answer* it. They want *our* opinion on it, too." This student also appreciated the way adult teachers asked him clarifying questions and invited his own responses and opinions. Rather than shutting learners down, he appreciated teachers who responded with comments like, "Yeah, I understand where you're coming from."

One group interview conducted by our research team centered on teenagers' appreciation for the respect adults showed them in their High School Theology Programs. One young woman reflected, "Sometimes when you're in your teens, I feel like you're in between the kid and the adult and you're not really sure where you fit. Some people still treat you like a kid, but *here* we're like full-on adults. They bring that out of you, bring the adult out of you. They make you think." Another participant agreed, grateful for the

11. Huebner, "Curricular Language," p. 231.

12. Huebner, "Curricular Language," p. 231.

13. Huebner, "Curricular Language," p. 229.

quality of instruction the HSTP offered: "Yeah. Cause you can only learn so much from your church and, like, here we actually have PhD students." The first commentator nodded: "Not only for the fact of PhD students, but you learn from other people based on . . . other questions they'll bring up in class, and even the PhD students will be like, 'Wow.'"

The excitement evident in this exchange stems from the young person's first taste of respect as a mature contributor in a theological community. A common theme in our interviews was young people's amazement at being treated as fellow theologians, co-journeyers with authority figures in an educational enclave. This respectful collegiality quickly informs youth's interactions with one another as well, as they become peer mentors in various learning cohorts. In our program at Lancaster Theological Seminary, we have found that those with previous experience as students in the program serve as excellent, and essential, peer mentors — not only because they help create a collegial culture, but also because they help sustain the incarnational Christian community that serves as the foundation for every other learning activity.

Adults show respect for youth in order to honor them as individuals, but also in order to model a way of becoming a mutual, beloved community that reflects Jesus Christ. High School Theology Programs strive to include young people from diverse racial and ethnic backgrounds, social class, gender identities, theologies, and developmental stages. In some programs, this diversity is deliberately cultivated; in others, diversity is simply a byproduct of the cultural moment in which we live. Either way, difference always risks conflict, and often leads to divisions within a community.

Amidst such diversity, adopting collegial learning practices can be difficult, even for adult leaders. As Beth Corrie, director of the Youth Theology Initiative at Candler School of Theology (a program that approaches diversity quite intentionally), explains, the importance of adult mentors who model a reconciling and boundary-crossing collegiality is crucial:

> You know, [as a staff member], you have to keep reaching out to people that you don't even agree with. You . . . can't just keep plopping down next to the kids that you already get along with; you can't keep plopping down with the staff people that you already know really well.

She adds: "We [adult mentors and teachers] have to be very intentional about constantly showing a different way of being. You've got to go sit down and eat with somebody that you know is going to be an awkward conversation, but you have to do it anyway."[14]

Peer Mentors: Let's Walk Together

When an incarnational community comes into being, its culture begins to take on a life of its own. The community that is a circle, when it is healthy and vital, soon morphs into an expanding spiral, opening out into the world and renewing itself by drawing others in. Participants in the High School Theology Programs form communities in which their gifts are valued and their voices honored, and they then return to their churches and — if all goes well — they begin to help build up that type of community in the church.[15] Some youth then come back to their programs-of-origin as peer mentors, or later as adult mentors, and they bring new friends with them. Grace, whose story began this chapter, learned to trust the community she experienced through the encouragement of peer mentors and adults who modeled a community of trust for her. As an adult mentor, she is now a model for others of how to live in a community of betrothal — a community whose truth is found in relationship with Christ and with one another. And so the story will repeat. The circle turns into an expanding spiral, in which the community teaches youth how to be community by being in community.

While this self-renewing process can (and often does) occur through informal social influence, as Anne Wimberly points out in chapter 4, many HSTPs have formalized the process by recruiting and training peer mentors. The effort to train peer mentors developed out of the shared conviction that the best way to help churches and pastors empower young people for leadership is to give them substantive leadership roles and experience in their programs. As one director, whose program explicitly cultivates youth leadership for future program years, told our research team: "The benefit we didn't know would come with this — and that has become the most important way that we establish our community — is that the young people experience youth leadership and safe community themselves during the academy."

14. Beth Corrie (director, Youth Theological Initiative, Candler School of Theology), interviewed by Christy Lang Hearlson, July 2012.

15. See chapter 6 in this volume, where Christy Lang Hearlson describes various ways in which programs engage youth's process of separation from and reintegration into home communities.

> They come back as peer mentors, and they immediately begin to establish that type of living that they have valued. . . . They show and exhibit and model safe and intentional communities of theological diversity and questioning. So when the new students arrive at the academy, the peer mentors welcome them into this new, yet similar variant of our already existing community. [As a result], they gently nudge, teach and mostly model exactly what we hope the community will be.

Despite this self-renewing effect, creating communities anew each year is still a challenge. Communities are living, breathing, evolving entities, and they must revisit and renegotiate community norms at each annual gathering. In fact, one sign that these programs serve as active expressions of incarnational community is their fluidity; even when new adult and peer mentors have imbibed the spirit of "safe and intentional community for theological diversity and questioning," participants' unique personalities and social locations create changes in how the community is constituted. As Bonhoeffer notes, relationships within the Christian community mean we must treat one another "only as the person that he [or she] *already is* in Christ's eyes," which calls for every person's active participation in setting the community's expectations. Honesty before God and one another is a precious gift that must be incarnated over and over again. When Grace returns to her church, and then again to her program as a peer mentor, her transformed life will be a gift to a new group of young persons, who will, in turn, offer others the good news that because "Christ has long since acted decisively for [us]" we are free to be who we are in Christ.[16]

Committing to Collegial Education for Christian Leadership Formation

For Christians, the truth of Christ is embodied in relationship, which means that Christian community grounds every other incarnational practice of the church. Indeed, divorced from this sort of community, pedagogies that seek to form Christian leaders are unintelligible. Grace's story points to the transformative power of the caring community of mutual support and accountability youth experience in the High School Theology Programs. Christ's mercy and grace, encountered through these relationships, had agency in forming Grace into someone capable of embodying mercy and grace for others.

16. Bonhoeffer, *Life Together,* p. 26, emphasis mine.

The community-centered, holistic pedagogies of HSTPs are suggestive for theological formation generally. In these programs, community is more than a "context" in which learning takes place; community is a learning space with *pedagogical agency,* which calls the whole self to engage ideas and practices for the sake of spiritual and vocational formation. As Bonhoeffer insisted, Christian community sets young people free to be who they are *in Christ,* and to experience what it means to bear their true image as Christ's own. If next-generation churches are actually to become life-shaping, incarnational communities, then those who lead them must learn to engage a community's life-shaping, incarnational power.

The HSTPs testify to a community's catechetical role in several ways. First, they remind us that the community we have is the one we must work with — it is already the gift given to us by God in Christ. It is tempting, for example, to imagine community as a by-product of our work as theological educators, rather than as a living, incarnational space where Christ meets our students. We protest that our institutions do not contain the right people, or have to deal with all the wrong people. Yet if it is true that God places us in community and calls us to see Christ at work in the midst of that particular set of relationships, we cannot approach Christian community as an imposed "ideal," accomplished by recruiting better members, exiling annoying ones, and shaping up the members we have, all of which undermines our own conviction that Christ is *already* present in our institutional communities. This does not mean that we should not work toward more faithful, more connected, more vital communities. But it does mean that the first step in acknowledging our communities' formative potential is to help one another look for Christ's presence in the midst of existing relationships, as we grow together into a beloved community.

Second, those of us who teach Christian leaders must have the courage and the freedom to employ holistic, relational pedagogies that allow our students (and ourselves) to experience — not just analyze — God's truth in community. The Christ-created *koinonia* has discursive, personal, and interpersonal expressions, and a primary experience of grace and mercy touches all of these. While acquiring intellectual knowledge about the church's texts and traditions is necessary for church leaders, countless spiritual leaders, from Luther to Wesley to Mother Teresa, have attested to the fact that this knowledge is not *transformative* until it takes on an event quality. For many learners, that event — the experience of a God who "happens" — happens in the context of conversation and relationship.

Young people attending seminary after a High School Theology Program (or who have had similar experiences that successfully translate theological information into experience) will have high expectations for formative conversation in the theological classroom. They will be disappointed by faculty who sacrifice dialogue for "getting through the material," and by institutions that confuse data transmission with teaching, or that adopt the wholly false assumption that integrative, communally based pedagogies employing conversation, imagination, personal engagement, and embodiment are substandard intellectual practices.[17] The HSTPs confront this misunderstanding directly, and challenge it with scores of theologically nuanced program alumni.

Third, High School Theology Programs' emphasis on intense community as a learning vehicle challenges those of us in theological education to reconsider the schooling model that structures most contemporary higher education. Echoing the industrial age that gave rise to so-called schooling models of education, schools were designed for efficiency of production (presumably, of knowledge), not for community formation, relational integrity, or conformity to Christ. In the schooling model, community is a by-product of the educational production process, not a formative educational element. Yet dividing learning communities into temporary units (think semester-long courses, credit hours, etc.) can make community more difficult than, say, time-intensive retreats or residential, short-term courses that students share while living together. The HSTPs, unencumbered by an educational "mold" into which their curricula must fit, offer educators an extraordinary window into what theological formation might look like that utilizes some aspects of the schooling model, but is not constrained by it.

Finally, the community-based learning models of the HSTPs call us to pay close attention to the motivation learners experience when their teachers show them respect and take their ideas seriously. As Katherine Douglass

17. Educators like John Dewey, Lev Vygotsky, Benjamin Bloom, Parker Palmer, bell hooks, and others — representing a range of educational theories — for more than a century have argued in favor of the superiority of imagination and holistic engagement as formative for the most complex and integrative forms of thinking. This cause has been taken up in various ways by the Carnegie Foundation for the Advancement of Teaching in the United States and the European University Association in Europe. Cf. Pat Hutchings et al., *The Scholarship of Teaching and Learning Reconsidered: Institutional Integration and Impact* (San Francisco: Jossey-Bass), 2001; the recommendations of the European University Association report, *Creativity in Higher Education* (Brussels: European University Association), 2007; and (specific to Christian leadership) Charles Foster et al., *Educating Clergy: Teaching Practices and Pastoral Imagination* (San Francisco: Jossey-Bass), 2005.

and Brent Strawn each point out in this book, even the subtler practices of the HSTPs — like intentionally addressing learners as "scholars" rather than as "students" — help the programs demonstrate the Christian community's ability to decouple status from roles. While the roles participants play in these programs are clear (program director, adult staff, peer mentors, participants, and so on), persons in each role share identical status: they are children of God. Just as the early Christian community recognized that, in Christ, there was "neither Jew nor Greek" and accorded equal status to slave and free, the HSTPs employ practices that communicate status as God-given, in equal measure, to every human being. By cultivating mutual respect between youth and adults, these programs demonstrate the enormous positive effect that mutual respect plays in human motivation. Creating supportive communities where learning is viewed as a relationship of mutual accountability, undertaken by partners on a shared journey — even when one partner is more familiar with the terrain than the other — turns out to be a highly effective way to motivate learning, as well as a way to encounter the truth of Christ.

The reason is simple. Community, that matrix of relationships of support and care in which we live exposed to God and to one another without fear, frees us to become who God created us to be. It is where, as Howard Thurman wrote, we find the relationships we long for "in which it is no longer needful for us to pretend anything."[18] Christian community catechizes us through the freedom of Christ, a role fully recognized by teenagers like Grace. What transformed Grace into a bearer of Christ's love and mercy was not her exposure to theology or her understanding of Christian tradition. What empowered Grace, and what empowers other young people in High School Theology Programs — is the presence of a community through which Christ takes human form, accepting young people fully so they no longer need to pretend to be anything but the wildly promising human beings God made them to be.

18. Howard Thurman, *The Inward Journey* (Richmond, IN: Friends United Press, 2007), p. 120.

CHAPTER FOUR

Give Me Mentors

Pedagogies of Spiritual Accompaniment

Anne Streaty Wimberly

Mara: Transformed through Mentoring

When Mara came to the Youth Hope-Builders Academy, she did not love life or herself. Carrying heavy burdens, she cried often and retreated to her room. Slowly, through patient conversations with caring adult mentors, she began to tell painful stories of being deeply hurt, ignored, and silenced, and how she hated everything about herself. Mentors prayed with her, offered guidance around anger, and affirmed her beauty and gifts of worship leadership, music, and empathy. Indeed, other participants gravitated toward her because of those gifts. In this caring community, Mara gained a stronger sense of self, determination, and life direction. She went on to college, where she studied with the aim of serving young people who had experienced trauma. When she later returned to the YHBA program, she came as an exceptional leader and caring presence for participants in pain, and her current vocation centers on child welfare in addition to youth ministry leadership in her church. As Mara tells it, her life was changed through the experience of mentoring at YHBA:

> Because of my mentor, I am in a place today of loving life and myself; and I'm in the process of doing all I can to make a difference in the lives of the next generation. My mentor listened to me as I talked about my struggles with so many things and where I was headed. I could tell it all, complete with yelling and crying! It wasn't always easy being pushed to own up to my abilities. I hadn't given much thought to having them or where and

> how I as a Christian might use them. I found myself, and there was no giving up. I received encouragement. I still do. I can count on my mentor even now. The word has always been that God has a plan for my life. It's true! God does! I'm so grateful!

As Mara's story of pain, healing, and ministry shows, the practice of mentoring responds to a real need: many youth feel that no one listens to them or cares about them, and they desperately desire spiritual companionship. They long for mentoring that reveals to them a model of the Christian life that can catalyze life-changing faith.[1] They desire mentors who will help them act in spiritually anchored and purposeful ways, and who will do so in the face of time constraints and wider cultural "tutoring" that runs counter to Christian spirituality and values. Youth seek this up-close and safe relational space in order to share openly their stories of trial and triumph to caring persons who receive them as gift and who act as story-sharers, freely giving back the gifts of self, guidance, and wisdom. Young people long for the countercultural ministry of spiritual mentoring that has at its center companionship guided by God and that demonstrates the caring, guiding qualities of Jesus Christ.

One participant said appreciatively of the mentors in his program, "They're there to help us to focus and stay on the right path." His reference to a path helps us name the relational space that youth seek as holy ground where they experience God's love, hope along the way, and a life direction patterned on the values revealed in the ministry of Jesus Christ. This is the kind of spiritual mentoring Mara experienced, and it is a pivotal practice across the High School Theology Programs. Drawing on firsthand observations and testimonies of leaders, mentors, youth participants, and parents in the HSTPs, this chapter explores the urgent need for mentoring, its theological bases, and ways to foster such spiritual companionship. The chapter concludes with suggestions for theological educators who want their students to glean the benefits of such relationships.

1. One of the contexts most likely to serve as a crucible for faith formation is in mentor relationships (other contexts include families and congregations). Cf. Kenda Creasy Dean, *Almost Christian: What the Faith of Our Teenagers Is Telling the American Church* (New York: Oxford University Press, 2010), p. 11. Gil Noam and his colleagues also stress that mentoring relationships with caring adults serve as effective means of youth development since development invariably takes place in the context of significant relationships. See Gil G. Noam, Tina Malti, and Michael J. Karcher, "Mentoring Relationships in Developmental Perspective," in *Handbook of Youth Mentoring,* ed. David L. DuBois and Michael J. Karcher, (Los Angeles: Sage Publications, Inc., 2014), p. 100.

Listen Up! The Need for Mentors Is Real

Mentors play a crucial role in the vocational formation of young Christian leaders in every High School Theology Program. Leaders in these programs confirm that high school youth long for caring mentors, are ready to engage in mentoring processes, and have the skills necessary for in-depth collaboration. In spite of this, most young people have little experience with mentoring. They — and the adults around them — arrive at the mentor-rich environments of HSTPs from individualistic, productivity-oriented, and tech-saturated cultural milieus in which people give little time to listening, substantively caring for, or guiding young people along their journey through adolescence and into adulthood.

Young People's Longing, Readiness, and Skills

The desire to be seen and heard is a basic human longing. Youth long for meaningful and authentic relationships in which they are seen and heard as valuable people, where they can voice their questions about faith and life in the presence of listeners who care and who take them seriously.[2] Particularly for youth of color, whom my own program predominantly serves, this acceptance means seeing youth as more than a problem to be solved or potential yet to be discovered.[3] Focusing on the primary need to be heard and loved corrects a common misperception of mentoring: mentoring is not just about teaching, modeling, or directing. Instead, good mentors listen, take young people seriously, and affirm them before giving guidance — though guidance is also needed.

Longing for vocational guidance

Young people especially express a need for guidance around purpose and vocation. Reflecting on her experience at the Youth in Ministry Program at Emmanuel School of Religion, Phyllis Fox writes that young people long to

2. Sean Lansing, "Reflections" (unpublished report, High School Theology Leadership Consultation, Indianapolis, IN, February 23-25, 2012).

3. Lansing, "Reflections"; also Jeff Kaster, "Reflections" (unpublished report, High School Theology Leadership Consultation, Indianapolis, IN, February 23-25, 2012).

"know who they are and what their purpose is. . . . [They] have big dreams, deep loves, courage to take risks, and radical idealism" that need to be "directed to the right goal, the right object, the right call."[4] Young people are often anxious about the future and want someone with greater life experience to help them prepare. One teenager commented on the way mentors help youth get ready for the rest of life:

> They're teaching us to prepare for life, and I feel as if they have done an outstanding and wonderful job, because they've been there. We haven't been there yet. I'm only going to be a senior in high school. What do I know? . . . I feel as if the mentors have been the biggest blessing that I've received in a long time, and for that I am forever grateful.

In a culture that rarely frames experience theologically, it is no small thing that this participant regards the presence of a mentor who offered guidance as a "blessing."

Concern about the future also translates into concerns about vocational direction, in which youth wrestle with the authenticity and meaning of their call.[5] For example, in the Ministry Quest program at Tabor College, a young man perceived an audible call from God to become a medical doctor. Upon hearing call stories of mentors in church ministry, he grew anxious about what this experience meant. When his mentor clarified the diversity of God's call, he expressed relief, saying, "I was worried that the only way to fully live out my calling was to be a pastor or missionary. That's what was troubling me. But now I realize that I can still be faithful to God's call as a doctor."[6]

Longing for authorship and agency

Further, youth long for mentors who help them respond to and make sense of their suffering, the world's messiness, and the difficult realities of society. They experience or observe instances of abuse and are aware of racial and cultural tensions. Many face broken relationships, loneliness, alienation, and

4. Phyllis Fox, "Reflections" (unpublished report, High School Theology Leadership Consultation, Indianapolis, IN, February 23-25, 2012).

5. Wendell Loewen and Jules Glanzer, "Reflections" (unpublished report, High School Theology Leadership Consultation, Indianapolis, IN, February 23-25, 2012).

6. Loewen and Glanzer, "Reflections."

depression. In the midst of these struggles, mentors give teenagers space to share their experiences safely while helping them frame their experiences theologically and make decisions to act as people of faith.

In this sense, mentors help young people author their own stories and become decision-makers in their own lives of faith. Tonya Burton at Perkins Youth School of Theology points out that young people are capable of thinking theologically, exploring their faith deeply, and working through challenges to their beliefs, their character, and their present and future actions as unapologetic Christians.[7] In the mentoring relationship, youth become equal partners with spiritual companions who encourage their agency in fulfilling important goals for others' good, in exploring their religious experiences and traditions, and in making connections between faith and life, theology, and practice.[8] In the end, these young people long for a deepening relationship with God, rather than mere information about God, and they seek mentors who can help them reflect critically as they exercise their own abilities to frame their lives in light of faith.

Many congregational youth ministry programs have sought to provide young people with caring, Christian-centered, and faith-forming mentoring relationships. Yet many of these well-meaning programs — fearful of "turning off" teenagers — have inadvertently re-cast them as consumers of experiences rather than as critical thinkers who are actively engaged in constructing their life worlds. Youth long to be invited into respectful, non-condescending mentoring relationships with people who, as Fred Edie from the Duke Youth Academy writes, do not regard them as "strangers, aliens, or imbeciles."[9] In addition, youth seek mentors who recognize their high ideals and vision, and their desire to make a difference in the world. Young people want opportunities to exercise their abilities to "think, judge, act and create [and] discover themselves as agents of change," and they seek mentors who

7. Tonya Burton, "Reflections" (unpublished report, High School Theology Leadership Consultation, Indianapolis, IN, February 23-25, 2012).

8. Karcher and Hansen refer to *authorship* as a necessary aspect of mentoring activities and interactions. This aspect affirms youths' readiness to be put at the center in decision-making in the mentoring relationship and becomes a basis on which empowerment, meaning, and hope occur. A discussion on authorship appears in Michael J. Karcher and Keoki Hansen, "Mentoring Activities and Interactions," in *Handbook of Youth Mentoring,* 2nd ed., ed. David L. DuBois and Michael J. Karcher (Los Angeles: Sage Publications, 2014), p. 69.

9. Fred Edie, "Reflections" (unpublished report, High School Theology Leadership Consultation, Indianapolis, IN, February 23-25, 2012).

recognize and honor their uniqueness, and give them space in which their unique gifts can blossom.[10]

Christian Companionship as a Countercultural Activity

The incarnational, relational nature of spiritual mentoring serves as a countercultural alternative to individualistic, achievement-oriented, and techno-centered relationship patterns that engulf North American young people. The commercial sector promises a perfect life, available through material items that make us feel good, look good, and live better than others — paving the way for relationships marked by competition and interpersonal estrangement. Technologically mediated relationships produce a sense of anonymity, even sequestering family members away from one another as father, mother, and child pursue their individual social media interests. These cultural pressures not only obscure our abilities to connect with others; they damage our relationship with God, creating a sense of deep relational hunger that Skype and FaceTime cannot satisfy.[11]

In this context, in-person mentors who come alongside both parents and young people offer youth an entirely different kind of relationality. One young person interviewed spoke about the mentors from a High School Theology Program in this way: "I think they're more understanding. It feels more comfortable talking to them." Such mentors help adults and youth move beyond the cycles of busyness, shouting, silence, and isolation in order to create space for questions about life and faith, deep and fearful feelings, aspirations, and hope. As they are "listened into being," teenagers feel their own agency taking shape. As one young person said, "[Mentors] are there to listen to us. That's what also builds great leadership. My mentor would always remind me when I wouldn't know what to do. He'd offer ideas or stuff. . . . He'd also remind himself to back off, [saying] 'I forget that this is your project.'"

10. Andrew Duran, "Reflections" (unpublished report, High School Theology Leadership Consultation, Indianapolis, IN, February 23-25, 2012); Claire Smith, "Reflection" (unpublished report, High School Theology Leadership Consultation, Indianapolis, IN, February 23-25, 2012).

11. Kaveri Subrahmanyam and Patricia Greenfield, "Online Communication and Adolescent Relationships," *Children and Electronic Media* 18, no. 1 (Spring 2008): 120, www.futureofchildren.org (accessed February 12, 2012).

Mentoring as Hospitable Spiritual Companionship

Theologically, mentoring relationships in Christian community depend on the reality of the household of God, where people experience God's purposes of abounding love in relationships. God's household connotes a personal environment that Archbishop Desmond Tutu calls *ubuntu.* In Archbishop Tutu's words, the Bantu term *ubuntu* means, "My humanity is caught up, is inextricably bound up, in yours. . . . A person is a person through other persons. I am human because I belong, I participate, I share."[12] The mentoring relationship that occurs through spiritual companionship exemplifies this understanding of relationships in the household of God. In God's realm, in this household, youth are not foreigners; they do not experience relational estrangement. Instead, the spiritual companion sees, accepts, and embraces the young person as kindred. God's love becomes a felt reality in the hospitality of the spiritual companion. In a hospitable relationship, youth reconnect with others and experience joy, celebration, and healing.

Scripture provides a guide for such hospitality. Hospitality is first of all an extension of the ministry of Jesus. As the Apostle Paul wrote, "Welcome one another, therefore, just as Christ has welcomed you, for the glory of God" (Rom. 15:7). Hospitality is also a proper response to divine grace. As 1 Peter 4:9-10 says: "Be hospitable to one another without complaining. Like good stewards of the manifold grace of God, serve one another with whatever gift each of you has received." Further, in hospitality, Christians open themselves to a larger spiritual reality. Hebrews 13:2 (KJV) refers to those who extend hospitality as entertaining "angels unawares," while Matthew 25 suggests that in showing kindness to others, Christians show kindness to Jesus himself. As spiritual companions welcome youth, they welcome Jesus. Hospitality is the mark of the household of God, binding spiritual sisters, brothers, mothers, fathers, and children to one another in love.

Such "kinship hospitality" has several important effects. First, it creates a process of respectful mutual exchange in the mentoring relationship. In this process, the spiritual companion attends to the quality of welcome young people receive so that trust builds and what Anthony Gittins calls "gift exchange" can occur.[13] In gift exchange, the youth and the spiritual companion reciprocally speak and listen, sharing voice and perspective. Second, hospitality

12. Desmond Tutu, *No Future without Forgiveness* (New York: Doubleday, 1999), p. 31.

13. Anthony J. Gittins, *Gifts and Strangers: Meeting the Challenge of Inculturation* (New York: Paulist Press, 1989), p. 102.

means that a mentor is careful to ensure that each person can enter the conversation from his or her own perspective, which in turn affirms appreciation for the elements of "positionality" — the way in which youths' social, gendered, ethnic-cultural, and religious identities locate them and give them perspective in a conversation.[14] Finally, hospitality in mentoring teaches young people hospitable behaviors by modeling love, care, and respect in a process of "mimetic moral work." In such mimesis, youth internalize and translate into their own behavior the hospitality they experience and witness.

Spiritual Companionship as a Mutual Process of Doing Theology

Mentoring carried out by spiritual companions is a form of discipleship and spiritual direction. The spiritual companion journeys alongside a young person in her unfolding story, hearing and assisting her in exploring life's questions and giving wise counsel that promotes her decision to live faithfully as a Christian. The mentoring relationship extends hospitality to youth in a safe space — *holy ground* — where a mentor listens to a young person's stories and helps him or her connect those stories to God's story, considering what such connections mean for everyday life. On such welcoming holy ground, spiritual companionship involves a "holy conversation"[15] that becomes a mutually active process of doing theology. This form of theology, instead of being purely verbal or academic, is personal and embodied, relying heavily on eye contact and body language. In holy conversation, mentor and mentee deal with existential questions: "Who am I?" "Why am I here?" "Where am I going in life?" "Why is life so hard?" "What should I do in this situation?" "What's God got to do with it?"

This embodied, personal approach to theology-as-conversation builds on the biblical model of Jesus as Mentor of the disciples. Jesus offered personal relationship with the disciples, and as spiritual companion, he posed and an-

14. An exploration of "positionality" is used most particularly to set forth an understanding of gender issues in education. See Mary Kay Thompson Tetreault, "Classrooms for Diversity: Rethinking Curriculum and Pedagogy," in *Multicultural Education: Issues and Perspectives,* 2nd ed., ed. James A. Banks and Cherry A. McGee Banks (Boston: Allyn and Bacon, 1993), pp. 164-85.

15. Margaret Guenther uses the term "holy listening" to describe the spiritual director's love of the Holy Spirit and being led by the Spirit to be present and listen attentively to the seeker. See Margaret Guenther, *Holy Listening: The Art of Spiritual Direction* (Lanham, MD: Rowman and Littlefield Publishers, Inc., 1992), p. 1.

swered deep questions of life. He dealt with questions about healing (Mark 9:28), signs of the end (Mark 13:4), and issues of faith and the need to understand (Mark 4:10, 4:38, 4:41).[16] Other biblical figures also engaged in mentoring relationships, learning from one another and facing difficult questions or situations together.[17] Scripture supports mentoring as an activity of doing theology that involves raising deep questions and struggling with the answers.

Setting Spiritual Companionship in Motion

Sanders entered the Youth Hope-Builders Academy (YHBA) Summer Residential Program shortly after the death of his father. During the opening days, his unusually quiet and withdrawn demeanor pointed to his grief. In a small mentoring group called Heart-to-Heart, he gradually began to open up about parts of his story and related concerns. He was the only child in his family; and, now with his dad gone, he was grieving deeply. The Heart-to-Heart mentor met with him individually to provide comfort, care, and conversation about his grief, and to explore his questions about who and how God is in situations of life and death. In the small group meetings, Sanders expressed worry about his mother and how she would cope. He wondered about his role in the family, what would happen to him, and if he had what it would take to honor both of his professional parents' expectation for success in life as a Black male. His peers rallied around him. In the process of story sharing, they too told of their painful experiences of loss and of worries about their futures.

In ongoing Heart-to-Heart conversations, and in the whole group Exploration Sessions, questions about the meaning of success and Christian vocational direction arose. Sanders described his understanding of success as a high-paying leadership position, but he was unsure of the kind of position that appealed to him. Neither he nor the rest of the group had given much thought to Christian vocation because they connected it to being a church pastor. Sanders completed a gifts inventory and said that it was helpful, but not until after he completed the High School Theology Program did Sanders tell a remarkable unfolding story. He said,

16. See Elizabeth Struthers Malbon, *In the Company of Jesus: Characters in Mark's Gospel* (Louisville, KY: Westminster John Knox, 2000), pp. 93-94.

17. For example, Jethro's mentoring relationship with his son-in-law Moses (Exod. 18); Moses' mentorship of Joshua (Deut. 3:28); David's and Jonathan's peer mentoring relationship (1 Sam. 19 and 20); Peter's and Barnabas' mentoring relationship (Gal. 2:11-13); and Paul's mentorship of Timothy (2 Tim.).

> My whole perspective of my purpose and why God has placed me on this earth is totally different as the result of being in YHBA. I was able to tell my story about my dad's death. . . . I received comfort and assurance from the leaders and, through them, from God. But I also heard stories from others that seemed far worse than mine. From them, I thought, "It's not about me. God has something for me to do to help others." I have been fortunate in so many ways — where I live and what my parents have given me. I plan to help others as much as I can.

Sanders has since completed undergraduate studies, is in leadership in a community service organization with youth, and is preparing to enter law school. Sharing his story was the beginning of a new life for Sanders.

Sanders' experience of story sharing points to a key aspect of mentoring in YHBA and in other High School Theology Programs: treating youth as whole persons. Emphasizing young people's whole selves reflects the belief that God creates whole persons who live out multifaceted, evolving stories. Moreover, youth want and need to share their complex stories. When spiritual companions tend to these stories, they treat the "sacred texts" of young people's lives as essential parts of the gift exchange between themselves and young people. They allow young people to explore their thoughts and feelings about life, to discuss their recognition of or hope for God's activity, and to wonder what God's activity means for their unfolding story. Shared stories transform and deepen young people's faith.[18]

For mentors to honor the whole of young people's lives requires attentiveness to the many elements of their complex *identities,* such as their ethnicity, socio-cultural location, gender, and religious affiliation. It requires an awareness of how youth perceive themselves in relationship to their immediate surroundings and in the wider culture and world. Sanders, for example, referred to his ethnicity and gender as a Black male. He also described his fortunate circumstances — having two parents who had loved and nurtured him and encouraged him to succeed. When mentors attend to the *social contexts* of youth, they are listening through young people's stories for clues about where they live, attend school and church, play, and work, as well as the qualities of these environments as informed by available resources. As

18. In my own work, I draw on Peter Gilmour's emphasis on story as sacred text. See Anne E. Streaty Wimberly, *Soul Stories: African Christian Education* (Nashville, TN: Abingdon, 2005); and Peter Gilmour, *The Wisdom of Memoir: Reading and Writing Life's Sacred Texts* (Winona, MN: St. Mary's Press, 1997).

Sanders' story revealed, mentors also must attend to young people's *networks of relationships.* Sanders' story was shaped by his relationship with his parents, but also by his relationships with other family members; school peers and friends; and others in church, community, and workplace; as well as those with whom he connected in social and mass media. The nature of Sanders' connection with God is also part of his relational network. Such networks, of course, change over time. Various *events* taking place in the family — such as the death of Sanders' father — or that happen in school, church, and beyond alter their relationships, and add to the stories young people bring into the mentoring relationship.

Moreover, mentors help young people recognize that their stories are laden with *life meanings.* Teenagers' thoughts, feelings, attitudes, and values reveal what goes into the way they make sense out of their lives, and these meanings may extend to their views about the future.[19] Sanders had definite thoughts about a future of success based on internalized parental expectations. But he later spoke of an alternative view of his future, transformed through interactions with peers and the outcomes of his theological reflection on God's purpose for his life. All of these aspects of identity factor into the stories youth tell, and mentors do well to attend to their interrelation.

Purpose-Driven Mentoring in the High School Theology Programs

Mentors in the High School Theology Programs have the overall goal of providing spiritual accompaniment that helps catalyze young people's positive development as persons, and helps them form life-changing faith. In surveying these programs' use of mentoring, four specific purposes stand out.

Purpose One: Giving Youth a Voice

The first purpose of mentoring in the HSTPs is to give youth a voice in a world where youth often feel no one listens to them. The mentor who seeks to give a young person a voice must take on three action roles: *listener, inquirer,* and *spiritual resource.* The mentor as listener addresses the prevalent

19. The various aspects of the stories of the lives of youth are the same as those comprising the lives of all human beings. These aspects of human life stories are described in Wimberly, *Soul Stories,* pp. 26-29.

complaint of young people that nobody listens to them. In order to give the young person a voice, the mentor provides an inviting space for the mentee to talk about whatever he wants without being judged. As one young person said of mentors, "They want to listen to you. They want to hear your side of the story, too. It is very encouraging to know that adults will listen and adults will take you seriously."

Yet listening without judgment does not mean passivity. In order to help youth wrestle with the meaning of their life, their beliefs about it, and their place and action in the world, the mentor becomes an inquirer, asking hard questions and again listening carefully. They help the young person ask herself questions like, *Do I see myself as beautiful? Damaged? Lovable? Do I live a life of grace? Do I choose to see the world as hostile or affirming? How does God see me? How does that change how I see myself and other people and, in turn, how I act in the world and the choices I make?* Youth respond well to this kind of inquiry when it does not function as a veiled attempt to simply convey what the adult already believes. One participant said with appreciation of the mentors, "They actually asked me what I thought."

Third, in seeking to give youth voice, the mentor takes on the role of a spiritual resource, becoming aware of and responding to young people's questions and concerns about Christian faith and life, including its doctrinal tenets and scriptural sources. In their search for certainty, youth ask questions like, *Is there a God? What is God like? Is my grandma in heaven? What's the difference between a Christian living their life wrong and an atheist living their life right? Why do many Christians condemn homosexuality and premarital sex?* To function well as a spiritual resource to young people, a mentor must actively invite hard questions and encourage youth to talk about their view of Christianity and their experience of themselves as Christians. Being a spiritual resource does not mean that mentors must have all the answers, but only that they are willing to point young people to other resources that will help young people make sense of their questions, and to wrestle with them more deeply as they find answers . . . or more questions.

Purpose Two: Collaboration and Relational Co-Authorship

Mentoring also creates collaborative relationships with young people as it helps them take on authorship of their own lives. For this reason, the mentor remains flexible, taking on a variety of roles — e.g., *friend, self-revealer, learner* — depending on what the context demands. The friendship a mentor gives goes beyond instrumental support by offering real care, keen interest in the present and future well-being of youth, and collaborative involvement in activities of leadership. As a friend, the mentor attends to the emotional state and needs of youth; gives encouragement, praise, support, and truthful advice when necessary; and plans activities with the young person, drawing on the young person's skills and giving increasing responsibility to youth. Youth appreciate the friendship they receive from their mentors. One young person reflected, "They seem like they really care about *all* of you." They also respond well to the collaborative, reflective spirit. One participant said, "Your mentors, they're usually higher than you, [and] you just listen to what they say, and [they] try to do all these things to make them like you . . . but here, you're talking face-to-face."

In the context of such trusting, collaborative relationships, a mentor can reveal details about his or her own life, using judicious self-disclosure to show care and warmth, build positive connection, and encourage their mentee's own self-disclosure. The mentor might reveal thoughts and feelings about the mentoring relationship, personal experiences akin to those of the young person, stories of struggles and how they were resolved, and stories of the Christian faith journey and calling. This has the effect of making the relationship mutual, which can remove clinical distance. As one young person commented, "Yeah, [mentors] share their own stuff too, so it's not like they sit back and watch you."

Further, to foster a collaborative relationship and model the Christian life, the mentor is also a *learner*. Like the mentee, the mentor grows in awareness of personal strengths, growing edges, and sense of call. One mentor, reflecting the experiences of many others in the HSTPs, said of the experience of mentoring, "I have reaffirmed my youth ministry calling." In order to act as a co-learner, the mentor invests in his or her own process of spiritual discernment in order to become more aware of areas of learning and needed growth. She might also express gratitude for what she learns from her mentee. Youth show surprise and appreciation for mentors who disclose that they continue to learn, saying, "My mentor will say, 'Man, I'm learning everything,'" or, "He likes learning things from young people."

Purpose Three: Learning and Personal Development

A third purpose of the spiritual companion is to respond to young people's desire for personal and vocational development. In seeking this goal, mentors take on the action roles of *teacher, counselor/sage,* and temporary *surrogate parent.* As a teacher, the mentor seeks to activate young people's knowledge, feelings, values, and actions regarding Christian faith and life. To do so, the mentor provides information and tools such as Scripture, stories of faith exemplars, historical material, and media, and uses these materials to engage youth in inquiry, critical analysis, discussion, and Christian values clarification. Youth commonly voice appreciation when they experience a mentor who is well equipped for the task of teaching; as one young person said, "In almost every one of the small groups we have, there's someone . . . teaching us, so it's like we have a professional to help us out." Or, as another youth commented, grateful for the relevance of teaching in the high school theology program he attended: "They're teaching us to prepare for life."

Sometimes youth share stories that reveal serious life disruptions, mental health issues, and problems associated with trauma. In these cases, mentors must act as sages with life wisdom to share, and sometimes as informal pastoral counselors. Mentors frequently collaborate to discern needs among youth that require more specialized training, and many High School Theology Programs involve some mentors who are certified to deal with mental health or trauma issues. Mentors also find themselves in bridge roles, filling "gaps" left by fractured family systems. One young person said, "My dad's death left a hole in my life. I didn't want to replace him, but, still, I needed somebody. My mentor has been there for me." By clarifying her role as surrogate (and not actual) parent, this mentor was able to offer a supportive and advising presence as the teenager learned how to seek out networks of love and support.

Purpose Four: Youth Agency and Action

High School Theology Programs also use mentoring to promote agency and action in young people. Teenagers long to address suffering — both their own suffering, and the world's. To this end, the mentor becomes a *spiritual guide* or *coach,* as well as a *challenger.* As a spiritual guide or coach, the mentor recognizes young people's need to make their own decisions about the kind of disciples and church leaders they are becoming. By providing teenagers in the HSTPs with a variety of opportunities for leadership, and by engaging youth in exploring their spiritual gifts and talents, mentors help young people imagine how God's call to them may unfold now and in the future.

As challengers, mentors recognize young people's penchant for reacting quickly to issues as they try to change the world in a day. Mentors in the HSTPs help the "now" generation try out methodical approaches for the sake of long-term change. Working alongside youth on various ministry projects, mentors challenge youth to take responsibility for all aspects of preparation and implementation. For example, one young person reported the planning process for a big project: "You have a whole meeting with the counselors. . . . [I'd say] I'm thinking I would talk about teen homelessness. They'd say, 'Okay, go deeper, what's the need? What's the need?' I'm thinking, 'Oh, I'll do a food drive.' They say, 'Okay, what's the need you're filling?' "

Do I Have to Do It All?

Effective mentoring requires quality relationships and interactions, but of course no single mentor can fulfill every role. Rather, the HSTPs create a *culture* of mentoring, where mentors are available to teenagers in multiple contexts, with different roles, personal abilities, and levels of preparation. For example, the mentor as *listener* is a role in which almost anyone — even peers — can become adept with training. The mentor as *spiritual resource* requires special preparedness. High School Theology Programs fill these mentor roles with adults who are theologically prepared, who feel comfortable fielding tough questions about faith and life, and who can reflect critically on their own motives, needs, and emotional states. This form of mentoring requires a self-awareness that allows mentors to act as a friend while acknowledging the reality of power imbalances and maintaining appropriate boundaries. Adult mentors who play the roles of teacher, counselor/sage, and temporary surrogate parent constitute another group of mentors who might be called *skilled helpers.* These adults have highly developed relationship skills, as well as professional or experiential training that help them carry out instrumental tasks. These tasks include engaging young people in formal, outcome-based classroom activities, as well as in follow-up sessions that aim toward more long-lasting learning, personal development, and change.

All of these kinds of mentors need ongoing support and development. Directors of the HSTPs have learned the value of initially assessing potential mentors' special gifts, strengths, experiences, passion, and commitments, and then helping them engage in self-assessment during the mentoring process. One mentor in the Youth Hope-Builders Academy reflected:

> This was not my first time as a mentor. But this time reminded me that mentoring is not always easy. In fact, it can be really tough! There were some breakthroughs. I celebrate them. But I needed more help with knowing what to do with youth who are in what seems like unsolvable situations. I learned that the task of mentoring is not about solving everything. Sometimes, simply being there, listening, and asking the right questions is enough.

Comments like this one can help program leaders discover areas to further prepare all their mentors, as well as places where individual mentors need support and attention.

Mentoring Patterns in the High School Theology Programs

By creating cultures of mentoring, young people in the High School Theology Programs have access to many levels of mentoring beyond the one-on-one mentoring that occurs over (and sometimes beyond) a specified program period. The most common pattern is the use of *small mentoring groups,* often called "covenant groups," where mentoring is carried out under the heading of theological reflection. In these small group settings, spiritual companions may come in the form of adults or youth peers, staff counselors or pastoral caregivers, professors, pastors, spiritual directors, or seminary students. Periods of reflection are often organized according to specific topics and include activities such as story sharing, *lectio divina,* prayer and other liturgical practices, journaling, art and other expressive modes in concert with other approaches.[20]

Multi-layered mentoring is also common. We designed this sort of multilayered organizational structure for the Youth Hope-Builders Academy in order to respond to major breakdowns in intergenerational relationships and to the dire need of both youth and parents for mentors and guidance. This structure includes group mentoring of youth by adult mentors, one-on-one

20. Notable examples of these organizational plans are described by Elizabeth Corrie, "Reflections on Pedagogies of Vocational Discernment" (unpublished report, High School Theology Seminar, Indianapolis, IN, November 11-13, 2012); Jeff Kaster and Craig Gould, "Pedagogies of Theological Education, Theological Reflection" (unpublished report, High School Theology Seminar, Indianapolis, IN, November 11-13, 2012); Anabel Proffitt, "Building Intentional Community *(Koinonia)* Towards Formation" (unpublished report, High School Theology Seminar, Indianapolis, IN, November 11-13, 2012).

mentoring by caring, committed adults working with teen mentees, peer mentoring among adult leaders, and cross-age mentoring carried out by high school teens with middle school mentees. For example, group mentoring carried out by adult mentors with teen mentees takes place in small, gender-specific Heart-to-Heart Clusters — "family-like pods" of six to eight youth that meet for one-half to two hours daily during the YHBA Summer Residential Program. The adult mentor typically creates significant time at the outset of the group meetings to build a safe space for sharing. These times entail relationship-building games, bonding experiences, setting rules of engagement, and discussing and committing to confidentiality agreements.

As part of the group-mentoring process, youth freely frame the conversation, typically focusing on group or personal issues, or past and present problematic experiences with family, school, church, or community. At times, the adult mentor also proposes a topic for group discussion and reflection based on observations of the youth over the days of their academy participation, including biblical stories and passages and personal story sharing by both mentor and mentees. Over the course of the Heart-to-Heart mentoring process, the mentor structures time for "praise reports" and "prayer concerns," and may introduce case materials, journaling, and artistic expression as vehicles for critical reflection. All of these activities help youth reflect theologically on God's presence and activity in all their lives, and enable them to discover prayer as a spiritual resource to be used individually and collectively.

A key movement in the mentoring process is the invitation to youth to move from a problematizing stance to a problem-solving position through concrete decision-making. The mentor frames the transition with questions like: "What will you do with this concern? How will you handle that issue? What might this suggest for your actions with others here and after you leave YHBA? What has happened here that gives you some ideas for vocational direction?" Peers may also offer recommendations for reflection and potential decisions. Particularly for young people with expressed or apparent low self-esteem, the mentor may give personal affirmation or invite youth to repeat the affirmation in the first person: "You are a valuable creation of God. You are a valued and handsome human being. Know that you are loved by God and loved by me." They may also add biblical passages, such as Psalm 139:1-18.

Cross-age mentoring by high school teens with middle school youth began at the Youth Hope-Builders Academy in 2009 with an initiative called TAPs (Teens And Pre-Teens). In this initiative, each high school youth was paired with a middle schooler whom he or she mentored with adult supervision over the program year. High school mentors were prepared for their role at a week-long, post-residential program intensive. Each day began with teen-led worship, followed by program activities interspersed with recreation and arts experiences — all designed to form leaders who embrace responsibility for giving back to their community, modeling Christian character for middle school youth, helping guide their Christian formation, and engaging in community service with mentees. To this end, the mentoring pairs were selected in conversation with the young people involved, their pastor(s) or youth pastor(s), and the parents or guardians of both the mentor and the mentee — who, Tuesday through Thursday during the training period, brought their middle school youth on site to participate in targeted activities to prepare them for the year-long cross-mentoring activities. Parents also attended sessions to explore supportive parental roles.

Once the mentoring relationship was underway, an adult liaison maintained monthly contact with the youth, receiving testimonies from the high school students about their experiences with their mentees, including responses from the parents. One high school mentor's story shows the power of modeling and *mimesis* mentioned earlier in this chapter:

> At church, I am an altar server. During one of our conversations, she [the mentee] told me that she was interested in serving. So I contacted the leader of the altar servers and asked if she could serve with me, even though she hadn't gone through the training. [The leader] agreed. We arrived at church thirty minutes early in order to prepare and set up for the Mass. During Mass, I guided her through the proper reverence, the holding of the book, the washing of the hands, the correct protocol, etc. After Mass, while we were cleaning up, she told me how much fun she had, and it was just a wonderful experience.

Another teen mentor's story expresses the way a mentor can offer support and challenge to a mentee: "We had a youth conference that our church hosted. I encouraged my mentee to step out of her comfort zone and fellowship with different people. She did it. It was a wonderful day." These mentoring relationships provide opportunities for the mentors to show maturity and to establish their own sense of self in the midst of collaboration. One eleventh grade mentor reports,

> After my homecoming football game, my mentee told me that he was proud of me for winning Mr. Eleventh Grade. He also told me that I'm not

> better than him, because he won Mr. Eighth Grade. I told him that my goal is not to be better than him. I'm just trying to lead in a positive way. He responded and said, "Yeah, I know." To sum up that whole conversation, I just basically told him that you have a chance to be the best you can be as an African American male; but it's your choice to take the responsibility and make the right choices.

Overall, the cross-age mentor relationships prove a valuable source of support and affirmation for younger mentees. One mentor remembers,

> I attended my mentee's step show performance. We met up prior to the show. I wished her luck and told her that I was going to be rooting for her on the front row. She was very excited and ready to go on the stage. She had on this really cool jacket that I later found out was for the act. She did a superb job and I congratulated her.

Two other forms of mentoring are worth highlighting. *Parents* play an essential role in the lives of youth, but they often desire and need opportunities to explore their role and receive guidance on how to enhance the faith and leadership formation of their children. We hear parents say: "I really don't know how to raise my teens in today's world. I want to help. I want to make a difference. I have lots of questions. Just as the youth need guidance from others, so do I." YHBA's response has been to provide forums focused on key issues identified by parents that include panels of parents who share stories and strategies around targeted topics, facilitated by professional counselors and pastoral caregivers who provide concrete input.

In addition to parents, *mentoring through technologically supported connections* is gaining in popularity in High School Theology Programs. Given the reality that young people's technologically mediated friend networks, relationship-tending and faith-building practices need not be confined to face-to-face contacts.[21] While HSTP directors recognize the downside of our tech-saturated world, some programs also leverage these connections to support the mentoring process. The Youth in Theology and Ministry program of Saint John's School of Theology and Seminary creates a year-round online community for the purpose of hearing and responding to young people's

21. An entire chapter on the nature and importance of tech-connections with youth appears in Anne E. Streaty Wimberly, Sandra L. Barnes, and Karma D. Johnson, *Youth Ministry in the Black Church: Centered in Hope* (Valley Forge, PA: Judson Press, 2013), pp. 132-48.

issues and questions.[22] Huron University College's Ask & Imagine program incorporates Facebook for purposes of engaging youth in peer mentoring, while adults guide youth in how to use Facebook to foster peer support, affirmation, and community-building.[23] Likewise, Emmanuel Christian Seminary's Youth in Ministry program (a partnership with Milligan College) also uses Facebook to encourage peer mentoring, as youth post prayer requests and offer support.[24] For all of these programs, online connections help continue relationships beyond the intensive program experience, and remind young people as they return home that they are not alone.

Expanding the Reach of Mentoring

Mentoring programs go a long way in addressing young people's need for safe spaces and trustworthy adults, both of which are critical as they develop into teachable, but unapologetic, Christians. There are, however, risks involved in the undertaking. Young people come to the High School Theology Programs — not to mention to churches, colleges, and seminaries — with troubling stories, doubts, and frustrations. They bring questions that challenge the most confident and skillful mentor. In addition, transformation seldom happens quickly, which can leave mentors feeling disappointed in the process or doubtful of their own abilities. Further, because mentoring requires energy, time, and ongoing engagement, some people find mentoring challenging, even overwhelming. Finally, setting up and sustaining mentoring programs requires significant time and energy, since recruiting, screening, training, communicating, and supporting mentors is necessary to their success in this role. Mentoring is demanding.

Yet if the HSTPs are any indication, the relationship-intensive programs and structures that create mentoring relationships are a worthwhile institutional investment. The world and the church urgently need leaders to offer an incarnational, countercultural response to individualistic, achievement-oriented, and technologically centered cultural patterns, making spiritual friendship a primary means of doing theology. Young people report how powerfully formative the mentor relationship is in terms of faith, vocation,

22. Kaster, "Reflections."

23. Judy Steers, "Reflections" (unpublished report, High School Theology Leadership Consultation, Indianapolis, IN, February 23-25, 2012).

24. Fox, "Reflections."

and personal development; mentors also report growth in both their confidence as leaders and in their own thinking about faith. In every stage of the discipleship process, mentorship fosters growth and transformation for both the mentor and the mentee.

The High School Theology Programs demonstrate that mentoring requires intentionality. While a mentor relationship sometimes blooms spontaneously like a solitary wildflower on a mountainside, creating a larger culture of mentoring requires communities that serve as "greenhouses" for mentoring: nurturing its early growth; intentionally structuring relationships; providing support, preparation, and self-assessment opportunities; and inviting young people to be mentored or to mentor — or, in some cases, to do both. Admittedly, the HSTPs have access to a stellar group of well-equipped mentors, and they show how powerful such a constellation of caring adults can be. Yet the programs also demonstrate that effective forms of mentoring do not always require "religious professionals," or even adults in general. Mentoring can occur between same-age and cross-age groups under adult supervision — patterns that are often quite powerful for all involved, especially when those involved are encouraged to make mid-course corrections in response to feedback and experience. Creating a culture of mentoring is demanding, but not impossible.

The significance of mentoring in the formation of Christian leaders requires us to take it seriously as a means of theological formation, and not relegate it to the margins of formal theological education — as a non-academic practice of personal support, something extraneous to the practice of theology. High School Theology Programs demonstrate how embodied, living theology emerges in the midst of holy conversations between mentor and mentee, in a context that more closely resembles relationships in a congregation than theological discussions in a classroom. If the educator's truism is accurate — that people teach as they are taught — then seminaries, denominations, and congregations have every reason to mentor the future Christian leaders in their care, for a world that desperately needs what mentoring gives.

CHAPTER FIVE

Holy Noticing

The Power of Nomination and Commissioning for Missional Formation

Katherine M. Douglass

Joyce had never heard of a High School Theology Program before her interim pastor brought one to her attention. Joyce grew up in the small town of Lowland, Indiana, in the northwest corner of the state. In her teens, she was feeling a call to ministry, but she had never seen a woman pastor lead worship or offer pastoral care — that is, until she encountered the new interim pastor at her church. In the three months this pastor had been serving Joyce's church, she had become a mentor to Joyce. One day, the pastor handed Joyce a pamphlet for the Summer Seminary Sampler, the High School Theology Program at Trinity Lutheran Seminary — a program the pastor herself had just heard about — and said, "I think this is something you need to do." Joyce recalls,

> I was also invited to another leadership program later in the summer, and I wanted to go to both, but for both it required the congregation support me in some way. Either the pastor had to recommend that I go or financial aid was needed. So she looked at the congregation and said, "I think that Joyce would be really good for both of these opportunities," and within a matter of three weeks, they not only had the money to pay for both camps, but they had spending money for me and gas money for my parents, and it was just incredible the amount of support I got. So I said, "Okay, I guess this is something that I am supposed to do." I came to Trinity and fell in love with it.

In the advocacy of her interim pastor and congregation, Joyce found her leadership potential named, called forth, and supported in powerful ways. Joyce not only went to the Summer Seminary Sampler; she also later attended Trinity Lutheran for seminary. The Summer Seminary Sampler was so formative for Joyce that she decided to volunteer as a leader with the program for several years after her involvement as a teenager. Joyce's decision to enter ministry emerged from an inner sense of call that was reinforced from multiple directions: it was first affirmed, named, and supported by the minister at her church, then by her congregation, and then by the High School Theology Program at Trinity. And Joyce is not alone.

Our research team heard Joyce's call story, in one form or another, many times at each of the thirteen youth theology programs where we conducted interviews. Regardless of the nature of the High School Theology Program, having a pastor "tap" young people for these programs and having a home congregation support, commission, and/or "send them out" with the congregation's blessing were powerful experiences by which many teenagers begin to discern a vocational path pointing toward Christian leadership. When they arrived at a High School Theology Program, they found their still-unarticulated gifts for ministry affirmed, advocated for, and encouraged. A large percentage of these young people returned home thinking of themselves as passionate Christian leaders, eager to participate in the mission of God.

By "mission of God," I have in mind theologian Darrell Guder's conception of the *missio Dei,* which involves the sense of being sent out from life in Christian community into the world to be a witness to Jesus Christ through one's daily life.[1] Teenagers in the HSTPs participate in the mission of God as they worship, pray, and build community together, as they feed the hungry, glean alongside the poor, share afternoons with adults who have disabilities, and engage in faith conversations with Muslim and Jewish youth. They learn to listen for the direction of the Holy Spirit, to recognize and subvert evil powers, to restore justice, and to embrace others. Such acts of reconciliation and restoration anticipate the Kingdom of God.

For many youth, participating in a High School Theology Program gave them a first glimpse of what a vocation in pastoral ministry, service, or justice might be like. We heard stories of countless HSTP alumni for whom this was true. Many now serve churches in various forms of pastoral ministry. One became a lawyer working on behalf of immigrants; another started an organic farm providing healthy food for the poor; yet another worked

1. Darrell L. Guder and Lois Barrett, *Missional Church: A Vision for the Sending of the Church in North America* (Grand Rapids: Eerdmans, 1998), pp. 3-5.

as a counselor for families with children with disabilities. Certainly, countless people who are not Christians work in such jobs, but HSTP alumni enter these vocations with the expressed belief that their work contributes to God's work in the world — and they name this conviction in startling numbers. They view their discipleship — their particular role in bringing about healing, reconciliation, and justice — as an answer to God's call. This is their purpose, their vocation.

Before they can respond, however, young people — like Moses before the burning bush (Exod. 3) — must become convinced that they are called and capable of such ministries. For many, this means developing radically new identities as they begin to think of themselves as being healed, gifted, and sent into the world as bearers of God's healing, justice, and reconciliation. For others, it means building on an inner sense of call and gaining confidence in what God can do with their abilities and vocation. After hundreds of hours of interviews and site visits, our research team concluded that one reason HSTPs are so effective at forming engaged and effective Christian leaders is that they commission and name young people as both *called* and *sent* by God and by the church, while providing significant space in which young people can reflect on and build a sense of Christian identity around this calling.

High School Theology Programs play a unique role in the practice of naming that happens as part of the Christian life. Their distinctive contribution is their ability to create intentional communities of naming, discerning, and reflecting upon young people's giftedness in light of God's mission in the world. Every HSTP continually challenges youth to reflect on how their particular gifts can contribute to the Christian community and to God's work in the world. While the face-to-face aspect of these intentional communities tends to last for two to four weeks, some programs continue the intentional relationships online, by phone, and through alumni reunions years into the future. The extended opportunity to observe young people in person — undistracted by students' prior social identities — gives program directors and mentors the opportunity to explicitly notice and name teenagers' gifts and graces, bolstered by the knowledge that the congregations who sent them have already noticed and named the good work God has already begun in these young people's lives (Phil. 1:6). For these directors and mentors, naming is a part of the theological and pedagogical formation of the next generation of Christian leaders.

The bold claim of this chapter is that the process of naming (and renaming) forms persons to participate in the mission of God as Christian leaders in the church and in the world. To unfold that argument, we will first explore some theoretical and theological claims regarding the power of language and naming as it creates reality and identity. Next, by placing the biblical narrative of the renaming of Abraham and Sarah beside concrete practices of the High School Theology Programs, we can see the theological and pedagogical power of naming for Christian identity. Finally, we will consider how adults (especially congregational leaders), congregations, and theological education can offer potential leaders the gift of naming, and what this suggests for the work of Christian formation.

A Predecessor and a Princess: Theological and Theoretical Perspectives on Naming

God's people have long known the power of naming. At the ripe old age of ninety-nine, after a lifetime of seeking to live in covenant with God, Abram was approached by God to form a covenant. The Lord said to Abram,

> "I will make my covenant between me and you, and I will make you exceedingly numerous." Then Abram fell on his face; and God said to him, "As for me, this is my covenant with you: You shall be the ancestor of a multitude of nations. No longer shall your name be Abram, but your name shall be Abraham; for I have made you the ancestor of a multitude of nations." (Gen. 17:2-4)

In the ancient world, as in some communities today, "a new name signifies a new phase in the life of its bearer."[2] Taken alone, "Abram" means father, but because the Hebrew word for "multitude" sounds similar to the name Abraham, the suffix expands the meaning to "father of multitudes." God had promised Abram many descendants (Gen. 12), prompting Abram to imagine and attempt to actualize the divine promise through his own efforts. The turning point came when God *renamed* Abram, confirming the earlier promise, changing Abram's identity and instantiating a new reality for him to grow into. God's promised future becomes a part of who Abraham is. Likewise, Abram's wife Sarai experienced a name change that altered her life and her identity:

2. Gen. 17:15-16, Walter J. Harrelson, *The New Interpreter's Study Bible* (Nashville, TN: Abingdon), p. 35.

> God said to Abraham, as for Sarai your wife, you shall not call her Sarai, but Sarah shall be her name. I will bless her, and moreover I will give you a son by her. I will bless her, and she shall give rise to nations; kings of peoples shall come from her. (Gen. 17:15-16)

The name Sarah, meaning "princess," linked Sarah to the royal lineage that she would produce. In short, Abraham and Sarah entered a new phase of life when God changed their names.

In changing Sarai and Abram's names, God did not cancel their old identities. Rather, their change in identity fulfilled and expanded upon what they had long hoped for. Abram and Sarai had lived with an inner sense that God was calling them to be parents; they had longed for a child and had gone to great lengths to accomplish this by their own devising. Their changed names did not cancel their desires and striving, but instead indicated a shift in their identity, powerfully altering the trajectory of their lives from desperate attempts to bear children toward a future of fecundity based in God's power. God's changing of their names was both a promise and a symbol that a new reality was unfolding.

Of course, Abraham and Sarah are not alone in receiving new names and new identities. Throughout the Hebrew and Christian Scriptures, we see evidence of transformed identities in name changes: Jacob/Israel, Hoshea/Joshua, Hadassah/Esther, Naomi/Mara, Simon/Peter, and Saul/Paul. In Judeo-Christian history names matter, and the practice of naming wields and bestows power. The practice of naming prods particular ways of imagining and living life in accordance with a name, especially a name that connotes a particular relationship with God. Names convey promises. They instigate new realities.

Both modern sociologists and contemporary theologians echo these ancient intuitions. In their classic work, *The Social Construction of Reality,* sociologists Peter Berger and Thomas Luckmann argue that identity is formed by society, specifically through the names that society gives to its children: "The child learns that he *is* what he is called."[3] Berger and Luckmann argue that language is the medium that transmits reality (and society) to an individual. In their words, "language constitutes both the most important content and the most important instrument of socialization."[4] In addition

3. Peter L. Berger and Thomas Luckmann, *The Social Construction of Reality: A Treatise in the Sociology of Knowledge* (Garden City, NY: Doubleday, 1967), p. 132.

4. Berger and Luckmann, *Social Construction,* p. 133.

to emphasizing the power of language to form identity, they also argue that language is the principle vehicle by which individuals can change reality.[5]

Our research of the High School Theology Programs underscores these sociological insights. Naming — both an activity in which youth are named and an activity in which youth are given opportunities to name — powerfully forms and transforms teenagers' self-understandings and their understanding of the world. As Berger and Luckmann explain, putting experience into language shapes the world and our shared sense of reality. When the church invites youth to name the reality of their experience — as well as God's activity in the world — using the language, symbols, and images of Christian tradition, they do not simply participate in a mental exercise. They exert force on society that, quite literally, shapes the world.

Because language, by definition, names our reality, it is not theologically neutral. Rather, to name a thing is to exert power: naming asserts the truth of an object or a phenomenon. It identifies God's movement in the self and the world. This power, of course, carries both risks and potential. Feminist theologians are among those helping us sort out the possibilities and challenges that language poses for identity formation. Theologian Sallie McFague writes:

> First, feminists generally agree that whoever names the world owns the world. . . . The feminist critique of religious language is an extremely sophisticated one, for it is based on a recognition of the fundamental importance of language to human existence. With Ludwig Wittgenstein, feminists would say, "The limits of one's language are the limits of one's world," and with Martin Heidegger, "Language is the house of being." We do not so much use language as we are used by it. Since we are all born into a world which is already linguistic, in which the naming has already taken place, we only own our world to the extent that the naming that has occurred is our naming.[6]

Here McFague uses the phrase "our naming" ambiguously to include both being named and the activity of naming. She claims that persons are only a part of a world insofar as they participate in the "naming" activities of that world: "New naming, changes in language, are . . . no minor matters, for if

5. Berger and Luckmann, *Social Construction*, p. 133.

6. Sallie McFague, *Metaphorical Theology: Models of God in Religious Language* (Philadelphia: Fortress, 1982), pp. 8-9.

one believes that language and 'world' are coterminous, then changes in the one will involve changes in the other, and such changes are often revolutionary."[7] The thrust of McFague's argument is a critique of the limits of the patriarchal language for God, but her insight has been widely applied by HSTPs for the broader purpose of identity formation in adolescents.

Yet Christian theology also challenges a simple constructivist view of reality in which language becomes the ultimate and defining force in the world. Distinguishing between human "reality" and ultimate "Reality," Christians maintain that while language does construct human reality, exerting real and shaping pressures and forces on individuals and their identity, God's Reality is beyond the limits of language. Human language always falls short of describing God, and cannot fully capture what God is doing in the world. Because God exists beyond human language, naming God does not control or create God. Nor does naming young people — important as it is — ultimately determine them or the world in which they live. Rather, naming proclaims God's intentions for the world and for us, providing us with what theologian Howard Thurman calls "a crown" that we grow into as we participate in God's transformation of all creation.[8]

Thus, the naming practices at work within the High School Theology Programs use language in ways that disrupt and reframe the disfiguring reality in which youth have lived, instead opening up perspectives on the divine Reality that defines the world according to the mission of God. HSTPs use naming practices to help youth see the world as a mysterious place where God gives sight to the blind, heals the sick, and brings justice where corruption has reigned — in other words, to help youth hear God's Reality as different from the world of labels they have been given. In these practices of renaming, young people hear themselves named by God as called, capable, powerful, whole, and beloved.

These theoretical and theological reflections help us see that words and names are not neutral; they are theologically loaded. Names have meaning, give power, and confer identity. They have the power to create, destroy, heal, and open new possibilities. As God changed Abram and Sarai's identities by giving each a new name, so young people experience the Holy Spirit's power through the High School Theology Programs' use of naming and renaming as formative practices.

7. McFague, *Metaphorical Theology,* p. 9.

8. Howard Thurman, *Jesus and the Disinherited* (Boston: Beacon Press, 1976), p. 106.

Practices of Naming and Renaming

The HSTPs are especially attuned to this nominative work of the Spirit, using intentional naming practices both explicitly and implicitly. A mentor or leader might say to a teenager: "I see this gift in you; do you sense it as well?" Or peers may reflect back to one another: "This is the you that I see." Or, naming can occur as youth are given the space and opportunity to say, "This is who I am, and this is what I believe." Naming might involve actually receiving a new name, but it also can simply involve hearing a gift or potential identified and called forth. In all these ways, the High School Theology Programs model intentional uses of naming to form young people's identities, and to commission them to participate in God's mission in the world. In our research, four practices of naming and renaming appeared prominently in most HSTPs:

1. Commissioning: "I Think You Should Try This"

Joyce felt an inner sense of call to ministry, but only when her pastor identified her gifts in a personal and public way, and when her congregation confirmed those gifts with their emotional and financial support, did she find the courage to take concrete steps toward exploring her call. These acts of support "commissioned" Joyce in the sense that they entrusted her with a kind of authority for the task of Christian leadership. Recognizing the powerful influence of adult mentors in the lives of young people, most High School Theology Programs require an adult or several adults to formally recommend a young person for participation. Program directors emphasize that the recommendation process is not designed to screen for only "the best and the brightest" students (in reality, in the HSTPs — as in most summer programs for adolescents — availability determines a large percentage of program enrollments); nor is the process primarily intended to ensure participants' readiness for the program (despite program directors' hopes that this would be the case). Above all, the nomination process is designed to assure the participant that someone else has noticed in them gifts for the ministry of Christian leadership. Often, the person who formally recommends a young person is the same person who had originally brought the program to the teenager's attention. Although a few young people stumbled across the HSTPs themselves, the vast majority attended after a parent, teacher, youth leader, pastor, or congregation member articulated their gifts, and after their congregation formally or informally commissioned them.

2. *Titles: "This Is Who You Truly Are"*

Another way naming functions at the High School Theology Programs is by bestowing on teenagers specific titles that reframe their self-understandings in relationship to God and the world. Berger and Luckmann's insistence that "the child learns that he *is* what he is called" rings especially true here. The Duke Youth Academy offers a case in point. At the DYA, adults challenge youth to consider how they are renamed in their baptism as one who belongs to Christ and — to paraphrase Martin Luther — as people called to be "christs" for others, i.e., people whose lives truly reflect Jesus Christ in the world.[9] They are reminded that in baptism they are claimed by Christ and that they become one with Christ in their resurrection out of the waters of death. DYA emphasizes that young people's new identity in baptism is God-given and therefore more authentic than any humanly given identity or name. It negates the pejorative and painful identities youth have taken on in the past; it gives them a renewed value, and it sets them on a path of participating in the mission of God. This theologically rooted naming calls young people who they already are (Christ's), as well as who they are becoming (christs).

Baptismal theology is not the only source of nominative pedagogies in the HSTPs. Some programs employ educational philosophies that seek to honor learners by calling them to live up to high expectations, and to recognize the value of young people's contributions to the church. At Candler School of Theology's Youth Theological Initiative, youth are called "scholars" rather than "students," "participants," or "youth," insisting that young people are called to become "public theologians" who identify injustice in the world and act to address it. Adult leaders at YTI report that the nomenclature of "scholars" and "public theologians" helps youth imagine themselves as practical theologians engaged in the crucial tasks of theology, and not as immature learners.

9. In Martin Luther's treatise *The Freedom of a Christian* (1520), Luther wrote: "(A)s our heavenly Father has in Christ freely come to our aid, we also ought to help our neighbor through our body and its works, and each one should become as it were a Christ to the other that we may be Christs to one another and Christ may be the same in all, that is, that we may be truly Christians." Available at http://www.fordham.edu/halsall/mod/luther-freedomchristian.asp (accessed October 18, 2013).

As the first youth theology program, YTI has influenced other programs. Huron University College recently adopted the language of "scholars" for teenage participants in the Ask & Imagine program; director Judy Steers reflected that this change in nomenclature immediately raised youth's expectations for themselves and made them more invested participants in ways that were profoundly positive.[10] Chelle Huth, the program director at Theological Education with Youth, affiliated with Lutheran Theological Seminary in Philadelphia, explained their program's decision to call young people "scholars" in order to create a contrast between CrossRoad and young people's usual experience in congregations:

> One of the key reasons that we call them scholars, because they aren't kids — well, they are kids, but we want them to understand that we honor them in a different way, in a way that they aren't used to being honored in an institution whose main foci are to teach faith and to teach people to teach faith, and to worship in faithful ways. And so to honor them by calling them scholars, I think, helps set a different tone.

Tonya Burton, program director at the Perkins Youth School of Theology, points out that the naming practices of her program are intended to call forth latent potential in their youth participants and make them aware of who they already are and can become. She explains,

> I come here . . . every year highlighting that [youth] are young leaders right off the bat. They may not know that, but we call them young scholars for a reason: to instill those callings [to be practical theologians] already through affirmations, and then [to give] them responsibilities that we deem are characteristics of leaders.

Like Abraham and Sarah, these young people experience renaming as both a promise of what they will be and as an actual inauguration of that new reality. They are already leaders; they are already theologians; they are already scholars; they already belong to Christ — and adults respond to them accordingly. Yet they are also *becoming* leaders, theologians, scholars, and mature Christians, living into the promise that has been opened by the new names they have received.

10. Personal conversation, Judy Steers, High School Theology Program Seminar #3 (February 5, 2013), Princeton, NJ.

3. Naming Particular Gifts and Callings: "I See This Gift in You"

A High School Theology Program tends to operate as an equal opportunity labeler: the same honorific language is used for each teenager in the program who is asked to take on certain tasks before his or her peers. All participants are called to ponder their faith, reflect in community, love God, serve neighbors, seek justice, and act as servant leaders or public theologians. Yet young people have differing gifts, and are called to different kinds of ministries — so the HSTPs also use language that names and reframes specific gifts and callings. Some programs, such as Youth Theological Initiative at Candler and Compass at Gordon-Conwell, explicitly challenge mentors and leaders to look for gifts in young people and find opportunities to tell young people what they see. A few programs design their entire curricula around the task of ferreting out and cultivating gifted new leaders for the church.

Most programs give youth opportunities to hone particular gifts for ministry. CrossRoad, for example, gives youth an opportunity to preach a five-minute sermon. After preaching, each preacher receives feedback from the group. When a teenager possesses a natural talent for preaching, the professor, mentors, and the program director take time during the week to affirm this gift explicitly, saying things like: "Wow, you really have a gift for preaching. I wonder if you have any opportunities to preach at home. Perhaps preaching might be a gift God has given you." Some youth may never have considered talent in public communication to be a God-given gift, explicitly valued by faith communities. Hearing this gift named (and many others) allows young people to begin to see their particular gifts as having a divine origin, becoming a way in which God has equipped them to serve Christ in the church and in the broader culture.

4. Youth as Namers: "This Is Who I Might Be, and This Is the World as I Know It"

The power of hearing oneself named as capable, gifted, and beloved cannot be overstated, but that power is amplified when young people have the necessary agency and creative space to name these emerging identities for themselves. As teenagers intentionally reflect on these new aspects of their identities, when they are allowed to ask questions about who they have been, who they are, and who they might become, they begin to own the vocations that others have noticed. Some of these opportunities for self-reflection come through formal practices and processes. The Interdenominational Theological Consortium's Youth Hope-Builders Academy in Atlanta works mostly with African American youth, and aims to build their confidence while strengthening their connections to their families and home churches. The first activity in the summer program each year asks youth to look up the meaning or story of their given names. The goal is to help participants feel solidly grounded in an inherited identity from which they can confidently move forward into the future, even as they experience Christ's transformation of that identity. The adult mentors at YHBA agree that throughout this process, as teenagers uncover affirming stories about their parents' dreams for them, they gain a sense of pride in their personal stories. This is particularly significant for those who have stories of distress, and had not previously thought of themselves as having a "goodly heritage" (Psalm 16:6).

Other opportunities for youth to reflect on their own identity — to name or rename themselves — tend to arise naturally when youth can explore, test, and refine their gifts in a discerning community that provides a welcoming space as well as peers and mentors with whom they can "try on" their identity in Christ, to see how it fits. A number of youth, for example, told us that coming to a High School Theology Program caused them to ask themselves, "All of these people think of themselves as having gifts for leadership as a Christian in the world or in the church. Do I have these gifts, too?"

A certain freedom seems to accompany the ability to name one's own identity. One female participant traced her changing career trajectory to her two-summer experience at CrossRoad: "If you remember, last year, I said I was definitely going to be a minister, but now I'm not sure. I am really feeling called to something else . . . " Her program, like many others, provided her the safe structure in which she could try on and take off the names and identities that her parents, friends, ministers, and peers had given her, so she could consider which "name" most authentically described her inner sense of the Holy Spirit's call.

Frequently, the space provided at the HSTPs for naming oneself allowed youth to claim an identity they would have been reluctant to admit prior to the program. A number of teenagers told us about the anxiety they experienced when claiming their religious faith at home or in school. Being immersed in a practicing, reflective community of faithful peers appears to encourage and normalize the expression of faith commitments. In the safety of these programs, populated by similarly religious peers, young people can practice Christian language without judgment, gaining confidence in their ability to articulate their faith identities. They gain the courage to say, "This is who I am. I am a person of faith."

Sometimes articulating a sense of one's religious self has the effect of making other identity statements possible as well. Lancaster Theological Seminary's Leadership Now program focuses on building a diverse, welcoming community, and youth frequently declare other identities in the context of faith: "This is who I am. I am a person of faith, and I am gay." Quite unexpectedly, leaders noticed that summer after summer Leadership Now seemed to provide a context where youth gain courage to discuss sexual identity, surprised to learn that two labels — "gay" and "person of faith" — need not be mutually exclusive. Leadership Now's program director Megan Malick observes that the safety of intentional Christian community seems to give teenagers permission to share dimensions of their lives that they have not shared elsewhere. In the holding environment of a safe social space away from home, teenagers feel free to take risks with their emerging identities, even entrusting these communities with information they had formerly held in private.

Effects of Pedagogies of Nomination

The pedagogies of nomination that occur in the High School Theology Programs form missional faith in a variety of powerful ways. When youth are named, renamed, or given opportunities to name, they participate in revolutionary and transformative practices that change them, and that change the world in which they live. In the HSTPs, naming had many benefits, including (1) opening vocational possibilities; (2) bringing about healing and reconciliation; (3) raising young people's awareness about their relationship with God; and (4) strengthening relationships with pastors and congregations.

Naming Opens Vocational Possibilities

In a society in which young people are constantly asked, "What do you want to be when you grow up?" — but are seldom made aware that their adult vocation can be a way of living out their Christian faith — naming practices provide crucial opportunities for youth to try on the identity of a Christian leader in the presence of peers and invested adults. Other youth experience High School Theology Programs as a chance to explore vocational possibilities apart from pastoral ministry that nonetheless flow from their faith commitments. For example, most programs introduce young people to Christian adults from an array of professions who explicitly connect their faith to their chosen vocational trajectory. Youth at Lancaster's Summer Seminary Sampler go so far as to job-shadow adults who do not work in churches, but who still view their jobs as "callings"; days prior to our on-site interviews, a conversation with a local funeral director had profoundly moved the teenagers we talked to. Meeting people from various walks of life who articulate faith as a springboard for their work as public defenders, city planners, homeless advocates, physicians, and so on prompts teenagers to imagine how they too might connect their lifework and their identities as disciples of Jesus Christ.

Naming Fosters Healing and Reconciliation

One frequent side effect of practices of naming and renaming is deep healing and relational reconciliation. Names have power to create, but they also have power to destroy, as the current climate of bullying makes bitingly clear. The nominative practices of HSTPs seem to disrupt these patterns in two ways. First, painful labels — instigated by others but repeated and internalized by young people themselves — are challenged by new names drawn from Christian tradition and the experience of Christian community. Instead of "You don't belong," youth hear: "You belong to God. You belong here." Instead of "You're not good at much," they hear: "You are uniquely gifted, and we value what you bring."

The HSTPs overtly challenge the social hierarchies and divisions teenagers have absorbed from media culture and the high school social order ("jocks," "preps," "geeks," "goths," etc.), disrupting this naming system with rituals of welcome and by offering liminal space where traditional stereotypes can disintegrate. Candler's Youth Theological Initiative, for example, directly confronts the unjust naming structures of young people's social worlds in their opening worship service, adapting Galatians 3:28 to proclaim to youth that in Christ, "there is no longer Jew nor Greek, Jock nor Geek." Likewise, Jessica Driesenga, program director of Calvin Seminary's Facing Your Future program, relates how one small group that she led, composed of five boys from the program, became a case study for reconciliation across the usual social dividing lines:

> One of the guys was one of those tan, very athletic . . . you could tell he was one of the popular kids at the school. He was quarterback of the football

> team; he was doing well in high school. Then we had another guy who had the long, dark shaggy hair and wore what you might call "Emo" clothing. You could tell that he was not going to be quarterback in high school, and he was not going to be a part of the popular crowd. He had expressed in our group a lot of the loneliness and isolation that he felt and . . . those feelings of not being worthy in his high school because he didn't have a ton of friends. And I remember the last day him coming to the quarterback in tears because they were *friends,* and he had never had someone that was in that [popular] group treat him like he mattered.

Such reconciling experiences help youth glimpse what a life beyond labels could look like, as they reimagine their relationships, identities, and values "back home."

Naming practices also help to heal deeply fractured self-understandings as well. Ken explained how Hellenic's CrossRoad program was one place where he was able to share his divided sense of self due to being adopted, and how vulnerable this made him feel. He described how this inward division made him feel defensive, lashing out at those who made fun of him. By naming this pain — and by worshipping with a community of peers who included, welcomed, and loved him — Ken used the faith practices of the Eastern Orthodox tradition to move toward healing, re-narrating his experience as an adopted child, forgiving those who had hurt him, and imagining how he might help others who feel like outsiders.

Naming Raises Awareness about One's Relationship to God

As young people hear themselves named through Scripture and Christian tradition in new, theologically rich ways, they arrive at more than just a clearer sense of self. They arrive at a clearer understanding of God and of their own spiritual longings. Naming our innate desire to be in relationship with God is a practice important to every Christian by helping us realign our priorities to become more closely connected to the One who made us. The ongoing National Study of Youth and Religion identified youth's tendency to think of God as a distant, helpful therapist rather than an active, sometimes disruptive, agent working in their lives. By contrast, youth in the High School Theology Programs are continually asked about what God is doing in their lives, and are expected to give an account of this experience — out loud — or at least pose questions about it in response. Hearing others name their perceptions of God's activity in their lives (i.e., "I think God is calling me to this" or "I believe the Holy Spirit has given me this gift") is a way of practicing a vocabulary of faith. Such conversations help youth gain facility with theological language that allows them to notice ways in which the Holy Spirit is at work within and through them.

Naming Strengthens Young People's Relationships with Clergy and Congregations

Paraphrasing Erik Erikson, Kenda Creasy Dean writes in *Practicing Passion* that adult guarantors (Erikson's own phrase) are "representatives of the adult world who embody worthy ideologies, and who respond to the adolescent's plea to be recognized as more than he seems to be, with unique potentials needed by the world."[11] According to Erikson, youth need adults present in their lives as models for what a life (including a Christian life) can look like, and also to provide solid claims against which youth can press. Unfortunately, as Dean claims, few youth have adults who are "there" for them, let alone present and invested in their lives in a role where they could be recognized as "more than [they] seem to be" and as someone with "unique potentials needed by the world."[12]

The High School Theology Programs swim upstream of this current by providing numerous adults, in multiple roles, who are explicitly commissioned to "be there" for youth, and to draw attention to God's presence in young people's lives by naming young people's God-given abilities and inclinations. These mentors also invite youth to talk about the way they perceive divine presence and direction. Practices of nomination help adults turn the spotlight of Christian vocation away from themselves toward the young people they love as they help them to recognize, just as their biblical forebears helped young people to recognize, that God loves the unlikely candidate for leadership. The Bible is full of stories about God's startling renaming of young people who, until the intervention of a divinely appointed messenger, saw themselves only as shepherds (David) or virgins (Mary). In each of these "renaming" stories, God first names young people

11. Paraphrasing Eric H. Erikson, *Insight and Responsibility: Lectures on the Ethical Implications of Psychoanalytic Insight* (New York: Norton, 1964), p. 125. Kenda Creasy Dean, *Practicing Passion: Youth and the Quest for a Passionate Church* (Grand Rapids: Eerdmans, 2004), p. 77.

12. Dean, *Practicing Passion*, p. 125.

as leaders and then equips them for the purpose to which they have been called.

While the professionalization of youth ministry since the 1980s has certainly had more benefits than drawbacks, the tendency to import leadership standards from corporate culture has also reinforced the tendency to see youth ministry as a distinctive "department" in the church.[13] The nomination and recruitment processes encouraged by High School Theology Programs blur easy compartmentalization, and strengthen young people's desire to connect with their pastors and congregations — and vice versa. The challenge of looking within their congregations for young people with interests or gifts for ministry gave ministers a formal "excuse" to talk with teenagers, not merely asking how their soccer team did in yesterday's tournament, but to actually see and name their gifts for the mission of God. As Joyce's story demonstrates, to feel noticed by a spiritual leader has a powerful effect on teenagers' sense of belonging to and purpose in a faith community. In a culture where youth are graded, scored, weighed, timed, and measured on a weekly basis in school and extracurricular activities, the effect of being noticed by an adult who is attentive to gifts of the Spirit is paramount.

Interestingly, practices of nomination were not only helpful on the "front end" of the HSTPs. Many youth described feeling a tension between their "before" and "after" identities — the person they thought they were "before" the program and the person they felt like they had become by the time they returned home. Naming on the part of pastors and congregations plays a pivotal role in helping teenagers to integrate their high school theology "selves" with life after the program. As Christy Lang Hearlson writes

13. Practical theologians tend to resist such compartmentalization, and a growing body of literature encourages churches to re-imagine excellent youth ministry as the healthy integration of youth deeper into the life of the church. This perspective has gained currency especially since the 1990s, as youth ministry has become more closely aligned with practical theology. Cf. David Ng, *Youth in the Community of Disciples* (Valley Forge, PA: Judson Press, 1984); Roland Martinson, *Effective Youth Ministry* (Minneapolis, MN: Augsburg, 1988); Mark DeVries, *Family-Based Youth Ministry* (Downers Grove, IL: InterVarsity, 1994); Kenda Creasy Dean and Ron Foster, *The Godbearing Life: The Art of Soul-Tending for Youth Ministry* (Nashville, TN: Upper Room, 1998); Joyce Mercer, *Welcoming Children: A Practical Theology of Childhood* (St. Louis: Chalice, 2005); Katherine Turpin, *Branded* (St. Louis: Chalice, 2006); Andrew Root, *Revisiting Relational Youth Ministry* (Downers Grove, IL: InterVarsity, 2007); Brian Mahan, Michael Warren, and David White, *Awakening Youth Discipleship* (Eugene, OR: Wipf and Stock, 2008); Amy Jacober, *The Adolescent Journey* (Downers Grove, IL: InterVarsity, 2011); also, Root and Dean's summary of this shift, *The Theological Turn in Youth Ministry* (Downers Grove, IL: InterVarsity, 2011).

in this volume, young people experience the return home in many ways, depending largely on the degree to which home congregations embrace the participant's new self-awareness about faith. Nominative practices proved to be significant for young people before, during, and after a High School Theology Program. A congregation's naming and commissioning of the newly empowered young leader at the conclusion of these programs proved to be exceptionally powerful, especially as churches deployed them for the church's ministry.

For the majority of the youth we interviewed, the time spent at a theology program was not merely formative — it was transformative. While nearly all High School Theology Program participants identify as Christians before leaving home, many if not most return with a renewed, refreshed, and invigorated understanding of what "being Christian" means — and what they might personally contribute to the church as a result. Thanks to the nominative practices of the HSTPs, these teenagers' invigorated understandings of their callings often include concrete plans rooted in their named gifts. Countless learning activities in the context of an HSTP — sermon writing, interfaith conversation, theological discussion, or just talking with roommates or mentors into the wee hours of the morning — were calculated to contribute to new understandings of teenagers' relationships to God and the church.

The Role of Congregations in Naming

The task of Christian communities on behalf of young people — in addition to protecting and empowering them — is to help them discern and name their gifts, and to commission them to use those gifts to serve God and others. We saw how one minister identified Joyce's emerging sense of call, and how her congregation — in three weeks' time — informally commissioned her by financially supporting her attendance at not one, but two leadership camps. Some programs take congregational practices of nomination even further, requiring congregations to work with young people on a ministry project at the conclusion of the program, or involving congregants as mentors with young people in between sessions of a multi-year high school theology experience. At Gordon-Conwell's Compass program teenagers may participate *only* if their congregation nominates them; there is no application process. While program director David Horn says that this has many advantages — including solidifying a teenager's a sense of call and identity as a leader — there are also unique challenges. As a result, some of the time at Compass is spent inviting young people to question their call, and discern whether their gifts really are for leadership in Christian ministry or elsewhere.

Congregational support and affirmation are key elements in practices of naming that are crucial to High School Theology Program participants. While HSTPs provide liminal space for healing, reconciliation, and identity formation, congregations remain the contexts in which young people must recalibrate their "camp highs" for the day-to-day work of Christian ministry. Teenagers quickly learn that the graced existence of a theology program, in which service, worship, reflection, study, and fellowship are orchestrated to flow into and out of one another seamlessly, is not replicable in the week in, week out rhythm of congregational life. It is entirely realistic, however, for congregations and parents to participate in this graced existence by listening to youth narrate their transformative experiences, inviting them into leadership roles within the congregation, and sending and receiving youth through practices of nomination, commissioning, and receiving.

Insights for Theological Education and Leadership Formation

For those committed to forming future Christian leaders for the church and beyond, helping young people discern, name, and nurture their gifts for ministry — long before they need a job — is a critical concern. Seminary education, of course, is graduate education, not catechetical instruction. Nowhere is this more obvious than in seminary intake systems, which rely somewhat on practices of nomination but much more decisively on formal applications, test scores, and undergraduate preparation. Yet the importance of seminaries, divinity schools, and theological institutions becoming organically involved in helping young people name their gifts for ministry *before* graduate school is, as we have seen, one of the chief benefits of sponsoring a High School Theology Program.

Similarly, the "exit strategies" that accompany seminary graduation are frequently an overlooked but formative element in young people's call stories. Unlike HSTPs, where teenagers return to congregations that often purposefully utilize these homecomings as opportunities for leadership formation, seminaries and divinity schools typically graduate people into the unknown, and hope that things turn out well. As this project makes clear, a more successful formula for establishing young people's identities as Christian leaders would make practices of naming and commissioning an intentional part of the curriculum. Theological formation must include intellectual as well as moral discipline, but nominative practices — before, during, and after seminary — serve as a "third rail" to guide missional formation by planting, cultivating, and reinforcing young people's understandings of their identities as participants in the mission of God.

Perhaps pedagogies of naming matter even more for church "systems" (congregations, regional judicatories, denominations) of leadership formation, since these practices cultivate vocational attentiveness for those who do — and don't — view their calls in relationship to formal theological education. In 1998, when the Virginia Annual Conference of the United Methodist Church "renewed efforts to strategically focus on encouraging vocational discernment among young people," conference leaders set out to identify and cultivate future clergy and lay leadership by integrating pedagogies of naming into every aspect of the conference's age-level ministries. At middle high camps and conferences, teenagers heard their gifts for spiritual leadership named and encouraged, and they were given multiple opportunities for primary leadership. Conference youth ministry personnel tracked these young people into high school, inviting them to discernment programs and leadership summits. In college, conference leaders requested these young people as volunteers at youth events and employed them as camp and conference staff. Those who attended seminary were also tracked; upon graduation, young pastors were commissioned and placed in peer groups with a mentor who attended closely to the needs of young clergy, helping them discern their future vocational trajectories. It is no surprise that the Virginia Annual Conference has the highest percentage of young clergy in the denomination, and generally boasts an extremely committed corps of lay and ordained young leaders — some of whom were first identified fourteen years ago, at a middle high camp.[14]

14. Beth Downs, cited in "Virginia Conference Fares Pretty Well in Latest Clergy Age Report," *Virginia United Methodist Advocate* (2012), http://www.vaumc.org/page.aspx?pid=2423 (accessed October 20, 2013). Data are available from the Lewis Center for Church Leadership, Washington, DC, http://www.churchleadership.com/clergyage/um_clergy_age_trends13.html (accessed January 20, 2014). This number reflects all categories of clergy recognized by the United Methodist Church (elders, deacons, and local pastors age thirty-five and under). The process for recruiting young clergy was explained to Kenda Creasy Dean by Beth Downs and Rhonda van Dyke Colby, personal conversation, Virginia Conference Ministers Convocation, Blackstone Retreat and Conference Center, Blackstone, VA, January 20, 2009.

The nominative practices of the High School Theology Programs create bridges that connect young people in congregations with broader, more formal systems of leadership formation. They reassure youth of God's confidence in them by demonstrating the church's support and confidence in their leadership. By helping teenagers discern their gifts, explore their calls, reconstruct their fractured identities, and name God's activity in the world, the HSTPs' pedagogies of naming are powerful vehicles for constructing adolescent faith identities. What's in a name? When it comes to engaging young people in the mission of God, a great deal.

CHAPTER SIX

Taking It Home

Separation and Reintegration as Teachable Moments

Christy Lang Hearlson

In Martin Gardner's 1973 novel, *The Flight of Peter Fromm,* a young man leaves his Pentecostal church and devout family to enroll at the University of Chicago Divinity School, where he hopes to change the school's secular ethos with his religious fervor.[1] Instead, theological education slowly corrodes his convictions and creates a widening break in his identity that can only be crossed at great psychological and spiritual peril. In a key scene, Peter returns home, where his mother begs him to pray. Knowing what she expects, he prays in tongues. Yet praying in tongues is a practice Peter no longer believes in, and his dishonest performance pitches him into despair that leads to the brink of madness.

A more recent novel by Barbara Kingsolver, *Flight Behavior,* opens with the central character hiking up a mountainside toward an adulterous tryst. Dellarobia is stopped short by a vision of orange flame that does not burn the forest.[2] Filled with awe and an overwhelming sense of vocation, she runs back home. When scientists arrive to study the phenomenon, they invite Dellarobia to work with them, and she becomes a translator between the scientists and her poor small-town community. Although her liminality is sometimes acutely painful, Dellarobia works hard to integrate her learning into her life, achieving a level of knowledge and freedom she had not imagined.

Peter and Dellarobia represent two ends of a spectrum. On the one

1. Martin Gardner, *The Flight of Peter Fromm* (New York: Prometheus Books, 1994).
2. Barbara Kingsolver, *Flight Behavior* (New York: Harper, 2012).

hand, an experience of separation from home and of education can lead to inward chaos and permanent dislocation. On the other, such experiences can lend new perspective and courage for daily life, as well as skills for translating between different communities. What makes the difference between these two? This question is acute for theological education, which often removes learners geographically from home, and invites students to undertake spiritual, intellectual journeys. This question is equally acute for the High School Theology Programs, since learners leave home in order to be immersed in a new community and formed in new ways — and then return home again. In some cases, learners skillfully reintegrate into their families and churches with a sense of vocation as Christian leaders. In other cases, youth simply cannot match up the seams of their home life with their experience in their youth theology program. What makes the difference?

In this chapter, I will seek to answer that question by first offering theological and psychological perspectives on the experiences of separation and return, drawing especially on the research of Jeffrey A. Kottler, who has explored factors that prompt lasting personal change. I will then turn to data collected by the research team of the High School Theology Program Seminar, which suggest that when teenagers return to their home contexts after a High School Theology Program, they are met by one of four basic orientations: *partnership, substitution, transformation,* and/or *opposition.* After describing and assessing each of these approaches as they relate to separation and integration, I will recommend two in particular and briefly suggest how they might inform theological education and congregational ministry with youth. What seems clear is that the catechetical impact of deeply formative vocational experiences like High School Theology Programs does not end with the car ride home. The homecoming itself may be decisive in a young person's ability to claim his or her vocational identity.

"Go from Your Country and Your Kindred": Separation and Transformation

In ancient agricultural communities in which most people stayed put, wandering was weird behavior, but the Bible is full of stories of people who went out from their "country and kindred." Adam and Eve, Abram and Sarai, Hagar, Ishmael, Jacob, Joseph, Moses, the Hebrew people, Naomi and Ruth, Esther, Jonah, Mary and Joseph, Jesus, Peter, James, John, Paul, Onesimus,

Priscilla and Aquila — they were exiles, sojourners, nomads, escape artists, wanderers, migrants, emigrants, refugees, and missionaries.

Away from the familiar, safe, and civilized, they met God. In the wilderness, the angel of the Lord gave Hagar a covenantal promise, and she in turn named God. Jacob dreamed of God's promise and wrestled God's angel. Joseph discovered God's faithfulness in the midst of enslavement. The Hebrew people experienced God's discipline and provision in the wilderness. Jonah had it out with God on the outskirts of Nineveh. Elizabeth and Mary felt divine life dawning when Mary traveled to see her cousin. Angels attended Jesus in the wilderness, the disciples saw God heal and teach in Jesus, and Paul heard the risen Christ speak to him. When people leave home, the biblical narrative suggests, holy things happen. Wrenched out of the quotidian, people encounter a wild God, the God of *elsewhere* and *everywhere,* and they can never be the same.

The Bible, of course, is not the only place where we witness separation from home as a time of transformation. Therapist and educator Jeffrey Kottler has spent his professional career studying experiences that catalyze personal change, particularly geographic travel, as well as the factors that sustain such change afterward.[3] Kottler suggests that people who set out on a geographical journey often already have a mindset ripe for change, but once they leave home, they also experience insulation from the usual influences of their lives, which sets them free to move in new directions and experiment with different identities.

Such disconnection from established networks of relationships is potent because our relationships are tremendously accurate predictors of our attitudes and behaviors. In *Connected: The Surprising Power of Our Social Networks and How They Shape Our Lives,* Nicholas Christakis and James Fowler show how the web of relationships in which we are embedded shapes our lives and pervasively affects — sometimes dictates — our emotional states, romantic lives, financial welfare, health, addictions, and religious and political views.[4] It should not be surprising, then, that geographic journeys that separate learners from established social networks impact their thoughts, emotions, and behavior.

3. Jeffrey Kottler, *Travel That Can Change Your Life: How to Create a Transformative Experience* (San Francisco: Jossey-Bass, 1997) and *Making Changes Last* (New York: Routledge, 2001), p. 130.

4. Nicholas A. Christakis and James H. Fowler, *Connected: The Surprising Power of Our Social Networks and How They Shape Our Lives — How Your Friends' Friends' Friends Affect Everything You Feel, Think, and Do* (New York: Back Bay Books, 2009).

In addition to removing the traveler from relational networks, separation from home also introduces disorientation, which Kottler argues incites change:

> More often than not, the most powerful and dramatic changes took place during a time when someone felt lost or literally *was* lost. . . . It is interesting to consider that it is often when you are most uncomfortable, most out your element, most confused and anxious, that the real action begins. You are forced to rely on resources that you never knew you had. You are required to solve problems in new ways. And often what you learned from these crises has helped you ever since.[5]

In addition to fostering such flexibility, resourcefulness, and proactive behavior, travel heightens our senses, sometimes inducing an altered psychological state. This strong emotional arousal, Kottler explains, sparks transformation, since it creates a clear memory and prompts action.

Drawing on the potential of travel to instigate change, the High School Theology Programs enable young people to "get lost" through a variety of practices, many of which David Horn describes in his chapter on pilgrimage in this volume.[6] Most notably, the programs physically remove young people from their home churches and families for a time of intentional growth, take away devices that connect young people to their routines and social networks, and transport them to new places and experiences. Many youth whom we interviewed expressed that their program gave them space to reflect on their lives as they would not have done had they stayed put. They also said their program challenged their assumptions, showed them new perspectives, opened up vocational possibilities, helped them make their faith their own, and gave them skills and courage for living out and talking about their faith. Their comments suggest that practices of separation allow for the development of critical distance, freedom to try out new identities, and the opportunity to personalize learning.

5. Kottler, "Change: What Really Makes a Difference?" *Psychology Today,* December 8, 2010, http://www.psychologytoday.com/blog/helping-yourself-helping-others/201012/making-changes-last (accessed November 27, 2013).

6. See especially David Horn's chapter in this volume: "Prepare Me for a Worthy Adventure: Pedagogies of Pilgrimage in the Compass Program of Gordon-Conwell Theological Seminary."

"Go Home to Your Friends": Possibilities and Problems of Reintegration

When people meet God on the road, their encounter with holiness often sends them back home changed and ready to effect change. Psalm 126 describes those who go out carrying seeds for sowing and come home singing songs of joy, bearing sheaves. When God's people go away from home, they come home bearing gifts — new songs to sing, new joy to share, new food to sustain themselves and their neighbors. But a sojourner's return does not guarantee a community's welcome. When the wild God of elsewhere sends us home to the here and now, reintegration is never simple.

Jacob finally returned home to the brother he had defrauded, but he came in fear for his life and was shocked by Esau's graciousness. Naomi returned home accompanied by a faithful daughter-in-law who would bless the whole family line, yet she was also a vulnerable widow who had to maneuver her way back into society. After the burning bush, Moses feared that the Hebrew people would scoff at him, and he needed his brother Aaron to partner with him. When Jesus returned to Galilee from the wilderness and preached in his hometown synagogue, his community tried to throw him off a cliff. We do not know what happened to the Gerasene demoniac whom Jesus instructed to go home and tell his friends what the Lord had done for him, but he must surely have faced surprise and skepticism. Return does not guarantee integration. How then can we equip those who return home to tell their stories, sing their songs, spread their joy, and feed others with the food they have gathered? How can we welcome youth who come home changed, helping them integrate what they have learned into the rest of their lives?

The task is not simple — there is no magic formula — and the challenges are real. In our research on the HSTPs, three challenges to reintegration predominated. The first challenge is the tendency for youth to take the path of least resistance and to jump into old ruts at home. Director Andy Brubacher Kaethler tells of a mother who remarked to him with some anxiety that her daughter had come home changed from her program. Her daughter had become committed to discipleship to Christ, zealous about ethics, questioning of consumerism — all disquieting behavior. But then, the mother reported with relief, soccer season began, and her daughter was "back to normal."

A second challenge is that youth go home to face others' apathy toward the ideas and practices they have become passionate about. Staff and directors told stories of youth who returned home and tried to convince their youth ministers to talk more about the sacraments, their congregations to address homelessness, or their friends to care about where they buy their clothes — and their efforts fell flat. Their home communities could not relate to their newfound passion and did not join in their work, so their gifts went neglected. Discouraging experiences like this led some youth and alumni to say that their High School Theology Program "ruined" them for churches that go about business as usual.

Third, youth sometimes face others' active resistance. One alumna of the Youth Theology Initiative at Candler School of Theology was changed by learning about systemic social injustice. Yet her new theological and political opinions wreaked havoc in her relationship with her father. Near tears, she said, "My dad called me 'you damn liberal' more than he called me by name for a whole year." While many youth meet a friendly welcome, others cannot overcome the apathy or resistance they encounter and respond by giving up on their vision, seeking a new congregation, or simply leaving church altogether.

Jeffrey Kottler's research on factors that make personal change likely to endure resonate with these stories. He names five factors, two of which relate to the initial learning experience, and three that relate to the learner and the learner's community. First, if the experience of learning involved *strong emotional arousal,* and second, if learning occurred in *multiple modalities,* especially in active, experiential learning, then it is more likely to prompt lasting change. Third, for change to endure, the change cannot simply be imposed or superficially experimented with; it must be *internalized* or personalized. Fourth, the learner needs a *community* that supports the change. Finally, change persists when learners' *interest and commitment are sustained* over time, which requires overcoming frustration, obstacles, and distraction.[7]

The High School Theology Programs generally do an excellent job of supplying the first two factors in Kottler's list. As participants experience intense community, thoughtful worship, and demanding service and academic learning, they are aroused emotionally. They also engage in experiential, active learning, worshipping in unfamiliar traditions, leading their own worship services, planning and carrying out projects, talking with homeless people, visiting civil rights memorials, backpacking in the wilderness, or praying alongside monks. Youth widely agreed that such active learning experiences changed them. The last three factors — internalized learning, supportive community, and commitment over time — are harder for High

7. Kottler, "Change: What Really Makes a Difference?"

School Theology Programs to control, but as we will see, some programs employ practices that make these results more likely.

Preparing Youth to Return: Four Orientations

The Princeton Theological Seminary team found that the High School Theology Programs oriented themselves in four different ways in relation to participants' home contexts, and that the orientations they chose appeared to affect how they went about preparing young people to return home. The four basic approaches are *partnership, substitution-compensation, transformation,* and *opposition.*[8] While some programs were nearly ideal types, others showed a mix of attitudes.

An Ecology of Faith Formation: A Partnership Approach

Some programs strongly emphasize the positive, interdependent partnership between their program and the home church or family. Directors and staff of these programs refer to a total "ecology" of faith formation, or to an "intergenerational village" that seeks to help young people understand themselves as belonging to the Christian faith or to a particular Christian tradition. They see themselves as playing a distinctive role in this ecology — whether it be helping certain youth explore theological questions, training youth to be leaders, or helping youth grow spiritually, ethically, and relationally. Drawing on the resources that seminaries offer, they offer an intense experience away from home that churches and families cannot give, while still depending on families and churches for recruitment of youth, prayer and moral support, and financial and human resources. Some such programs are specifically geared toward building enthusiasm about ministry vocations or church leadership, and others aim toward "denominational branding," helping youth understand and commit to their denomination.

The practices associated with this partnership orientation reveal a high level of trust between the program leadership and church leaders. Programs that fit this approach actively recruit youth from churches or parishes, re-

8. These categories bear a strong resemblance to the taxonomy H. Richard Niebuhr offers in his *Christ and Culture* (San Francisco: Harper & Row, 1951), though they were created without his work in mind.

quiring sponsorship or recommendation by a pastor or church leader. In some cases, pastors, priests, or bishops have sent cohorts of youth year after year, welcoming them back to significant positions of leadership or to ongoing projects. The programs in turn show that they value participants' home contexts and denominational identities, depicting youth as heirs of rich theological or cultural traditions. For example, the Youth Hope-Builders Academy asks youth to explore the origin of their name and what it reveals about their parents' hopes for them, and then connect their name to their identity as African American Christians. Likewise, through theological reflection and liturgical practice, the various Roman Catholic programs teach youth to participate meaningfully in Catholic Mass, and the Duke Youth Academy focuses on helping participants appreciate the significance of baptism and communion as practices that mark almost all Christian communities.

A partnership orientation also leads to intentional, ongoing communication with the home context before, during, and after the program. Besides asking for recommendations from the home church, certain programs assign a mentor at home to partner with the participant upon return, providing guidance, accountability, and encouragement. Other programs ask an adult from home to attend the program with youth from their church, or they offer training and information to home churches to help them welcome youth back. Stressing the critical role parents play in faith formation, some programs seek to aid parents in understanding and affirming their children's learning, so they provide websites and blogs where youth can update parents and post pictures, and they print out and deliver parents' emails to youth. Some programs afford yet more contact, setting aside time daily for youth to call their families.

Guided by the innovating vision of Dr. Anne Wimberly, the Youth Hope-Builders program goes even further, treating parents and families as an integral part of their program. They invite parents and families to attend opening and closing ceremonies and to formally release and then receive back their children. Parents and families are also invited to attend two talent shows, an all-day family recreation day, and subsequent reunions. This remarkable program has recently begun operating within three different congregations, seeking to strengthen partnerships even further. Wimberly points out that participants in her programs are often alienated from their parents or families (they are already separated in many ways, even if they are living at home), so the program seeks to repair this breach through intentional time spent as families, and through teaching practices of communication.

The strengths of a partnership model are many. Since programs oriented this way draw on the resources of other institutions, they do not have to be or do everything for participants, but can focus on what they do best. Since they build trust over time with churches and families and show themselves an ally to them, they may have an easier time raising financial support and becoming self-sustaining. They also set youth up to feel a sense of belonging to a church, denomination, or religious tradition, making for a more seamless transition between the program and the home. Further, since programs with this orientation are motivated to work for healthy connections to home communities, they invest time in finding adults who can offer mentorship not only at the program, but also in home contexts, thus increasing the likelihood that youth will return to a supportive community. As Kottler notes, such a supportive community can help sustain change because it offers help and accountability.

A partnership approach is most vulnerable where it is most dependent. Since it depends on families and churches as partners, it suffers when churches and families do not take responsibility for their role in the ecology of faith formation. Even with efforts to connect with home contexts, programs cannot always overcome the apathy, resistance, or abuse some young people meet at home. Further, when programs maximize continuity between home and the program, they may neglect the psychological benefits of separation from the home context, which include opportunities to individuate and to personalize one's learning, rather than uncritically assuming the beliefs, practices, and worldview of the home context. Despite these weaknesses, a partnership approach appears to be one of the more successful at preparing young people to return to their communities as gift-bearers, rather than as strangers or enemies.

"Going Deeper": A Substitution or Compensation Approach

In contrast to programs that see themselves as part of a larger ecology of faith formation, certain programs function as substitutes for or alternatives to the church or family, either as a short-term "home away from home" or a standalone experience of an ideal church community. While this is sometimes the case simply because programs want to offer youth a fulsome experience of faith formation in community, it is more frequently an attempt to compensate for the failures of family and church. Those failures can be quite real, with some youth reporting fractured or abusive families, churches in crisis, and youth programs that do not take young people's questions or leadership seriously. For some participants, their program becomes the first place they have encountered life-giving Christian community that deals with conflict constructively, honors their hard questions, and equips them for leadership.

In this substitution approach, the dominant theme is not continuity, but contrast between the program and the home context. Such contrast is often construed in terms of depth. Staff talked about wanting to give youth opportunities for deep conversation, penetrating exploration, and profound communion that are unavailable at home, and they faulted youth groups that serve up manic entertainment and facile answers, as well as distracted, busy, and ill-equipped parents and a culture of instant gratification and distraction. This is not to say that these staff had no sympathy for the challenges youth ministers and parents face, but that they had learned they could not rely on churches and families as dependable partners in faith formation, and so needed to supply youth with a whole experience of education, worship, and community.

Many youth also used depth language in interviews, expressing gratitude for the chance to "go deeper" in theological exploration and in community, and contrasting their High School Theology Program with boring or authoritarian teaching and shallow relationships at home. A few youth suggested that their youth leaders and parents were more interested in telling them what to believe than in engaging them in conversation around hard questions. Yet youth were not entirely negative about their churches and families. No youth blamed their youth pastors for lack of depth and admitted their church leaders tried to get real conversations going, but to little effect. They attributed such failures to the fact that church youth ministries involve less intense, less frequent time together and include a greater range of ages and commitment levels.

In this substitution approach, family language abounds: youth say (and are told) that they are brothers and sisters in Christ; mentors are referred to as older siblings, aunts, or uncles; directors and pastors are called or treated as surrogate parents, and the group engages in regular "family times." Youth also comment that they see their group as their new family, whom they will depend on when they return home. As this new family or mini-congregation develops its own rituals, worship patterns, prayers, and rules of engagement, youth express a deep sense of belonging. Yet unlike the previous approach, in which youth feel they belong to a larger faith tradition or community, they feel they belong to a smaller community that lives what they perceive to be a more authentic expression of the Christian life than they see at home.

While almost all the programs offer youth a bracing experience of deep theological exploration, exposing youth to new theological concepts and vocabulary, programs that take a substitution or compensation approach are more likely to urge youth to try on ideas and practices that are unfamiliar to or at odds with their home context. In this way, they encourage them to individuate from their received faith and to claim faith as their own. If the partnership orientation pictures youth as heirs of a rich theological tradition, this approach pictures youth as courageous miners or divers who go deep in search of treasure.

Since programs that take this approach do not entirely trust that a supportive church and family awaits participants, they approach reintegration by seeking to extend the program's community. They emphasize the power of social media groups, regular reunions, and ongoing contact between alumni and staff to keep the community going, and they stress to youth the importance of finding others at home who also want to go deep. They may also encourage youth to start their own groups at home modeled on their experience of ideal family and church.

The strengths of this approach are that youth are excited by the emotional intensity of belonging to their new "family," by the closeness and freshness of personalized worship practices, and by deep theological exploration. In Kottler's terms, they claim their learning as their own, they are alerted to the fact that they will face obstacles at home, and they are encouraged to seek supportive community. Yet since this approach does not stress partnerships with churches and families, it risks sending youth home without advocates or mentors to guide them and offer accountability. In addition, this approach sometimes encourages youth to identify a short-term, intense experience with authentic community or church but neglects to admit the special resources and planning required to pull off such a program (including seminary-trained mentors and seasoned theological teachers with doctorates) — resources that are often simply not available in home contexts. When youth start to believe that their home contexts should replicate exactly the ideal they have experienced while away, they risk becoming judges and critics rather than gift-bearers.

"You Can Change the World": A Transformational Approach

A third approach sees youth as change agents who can transform their church or family by offering leadership in their congregations and by "catechizing their families," in the words of one director. Like the previous pattern, this approach is realistic about churches and families and also stresses deep community life and theological exploration. Yet this approach wants to harness young people's zeal and dissatisfaction for the sake of change. In this pattern, youth are reformers and prophets who bring a balance of good news and wise judgment to share with their youth groups, congregations, and families. The goal is that they will remain committed to their churches and families, while developing critical distance and skills for effecting change.

Programs with a transformation approach try to offer youth a distinctive experience of Christian discipleship, encourage them to discern what aspects of it might enrich or transform their home context, and equip them with skills for making change happen. They train them by giving youth opportunities to plan, lead, and debrief events, thus raising their competency and confidence as leaders. They ask youth to envision themselves returning home to live out what they have learned. They practice role-playing around certain challenges or temptations youth will face and invite youth to write documents describing the change they seek, draft action plans, research organizations that can serve as resources, and name possible allies and mentors at home. They also bring alumni to speak with current participants about the challenges they faced — as well as victories won — at home.

This approach, when done well, can be quite effective at supporting the process of separation and reintegration. By modeling a different way of life and granting young people a prophetic identity, they help them separate and individuate from the home context. By teaching skills for effecting change at home, they help youth internalize learning and sustain their interest and commitment over the long term — two of the factors Kottler names as contributing to enduring change. In this approach, youth are given maximum opportunity to integrate what they have learned into their daily lives.

Yet the transformation approach has two major risks. First, it risks using young people as pawns in a colonizing scheme that disregards the integrity of the traditions from which youth come. Young people come from contexts that have their own unique cultures, traditions, theologies, and attitudes. While some of these patterns may be broken or corrupt, others simply differ from the dominant culture or theology of the High School Theology Program. In challenging young people to change their home contexts, HSTPs must be extremely careful not to hold up their program as the only viable pattern of Christian community or to impose ideological norms on young people. When programs impose norms on youth who will go home as change agents, they risk making them into insensitive colonizers, rather than equipping them as indigenous leaders who translate between traditions and cultures.

A second risk is that youth will try to transform their church or family without help from guiding adults who can interpret the theological and historical underpinnings of the practices youth encounter at home. For example, a girl from a church that does not ordain women might learn to preach at her program, youth from a praise-band church might embrace Taizé music, and a young man from a conservative congregation might befriend gay and lesbian mentors or youth. When such youth go home, they may be enthusiastic about transforming congregational practices and attitudes, but they might not see that those practices and attitudes are the visible tip of vast submerged icebergs. When they crash into the bulk of deep tradition, they need adult partners to help them understand what is happening and decide what to do next, or they may quickly find themselves out of their depth.

"Stand Strong": An Oppositional Approach

A final stance is more adversarial and is often the result of significant frustration with home contexts that have failed young people or rejected their leadership. No program we studied takes this approach alone; rather, certain programs occasionally depart from one of the other approaches and become openly oppositional to the family and church. For example, in various interviews, staff and alumni from different theological traditions lamented that the church has bought into a larger corrupt culture and forsaken a countercultural gospel, and that it is failing young people by infantilizing them, offering them poor substitutes for substantive education and formation, and refusing to heed their voices. Some churches and denominations, they explained, appear to be totally resistant to the change that High School Theology Programs represent, leaving the program no choice but to take an oppositional stance. Staff also described the role some parents play in keeping youth groups too safe and entertainment-oriented, worried about church programs that become subservient to such parents, and told of parents who were angered by how the program shifted their child's political or theological views or vocational hopes away from their own. Though youth were less likely to speak so critically, they occasionally expressed frustration with the rigidity, shallowness, or intellectual apathy they perceived at home.

If in the transformational approach youth were reformers and prophets, now they are separatists, puritans, and pioneers, bravely striking out from a corrupt church. In their program they learn to own a faith that may be quite different from what they learned at home, to engage in conflict honestly and unflinchingly, to act courageously when no one else agrees with them, and to seek faithful people outside their families or congregations.

This stance obviously affects communications between home and the program. Some staff, aware that their program's theological or ethical convictions conflict with what participants' churches and parents may espouse, stress the importance of being radically transparent with parents and church leaders, while others take the opposite tack, expressly *not* advertising in advance the more controversial topics youth will encounter. Since in this view parents, churches, and church leadership are not usually allies, they also do not make obvious recruitment partners, nor are they abundant sources of mentors. Instead, mentors in these programs tend to be critical of churches and families. From this perspective, the task of integration is more about integrating what one has learned into one's life, but not about reintegrating into church or family — for in that way lie frustration and backsliding.

The oppositional approach has real merit, given the fact that certain churches and families really do resist change, reject young people's leadership, or abuse their vulnerability. It is not naïve about the frustrations youth may face at home and can offer sympathy and support to youth who suffer rejection by their home context. But this stance risks becoming harshly puritanical, judgmental, or cynical. It does not give credit to those churches and families who are doing an excellent job with their youth (and these are often churches and families who have raised youth who want to attend a High School Theology Program to begin with!) or who have good intentions. Further, like the substitution and transformation approaches, this stance can unfairly hold home contexts to the standard of an intense experience away from home that has access to tremendous resources. If youth buy into that ideal vision, they can become disillusioned with families and congregations, where the tasks of daily living and mundane administrative matters demand attention, and where the journey of faith is walked at a slower pace. Finally, because an oppositional stance tends to be frustrated with compromise, it rules out the potential of partnering with "good-enough" mentors and institutions at home. The risk is that these programs will send young people home without adult advocates or partners, setting youth up for frustration.

Lessons for Theological Education and Congregations

High School Theology Programs have much to teach theological education and congregations about effective ministry with young people. All four of the approaches — partnership, substitution-compensation, transformation, and opposition — seek to honor young people's needs and concerns, foster spiritual and personal maturity, and give them skills for navigating life, exploring theology, and offering leadership. In all HSTPs, youth are central to the ministry of the church and can provide leadership and vision now and in the future. In contrast to popular culture depictions of youth as shallow consumers, wild animals, or vulnerable victims, HSTPs treat youth as beloved heirs of a rich tradition, members of a close community, capable explorers who can go deep, powerful prophets and reformers who can change their world, and social critics and activists who act courageously. For all their differences, these perspectives can fuel the imagination of congregations who struggle to hang on to youth past confirmation, form youth as disciples, or send youth out as leaders.

While all four approaches have merit, two of these orientations appear to be more helpful for the task of reintegration — the partnership and the transformation approaches. The substitution-compensation approach responds to real crises in the home and the church, but it too easily leaves youth without a supportive everyday community that can help sustain their work, and since it tends to be focused on the experience of ideal community, it does not usually teach critical skills for effecting change. Moreover, although the opposition approach is sometimes justified and can form dedicated activists and pioneers, it precludes the option of reintegrating into a home community, leaving youth vulnerable to loneliness and defeat. The partnership approach, on the other hand, fully expects from the beginning that youth will return to their communities, so it maximizes those communities as resources even as it offers them information and training. At its best, this holistic approach gives young people freedom to explore while also showing them the way back home, and it provides for mentoring relationships with caring adults. The transformation approach takes into account the crises and problems that give rise to the substitution and opposition patterns, but it does so in a more proactive, positive way that seeks a balance of criticism and commitment. At its best, this approach not only builds up young people's courage and confidence but also gives them skills to interpret culture, propose change, and lead transforming movements — all skills needed by leadership of the church in the twenty-first century.

As theological institutions seek to form church and community leaders, they might take lessons from the partnership and transformation approaches. Today an increasing number of theological students come from independent, non-denominational churches without processes that intentionally bridge the experience of the home context and seminary. Theological schools can choose to claim that this bridging activity is someone else's responsibility (the student's or the home church), or they can seek ways to partner with churches and community groups, making explicit the expectation that students will use their schooling to bless and transform congregations and communities.

One intriguing possibility comes from Andover Newton Theological School, which is preparing to pilot a cooperative MDiv degree program. Designed to eliminate seminary student debt and foster church connections, the five-year program offers students the opportunity to apprentice to a seasoned pastor while serving in a congregation through their whole seminary career. Students in this program receive academic credit for the work they do in church, build relationships in a congregational setting, and engage in action and reflection in an ecclesial community they come to know well. They learn skills for transforming communities even as they participate in them as committed pastors. As experiments like the one at Andover Newton proceed, they can look forward to receiving capable, prophetic students who have been formed by High School Theology Programs, students who already know that when they journey to encounter the God of elsewhere, they return to share what they have learned, singing new songs of joy, carrying sheaves of grain.

PART THREE

More Than Summer Camp

Adventures in Vocational Practices

The trouble with deep belief is that it costs something.

DONALD MILLER, *Blue Like Jazz* (2003)

CHAPTER SEVEN

Getting All Turned Around

Truth, Disruption, and Reorientation in High School Theology Programs

Andrew Brubacher Kaethler

Kristi participated in !Explore, the High School Theology Program at Anabaptist Mennonite Biblical Seminary, in 2005. Kristi is from a small town in rural southern Ontario, near Lake Huron. The people of her church are not particularly progressive or highly educated, but they are honest, hard-working people who want to do well by their children. Kristi was deeply involved in this congregation. While her church affirmed her, it did not push her to expand her world. Being adventurous, she took the risk of exploring the wider world of her denomination and theological tradition. Her parents facilitated her participation in denominational youth events, which afforded Kristi additional leadership opportunities within the Mennonite church. She credits the adults in her church and denomination with trusting her with leadership early on and for believing that when youth are given the opportunity, they rise to the challenge.

!Explore allowed Kristi to expand her world and to witness the diversity of the Mennonite church. Even though her hometown is only five hours, three hundred miles (500 km), and one international border away from Elkhart, Indiana (where Anabaptist Mennonite Biblical Seminary is located), spending eighteen days with Mennonite youth from across Canada and the USA, including African American and Hispanic Mennonites, launched her on a journey that would carry her much farther than the three hundred miles that brought her to !Explore.

At !Explore, Kristi encountered a context and structure for living into her questions of faith, and for discovering new sets of questions evoked by her encounters with other youth. Finding new questions, rather than new answers to *old* questions, energized her. Also exciting were the new vocabularies she learned that deepened and enriched her faith: the vocabularies of biblical theology, of ritual in worship, of service, and of other Mennonite groups, including African American Mennonites and Mennonites from Western Canada. Within the structure of this High School Theology Program, Kristi found a community in which to test her new vocabularies, and to explore what they meant for her own faith, identity, and emerging sense of vocation.

In this way, !Explore introduced Kristi to the joys of theological reflection, an activity that can (and should!) permeate our days as Christians. Kristi later reflected that she wished she had received fewer devotionals for youth about abstinence from sex and drugs, which was not her scene as a teenager, and instead had been invited into more conversations about Christian education of children and outreach to the community, where her emerging interests and passions lay. Like Kristi, many participants articulate that the most exciting thing about the program is meeting other young people who *want to talk about God and the church!*

Kristi grew in her identity as a follower of Jesus at !Explore. Theological conversations challenged her to build upon the foundation her congregation had provided. She commented that she had "always taken Jesus seriously," but hearing other youth articulate their faith gave her new terminology and new categories for understanding her faith. The fact that others listened to her theological questions and wanted her to contribute to theological conversations introduced her to the notion that to be a Christian is to be a theologian — to think deeply about God and God's call in our lives, individually and collectively; to reflect on the centrality of community in worship, fellowship, and service; and to contemplate the normativity of Jesus' life of healing and suffering for Christians today. In !Explore, these topics were discussed not only in formal class settings where professors and adult leaders guided the conversations, but also in informal settings between students at the dinner table or while driving to a learning site. Kristi met people who lived by a common purpose, and people who dedicated their whole lives — not just a weekend or night of the week — to service and reconciliation in Christ's name. These encounters expanded Kristi's horizon of what a fruitful Christian life could look like.

Disruptive Continuity: The Vocational Rhythm of Formation and Transformation

!Explore prompted Kristi to grow as a leader. It clarified her understanding of the work of a pastor, and it highlighted and expanded her repertoire of leadership gifts. Most importantly, this HSTP prompted questions about places where the work of a pastor and her own leadership gifts converged. In the years following !Explore, Kristi continued to teach Sunday school in her home congregation. She expanded the contexts in which she accepted leadership, becoming involved with chapel services while at university. While her congregation did not actively encourage women to consider the pastorate, they did encourage Kristi. After graduating from college, the campus chaplain encouraged Kristi to consider an interim youth pastor position, which precipitated an agonizing process of discernment. The short-term, part-time position did not scare her; rather, for the first time she identified patterns and themes in her life coalescing around pastoral ministry, and sensed she was on the verge of taking a big step toward claiming a particular identity and vocation. Kristi took a deep breath and jumped in. Today, Kristi is a "permanent" youth pastor in another Mennonite church in southern Ontario, with male and female pastoral mentors who empower her and help her solidify an identity as a young pastor. Kristi notes that beginning this long-term position forced her to confront new aspects of her identity and calling, even as it built on her prior leadership experience.

You'll notice a rhythm in Kristi's life that first became evident in her summer at Anabaptist Mennonite Biblical Seminary. Past experiences of faith are recognized and honored, while surprising encounters with God, self, and others give her new frameworks for thinking about faith, and launching her discipleship in new directions, as the cycle starts anew. Although !Explore was clearly a key step in the process by which Kristi became a young pastor, it did not effect a seismic about-face in her young faith, identity, or vocational aspirations. Yet that is what makes her story interesting: her journey demonstrates how the development of faith, identity, and vocation depend on both *formation* and *transformation,* two concepts that tend to be bifurcated and treated as binary options in leadership development and in ecclesial ecology.

Rather than standing opposed, formation and transformation wind through Kristi's story in a cyclical, symbiotic relationship. She was formed in her ordinary congregation through slow-paced, enduring practices and faithful adult companions, and this formation helped her open up to God's extraordinary transformation in intense experiences at !Explore. In turn, Kristi engaged in ongoing faith, identity, and vocational formation at university. This process of inquiry and development continues for Kristi even now. "I preached a lot this summer," Kristi said recently. "I don't like it when I have to preach so often. Like, really, who am *I* to preach the Word of God to all these people?" We can answer: she is a servant of God, formed by God through her community, transformed by God alongside her community, and ultimately, blessed by God and her community. She is still on a journey — a pilgrimage, as chapter 10 of this volume describes it — marked by a recurring cycle of formation, transformation, and blessing.

Imagining Kristi's story as a journey provides us two rich metaphors for formation and transformation: home and pilgrimage. Kristi's story illustrates that Christian pilgrimage begins at home. Having a home to depart from, physically and metaphorically, is the necessary prerequisite for the journey.[1] Home and pilgrimage illustrate that formation and transformation are complementary, not competitive, elements of the development of faith, identity, and vocation. Formation occurs at home, in the family or home congregation, but during experiences of pilgrimage we become especially receptive to the inbreaking, transformative work of God and the Holy Spirit.

This chapter will argue that both formation and transformation are essential for growing in faith, developing identity, and discerning vocation. Formation provides stability by underscoring the foundations of faith, while transformation occurs when encounters with truth disrupt our cultural assumptions and invite a reorientation toward the good news of the gospel and the Kingdom of God. This chapter offers a theological account of the disruptive nature of encountering truth, as well as a pedagogical account of the necessity of disorientation and disequilibrium. I will suggest that disruption and disorientation are not ends in themselves but rather are opportunities to displace cultural assumptions with commitments oriented around the good news and the Kingdom of God. Finally, I will suggest how we might incorporate pedagogies of disruption and reorientation into the church, home, and school — wherever Christian leadership takes root.

1. In this volume, my colleagues David Horn, Christy Lang Hearlson, and Brent Strawn discuss this rhythm in different ways. Horn stresses the importance of the journey in preparing us for God's inbreaking transformation in High School Theology Programs; Hearlson describes the necessary rhythm of "leaving" and "returning" in these programs; and Strawn emphasizes the priority of scriptural catechesis (formation) preceding biblical critique in these programs.

Holy Confusion: The Theological and Pedagogical Importance of Decentering

Formation is a process of centering. Transformation is a process of recentering. In between centering and recentering is the necessary stage of decentering. Pilgrimage allows us to leave the familiarity of home to explore new geographical, social, and existential places, creating a liminal space for cognitive, emotional, and spiritual discovery. The point of disruption and deformation, to be clear, is not simply to introduce chaos. The purpose is to unmoor comfortable, assumed, handed-down perspectives and to create a space into which God's inbreaking truth may be recognized in new ways.

Jesus engaged in a kind of centering, decentering, and recentering, as a number of prominent biblical examples demonstrate. He left his home in Galilee and, after being baptized by John, he journeyed into the desert to be decentered and recentered before facing temptations by Satan (Matt. 4:1-11). Similarly, Jesus regularly engaged in practices of withdrawal and return, culminating in his retreat to the Garden of Gethsemane where he decentered and recentered his ministry before his arrest and crucifixion (Matt. 26:36-46). This decentering and recentering allowed Jesus to confront his divine identity and embrace the truth about God's love and desire for humanity and for all of creation.

Getting All Turned Around: Truth and Decentering

Truth is always disruptive. The New Testament word for the disruptive nature of truth is *metanoia,* meaning a change of mind, heart, and behavior. It is the process of turning — not merely a turning *from,* motivated by guilt or shame, but a turning *toward,* drawn forward by the light of truth. *Metanoia* is the process of truth telling and healing that Jesus himself often initiated in those whom he encountered. The center of Jesus' teaching ministry was characterized by the call to *metanoia* (Luke 15:7), illustrated for his listeners and followers though numerous parables.

In the parable of the Prodigal Son, the son has a change of mind, heart, and behavior toward his father, spurred by his hedonistic excursion and subsequent desperation (Luke 15:11-32). In a later parable in the same section, Jesus confronts his listeners with an unsettling truth about how wealth distracts from the way of the Kingdom of God (Luke 18:18-30). Zacchaeus also responds affirmatively to the disruptive truth of God, changing his perspective and making things right with those he had cheated or oppressed (Luke 19:1-10).

Such encounters suggest that truth, in the New Testament view, is not best understood as a "thing," a possession, an idea, abstract concept, or a disembodied principle. It is, rather, an "event." Admittedly, it is possible to observe truth passively, but to do so misses both the transformative power of truth and the full impact of God's communication with us. According to the witness of Scripture, God confronts us with truth. God presents truth in such a way that it needs to be encountered and wrestled with.[2] Truth, when fully encountered, *moves us,* from one place and perspective to another. It is a disruptive event because it then forces us to reorganize our view of God, of humanity, and of the world, and it prompts us to relocate ourselves in relation to each of these.

John Caputo compellingly articulates this understanding of the disruptive nature of "truth as event." Caputo revisits Charles Sheldon's century-old question, "What Would Jesus Do?" Although this question has become a thoroughly domesticated and commodified cliché through the WWJD movement of the 1990s and early 2000s, Caputo claims this question was originally posed by Sheldon to disrupt the Christian's assumed and complacent view of things, especially social realities. When we are content with the "same" and with the familiar, Jesus, according to Sheldon, introduces us the "other," to the poor and to those who are on the social periphery.[3] By encountering the other, we are reminded that the good news of the gospel is always "good news for the other," not just for me, and while the gospel's truth may be disruptive, it is never "imposed coercively."[4] Truth, then, is not a gift we can give ourselves; truth is the disruptive gift of the encounter with the other.

This is why holding tightly to assumptions or preconceived conceptions of people, places, or situations can stymie us from fully encountering the disruptive nature of truth. In the first place, unchallenged assumptions simply prevent us from seeing disconnects between old perspectives and new ones. Moreover, we become fearful of the domino effect: What if accepting this new truth affects other perspectives, values, and behaviors we hold dear?

2. This view of truth is similar to Judy Steers' understanding of encounter, presented in chapter 11 of this volume.

3. John D. Caputo, *What Would Jesus Deconstruct? The Good News of Postmodernism for the Church* (Grand Rapids: Baker Academic, 2007), pp. 27-30.

4. Cf. John Howard Yoder, "Meaning After Babble: With Jeffrey Stout Beyond Relativism," *Journal of Religious Ethics* 24, no. 1 (Spring 1996): 135; "On Not Being Ashamed of the Gospel: Particularity, Pluralism, and Validation," *Faith and Philosophy* 93, no. 3 (July 1992): 292.

The Art of Truth-Telling: Recentering in the High School Theology Programs

These assumptions that we hold dear, but seldom acknowledge or seriously question, fall under the rubric of *culture.* In order to encounter the truth event of the gospel, we all need to be able to acknowledge and name the cultural assumptions by which we live. Many High School Theology Programs are transformative because they introduce youth, implicitly or explicitly, to cultural hermeneutics — the process of reading and interpreting culture, similar to the way biblical hermeneutics is the process of reading and interpreting the Bible. It is appropriate that Christians read and use the Bible to affirm and critique culture, but, as the African theologian Musimbi Kanyoro contends, without a critical awareness of how culture shapes our assumptions, and without the independent skill of being able to read culture, Christians are prone to respond to culture in quasi-Christian ways. Either we read the Bible as a blind confirmation of culture — including its destructive and harmful aspects, like material consumption, militarism, or nationalism — or we categorically reject culture, associating it predominantly with sin or with secularization.[5]

What elements of culture need to be named? From what cultural assumptions might young Christians need to be dislodged? Before we can be recentered in the gospel, we need to read culture in a way that disentangles the good news of Jesus as presented in Scripture from pseudo-gospels and ideologies of individualism, consumption, and entitlement.[6] These three "malaises of modernity," identified by philosopher Charles Taylor, are instructive. The first malaise, individualism, highlights the "disenchanted" nature of the modern world. Modern social, political, and economic orders allow little space for the divine presence, which means that humanity is no longer routinely viewed as part of a divinely ordained, created, cosmic order. The second malaise — the widespread employment of instrumental reason — considers solutions to economic, social, and political problems

5. Musimbi Kanyoro makes this point convincingly when she reflects on a return to her native Kenya and engaging in Bible studies with women in her home village. She observes that without the lens of a critical awareness of cultural assumptions, the women of her village inadvertently use Scripture to condone customs harmful to girls and women instead of speaking truth to them and challenging them. See Musimbi R. A. Kanyoro, *Introducing Feminist Cultural Hermeneutics: An African Perspective* (Cleveland, OH: Pilgrim, 2002).

6. This is not an exclusive list, but an attempt to name the dominant social, economic, and political narratives that characterize late modern Western Liberalism.

mostly on a "cost-benefit" calculus. Money and "efficiency" are prioritized over human lives and meaning-making tasks, reducing human identity to that of a consumer, instead of recognizing the complexity of persons being consumers *and* producers, family members, global citizens, stewards of creation, fellow creatures, etc.

The third malaise, ironically, is the loss of social freedom as people lose control over the narrowing strictures of politics, economics, and technology. Living "against the grain" is increasingly difficult. People feel alienated from the public sphere.[7] While Taylor celebrates the emergence of the modern "self," he laments its disconnect from social, epistemological, and political contexts. As a philosopher, Taylor argues that the self is not an autonomous self, but is always a self-in-social-context — a position Christians cannot help but recognize as a theological claim.

High School Theology Programs give youth language and tools for analyzing the human condition, and equally important, a community that does such analysis together. The themes of individualism, consumption, and entitlement are common themes addressed in these programs as youth subject them to prophetic critique. Chelle Huth, the Project Director of the Theological Education with Youth (TEY) program at Lutheran Theological Seminary, Gettysburg, articulates the importance of language, tools, and community like this:

> [TEY invites youth into] a deeper understanding of being Christ's, of being a child of God, to ask how do I live with that identity every single day. . . . The language we use is the contract language of the covenant. . . . [We ask,] "how do we live as people of the covenant?" Because God loves us, therefore I will feed the hungry, I will meet the needs of my neighbor, and I will sit with those who are the other. And so we use a lot of covenant language in TEY, and the response of the [youth] scholars has been that it has given them a clearer understanding of what it means to be a baptized child of God, [a fuller understanding] than any confirmation program that they have ever been in in any congregational setting. So, by giving them that deeper understanding and answering their questions, it is adding to the foundations that have already been placed by families or congrega-

7. Charles Taylor, *The Malaise of Modernity* (Toronto: Anansi Press, 1992), pp. 2-10. Taylor is not an antimodernist. He seeks a nuanced analysis of modernity, embracing valuable aspects of modern life, and Taylor would not want to jettison, most notably, the modern understanding of the "self."

> tions. . . . We are just adding more foundational pieces to it so that their foundation is stronger and broader and deeper.[8]

An alumnus (and eventually counselor) from Candler School of Theology's Youth Theological Initiative (YTI), reflects on the way YTI worked to provide youth with language, tools, and a community in which they could analyze entitlement, race, and class in America without silencing those who actually experience injustice:

> The private school white kids are the ones who are more likely (or, ironically, maybe not) to have vocabularies about privilege and structures of injustice. [Privileged youth] are able to *theorize* these things in ways that [less privileged youth] scholars who have been going to underfunded inner city schools have the *experience* to analyze. The youth from underfunded schools are certainly able to analyze structures of injustice, but maybe not with a sense of safety that the dominant group has.

As these reflections suggest, the HSTPs intentionally set out to help young people analyze culture in ways that encounter truth and, consequently, reveal God's intentions for their lives in new ways. These programs are not simply working against culture; rather, they are operating from an alternative center that is distinct from the foci of the dominant cultural ethos. Countering the dominant culture's focus on individualism and entitlement, YTI encourages youth to think about Christian theology's emphasis on liberation, diversity, and solidarity. Challenging the dominant cultural center of consumption, TEY focuses on the biblical and historic Christian concept of covenant.

Pedagogies of Decentering: The Spiritual Benefits of Disequilibrium

For many youth, the learning that occurs in the relatively short time span of a High School Theology Program is both formative and transformative. For some, the experience is immediately and radically transformative; for others, like Kristi, it is more like a tsunami wave forming far from shore, intensi-

8. Chelle Huth, "Reflections," Theological Education with Youth, Lutheran Theological Seminary (Gettysburg, PA), unpublished paper, High School Theology Leadership Consultation, Indianapolis, IN, February 23-25, 2012.

fying over time as it approaches land. Either way, an important step in the pedagogical process is disembedding young people from their accustomed perspectives by creating experiences of disequilibrium through which teenagers encounter the other and are confronted with the event of truth. Such encounters and confrontations can disrupt a young person's existing identity, schema of the world, and vocational aspirations. They pose a *disorienting dilemma,* to use the terminology of transformative learning theory, creating psychological, intellectual, and moral *disequilibrium* through constructed experiences that disrupt, sometime gently and sometimes more vigorously, inherited and familiar identity, convictions, and set of behaviors.[9]

Disequilibrium is neither an end in itself, nor simply an educational strategy — for many young people experience chronic disorienting dilemmas in the course of their daily lives long before arriving at a High School Theology Program. The point is not simply to be disruptive. The purpose is to prompt and precipitate affective, cognitive, and effective reorganization and reorientation, with the help of an intentional reflective process and a community of support that can "hold" the young person in the state of disequilibrium as new insights emerge. The purpose is to create space in which the Holy Spirit's inbreaking can be discerned more readily, and in which the Word of God, the good news that is truly *good* for all humanity and truly *new* for our time, can be encountered.

The HSTPs capitalize on numerous "disorientations" that young people confront in the course of these programs. One type is simply geographical disorientation: being transplanted from a familiar environment to an unfamiliar environment. By itself, geographical disorientation does not necessarily cause disequilibrium, but it is frequently a correlate to other unfamiliar experiences. Another type of disorientation is ethical or moral disorientation, where some previously held conviction or behavior is challenged and juxtapositions emerge that beg to be resolved. A third type is worldview or cultural disorientation, in which a disorienting dilemma prompts wholescale questioning of previously held cultural schemas. This can result from the accumulation of smaller dilemmas and disequilibria, or from major ones that are urgent and command deep attention.

9. Jack Mezirow, "Transformation Theory of Adult Learning," in *In Defense of the Lifeworld,* ed. M. R. Welton (New York: SUNY Press, 1995), p. 50; also see Mezirow, *Transformative Dimensions of Adult Learning* (San Francisco: Jossey-Bass, 1991), pp. 93-96 and *Fostering Critical Reflection in Adulthood* (San Francisco: Jossey-Bass, 1991), p. 168. Although Mezirow's work focuses on adult learning, the concepts of the disorienting dilemma and disequilibrium are relevant and applicable to adolescent learning as well.

Transformative learning theory emphasizes the roles that both educators and learners play in disequilibria. The educator actively and carefully cultivates an environment in which transformative learning can occur. Unsurprisingly, a strong correlation exists between students who experience healthy disequilibrium in HSTPs, and those who claim strengthened identity, greater vocational clarity, and renewed faith as a result of these experiences. Occasionally participants encounter a disorienting dilemma that is overwhelming, perhaps because it is unintentionally presented or is presented recklessly. Such moments underscore the fact that disequilibrium is not good in itself, and requires adult leaders who are sensitive to each individual participant so as to ultimately facilitate reorientation.

Take, for example, the students from Hellenic College's CrossRoad program, one of the sites where our researchers spent time with teenagers during the summer of 2012. As part of the CrossRoad program, teenagers spent a day with a homeless community in Boston, an experience that one counselor said was designed to help youth "go deep" and "grasp on to something real." By all accounts, the experience was jolting for the participants because it placed them in unfamiliar geographic, economic, and social contexts. Buying food for a homeless person was only initially difficult. What was an ongoing source of discomfort, however, was figuring out what to say to a homeless person, or how to respond to her or his story. When one homeless person rejected their help, youth were left feeling "shocked and confused." The physical, interpersonal, and cultural disequilibrium came as a result of teenagers trying to befriend and care for people in the very short term, while at the same time realizing that there are long-term roots to problems of homelessness, and also long-term processes needed to affect change. As the counselor put it, youth found it "heart-wrenching" to think about where a homeless person might get his or her next meal — but even more heart-wrenching to wonder when they might have their next conversation with someone who cares.

In Sunday School, the counselor noted, these youth did not really have to wrestle with vocation, but here, on the street, questions about their own faith, identity, and vocation were suddenly paramount. Young people were forced to align the stories of homeless people with their own stories, and with "stories of the Bible, [where] you learn that God loves everybody." One student, Cindy, reflected that the immersion experience was a way to "refocus" and to "practice the love that we are taught." John, another participant, observed how the experience challenged approaches to service that have their roots in consumer culture: "[Helping others] is not something you do to make yourself feel better, because that's not what serving is. You serve to care for someone, not to make yourself feel better." When young people realize that homelessness does not exist so that middle-class teenagers can consume another "experience," they are forced to rethink their own faith, identity, and vocation, reconsidering the good news of the gospel as good news for all, including the homeless men and women they met on their immersion day.

In the end, the test for disequilibrium's usefulness in vocational formation is not only that High School Theology Programs create space for reworking identity, faith, and practice, but also that they create the conditions for youth to be introduced to the other and to the event of truth. In other words, disorientation is not merely a psychosocial phenomenon prompting youth to a new developmental stage. It is also a theological phenomenon in which God is given the opportunity to speak a new truth into the life of a young person. The disorientation that HSTPs cultivate is not disruptive for the sake of being disruptive, but this disorientation instead strives to be directive. By directing youth into encounters with God in the other, the HSTPs position youth to struggle with concepts of justice, forgiveness, or grace, and to rely on certain sources, such as Scripture, Christian narrative, and the Holy Spirit, as they reorient their own lives toward Christ.

Call Me Weird: Nurturing an Ec-centric Faith

Singer/songwriter and Scripture evangelist Bryan Moyer Suderman writes, "When you learn to follow Jesus you will act a little strange. People stop and take a look." These lyrics capture the truth that, when Christians follow Jesus as if Jesus is truly Lord of all areas of our lives, we look odd from the perspective of broader culture.[10] Re-aligning their faith, identity, and vocational aspirations with the good news of Jesus is a countercultural act for young people. To begin imagining life "in sync" with the good news of Jesus Christ, but significantly "out of sync" with the dominant culture, requires a skillful sense of cultural hermeneutics, and the ability to identify, name, and analyze contemporary Western cultural values from the perspective of Christian faith. Experiencing life with a community of youth and adults for a

10. Bryan Moyer Suderman, "When You Learn to Follow Jesus (You Will Act a Little Strange)," *God's Love Is for Everybody: Songs for Small and Tall,* Toronto: SmallTall Music, 2002, compact disc.

short period of time — typically ten to thirty days — affords participants the opportunity to learn, test, and practice a new language of prophetic witness and cultural critique. This countercultural language is not at all *anti*-cultural. It is *counter*cultural, and the difference between these deserves explanation.

Encountering new languages and ideas can be discomforting or annoying. When that which we encounter calls us to *live* differently, it can feel dangerous. Challenging dominant cultural language, ideas, and lifestyles must have a purpose beyond being discomforting or threatening. Being countercultural is not simply a matter of doing the opposite of what dominant culture does. It is not primarily reactive. Rather, as Christians, a countercultural way of life means naming and practicing the central commitments to which Jesus calls us as disciples. It is about having encountered truth, and integrating the resulting new language, new ideas, and new forms of life into our daily life. When the central commitments of culture (individualism, consumption, and entitlement) do not align with the truth of Jesus Christ, followers of Jesus can be appropriately and positively described as being *ec-centric:* off-center, from the standpoint of dominant culture, but other-centered or Jesus-centered from the standpoint of a gospel-shaped people. Eccentric Christians will think, look, and act a little strange because they have been displaced from assumed cultural norms and centered on God and the other.

The "strangeness" that High School Theology Programs evoke is illustrated by Isabella and JoAnn, two recent !Explore alumna. Isabella discovered biblical and theological insights that enlivened her prayer life and deepened her care for creation. After the summer program, where she and three other participants learned the Lord's Prayer in Greek and (with the help of a New Testament professor) translated the Greek into English for themselves, she pushed her family and friends to new levels of attentiveness to prayer, encouraged them to begin buying locally, and to step up their commitment to recycling.

After returning home from !Explore, JoAnn became frustrated by the shallowness of theological conversation in her Christian high school. She began challenging her friends and classmates to take conversations about faith deeper. Undoubtedly, some of the strangeness of the HSTPs' formation wears off when youth return to the distractions — sports, clubs, lessons, etc. — that adults use to keep teenagers busy and fragmented. These activities are not necessarily bad in themselves, of course, but they often assume a commanding presence in our lives and divert our attention from God. What JoAnn found astonishing was that her encounter with the other, with God, and with truth through !Explore did have a long-term impact on her faith, identity, and vocation, allowing her to press for more mature discussion about faith with her peers, even after the novelty of the HSTP wore off.

Both Rooted and Odd: Learning from Disequilibrium

High School Theology Programs can typically name their central commitments. These central commitments are often relatively consistent with the denomination(s) or constituencies to which they are affiliated. But these programs are also able to risk more than typical congregational youth ministry programs. By practicing ec-centricity, they can pose difficult questions to both the dominant culture, and sometimes to the church itself. For example, Youth Theological Initiative (YTI) at Candler School of Theology, affiliated with United Methodism, creates space for youth to ask questions about sexual orientation and the value of other religions. The Compass program at Gordon-Conwell, an evangelical seminary, challenges youth to ask critical questions about the role technology plays in our lives, while Huron College's Ask & Imagine program encourages participants to ask provocative questions about tradition and exclusion in Holy Communion.

!Explore, a program of the Mennonite church, also espouses commitments central to Anabaptists: (1) making Jesus the center of our faith, (2) making community the center of our lives, and (3) making reconciliation the center of our work.[11] Yet these commitments are incommensurate with individualism, consumption, and entitlement, all dominant Western cultural values that even many Mennonites embrace. With foci that at times differ from and challenge their cultural context, and sometimes that differ from and challenge their denominations or constituencies, HSTPs may help reenliven the denominational vision among young people who attend them.

This has a big payoff. Leadership development programs abound in North America. Developing leaders for tomorrow is among the aims of schools, businesses, and extracurricular activities — not to mention churches, seminaries, and denominations. While High School Theology Programs must surely be counted among the groups nurturing leadership, what is unique about these programs is that they are intentional about developing *Christian* leaders: leaders who are vocationally compelled by the

11. Palmer Becker, Harold Stauffer Bender, and James R. Krabill, *What Is an Anabaptist Christian?* (Elkhart, IN: Mennonite Mission Network, 2008).

good news of Christ and who acknowledge a calling to use their gifts for ends other than economic gain or social prestige. Theological reflection on the disruptive event of truth, and pedagogical reflection on disorientation and disequilibrium, demonstrate the importance of forming Christians who are not just disoriented from the dominant values of the wider culture, but who are also reoriented toward the emerging Kingdom of God, in which all of creation has been reconciled with the Creator.

Leaders whose faith is shaped by Jesus, whose identity is shaped by a community of believers, and whose vocation is aligned with the Kingdom of reconciliation, have the capacity — by facilitating encounters with truth that decenter and recenter young people — to create communities that not only anticipate the Kingdom, but that proleptically embody that future for all of humanity. The High School Theology Programs model ways in which churches, denominations, seminaries, camps and conferences, and others committed to the formation of Christian leaders can create holy disequilibrium through geographical, moral, and cultural dislocation. The ultimate goal, however, is *re*orientation in a renewed commitment to the good news, revealed in the life and teaching of Jesus Christ.

The call in this chapter is to recognize that formation and transformation are both essential for encountering Jesus Christ. These two poles provide the launch-points for growing in faith, developing identity, and discerning vocation. For traditions that historically have emphasized formation, the call from High School Theology Programs is to acknowledge the importance of Damascus Road experiences (Acts 9:1-9) and facilitate *transformation* through disruptive encounters, even if these encounters lead to truth-telling about the complacency of Christian traditions. For traditions that historically have emphasized transformation, the call is to consciously value and facilitate *formation.* These Emmaus Road experiences (Luke 24:13-35) generally embody the slow processes and steady practices whose foundations embolden youth to venture forth and risk meeting God in the face of the other. The double action of formation and transformation are processes as natural as breathing in and breathing out; one is necessary for the other.

CHAPTER EIGHT

Fuel My Faith

Pedagogies of Theological Reflection in High School Theology Programs

Jeffrey Kaster

Samantha was a rising high school senior at her second two-week Youth in Theology and Ministry Summer Institute (YTM) at St. John's University. After her morning theology class, she approached me and announced, "Jeff, I'm really mad at you." Taken aback, I asked, "What's up, Samantha?" She replied, "I had my whole college academic program all worked out. I figured out all the classes I would need to qualify for a career in physical therapy. But now because you had us take these theology classes, I have to revise my entire plan. I love theology so much, I now have to figure out how to include theological study in my college coursework." Samantha in fact went on to minor in theology in college and spent the next four years not only studying theology, but also actively engaging in multiple Christian practices that deepened her faith over the course of her college career.

Samantha's story points to the fundamental question of how Christian discipleship is sustained. Samantha wanted to keep learning. Rather than simply speaking about an emotional or spiritual camp experience, Samantha was captivated by the theological exploration of the Christian tradition that the Youth in Theology and Ministry Summer Institute offered, and realized that she wanted to learn more. Like Peter on the mountaintop at the Transfiguration, she wanted to "stay a little longer."

Directors of the High School Theology Programs often tell similar stories in which participants approach them at the end of their program and ask, sometimes literally: "Can't we stay just a little bit longer?" These young people have had an encounter with God that touches their hearts and minds and, like Peter, they would like to build a tent and linger. We might say that youth have conversion experiences at these programs. They experience God's love and grace through a variety of pedagogical practices that incorporate service, justice, prayer, community, vocational discernment, creativity, and pilgrimage, and they want the experience to continue.

How can we help such youth move from a spiritual high to a sustaining faith so that, like Samantha, they continue to grow as disciples, both for their own sakes and for a church desperate for young leadership? Catechetical leaders must discern a combustible mix of elements that can fuel young people's discipleship journeys over the long haul.

Intellectual Community in High School Theology Programs

Despite the variety of High School Theology Programs, they all share one conviction: discipleship over the long haul requires familiarity with the texts and traditions that have fueled Christian faith for centuries. As a result, every HSTP plunges participants headlong into these resources, emphasizing a pedagogical practice typically missing from congregational youth ministry programs: robust theological reflection on Christian texts and traditions. The HSTPs develop "intellectual communities" of teenagers and adults in order to deepen their capacities for living theologically informed lives.

"Intellectual community" is a pedagogical strategy that is more often associated with graduate school than youth ministry. Indeed, the Carnegie Initiative on the Doctorate (2006) identified "apprenticeship" and "intellectual community" as the two signature pedagogies of excellent doctoral education, citing five essential elements that make such communities formative. In addition to being "knowledge-centered" (i.e., having as their goal the explicit purpose of generating understanding), intellectual communities are also "broadly inclusive," integrating young scholars fully into the practices of the community, viewing them as equal contributors to it. Furthermore, intellectual communities are "flexible and forgiving": they make room for creativity and risk-taking. They are "respectful and collegial," building camaraderie on "engagement, if not agreement." Intellectual communities are also "purposeful and deliberate" — they do not happen by accident, but have established structures, regular opportunities for students to lead as well as learn, and give students permission to ask unpopular questions. Finally, such communities are "relationship-based." Since all learning is social, students succeed best in communities that prize "thoughtfulness, attentiveness to the needs of others, a willingness to listen carefully and engage in meaningful communication across and in spite of differences, an ability to work collaboratively . . . and a commitment to the ethical treatment of others, especially those in disempowered positions."[1]

Every High School Theology Program director recognizes his or her own program in these descriptors. As it turns out, intellectual communities are as powerful for teenagers learning to reflect theologically on their faith as they are for doctoral students studying neuroscience. Engaging youth in a dialogic pedagogy of both theological reflection and experiential engagement in faith practices effectively helps them become Christian disciples for the long haul. Unfortunately, theological reflection on the Bible and on the teaching and practices of faith is an element frequently missing from adolescent catechetical efforts. This lack stymies the development of durable, "sticky" faith among adolescents.[2]

A key lesson of the HSTPs is this: *a holistic pedagogy that blends intellectual engagement with experiential learning improves the chances that young people's faith will grow with them.* In other words, as youth engage in a variety of Christian practices and participate in theological reflection on those practices through the resources of Christian tradition, they experience faith as intellectually substantive and practically demanding. Asking youth to intellectually reflect on the texts, traditions, and practices of Christian faith, while simultaneously immersing them in the doing of such Christian practices, is a combustible combination, igniting teenagers' desire to live as Christian disciples and equipping them for long-term faith.

In this chapter I will first present research data that suggest the positive impact of one High School Theology Program on participants' attitudes and vocational trajectories. I will then suggest that the HSTPs offer a third way between two previous models of religious education. This third way is a dialogical, praxis-oriented pedagogy that fuels faith over the long haul. Focusing on the intellectual engagement of young people in theological reflection, I will ground the pedagogical approach of the HSTPs in the doctrine of Holy Mystery and in Bernard Lonergan's concept of "intellectual conversion." I will end with several implications for the church and theological education.

1. Cf. George Walker et al., *The Formation of Scholars: Rethinking Doctoral Education in the Twenty-First Century* (San Francisco: Jossey-Bass, 2008), pp. 120, 122.

2. Sticky Faith research had been conducted by the Fuller Youth Ministry Institute. See Kara E. Powell and Chap Clark, *Sticky Faith: Everyday Ideas to Build Lasting Faith in Your Kids* (Grand Rapids: Zondervan, 2011).

Research Data: The Impact of One High School Theology Program

At the program I direct, the Youth in Theology and Ministry program at St. John's University, we conduct ongoing research on the impact of our curriculum on participants. Initial findings were published in the journal *Religious Education* in 2011.[3] The study conducted extensive telephone interviews with youth who completed the YTM curriculum between 2000 and 2004 (N=105) and gives a representative sample of this population (N=67). At the time of the survey, two-thirds were twenty-one years of age or older. It is not surprising that the faith of YTM alumni had durability; even though High School Theology Program participants tend to name these programs as decisive in their vocational trajectories, the influence of families and local parishes who send teenagers to such programs clearly factors into faith longevity. Predictably, in our research, those who completed the YTM program continued to be engaged Christian disciples as young adults:

- 74 percent continued to be excited about theological learning.
- 53 percent read theology books.
- 66 percent of the survey participants took at least one theology or religious study course in college: 45 percent took 1-3 courses; 5 percent took 4-5 courses; 5 percent took 6-10 courses; and 9 percent took 11 or more theology or religious study courses in college.
- 39 percent reported attending Mass once a week or more often (nearly three times the national average of weekly Mass attendance for college-aged Catholics).
- 58 percent reported praying about once a day or more often, while only 5 percent said they never pray.
- 25 percent reported reading Scripture once a week or more often.
- 90 percent reported involvement in some volunteer service.
- 79 percent reported involvement in political activity.
- 71 percent reported stewardship practices (donated $30 or more in the last year).
- 66 percent reported taking leadership roles in organizations.
- 19 percent majored or minored in theology in college.

3. Jeffrey Kaster, "Evaluating Adolescent Catechesis," *Religious Education* 106, no. 1 (2011): 63-81.

However, the research interview also asked participants to reflect specifically on the influence of the Youth in Theology and Ministry curriculum. The data suggested the following:

- 97 percent said YTM stimulated and nurtured excitement for theological learning.
- 74 percent said YTM influenced them to pray more often.
- 71 percent said YTM influenced them to participate more often in community service.
- 47 percent said YTM had a significantly positive influence on their leadership.
- 46 percent said YTM provided significant help in fostering serious reflection about vocation.
- 41 percent said YTM influenced them to attend Mass more often.
- 13 percent said YTM influenced them to be more politically active.

Such measures, while subjective, suggest that the program forms habits that in turn nurture long-term faith.

It is admittedly the case that students self-select into programs like Youth in Theology and Ministry and are thus be more likely than the general population to continue engaging in Christian practices or to pursue theological education. Yet a second study conducted at YTM showed that the program appears to affect a variety of participants' attitudes. All participants took a pre-test before they started the YTM program, and this same instrument was used as a post-test at the end of YTM's thirteen-month program. The following data represent four cohorts of youth (N=88) who started YTM in 2008-2011 and completed YTM in 2009-2012 respectively.

The most significant findings in this study are the changes that occurred in considering theological study in college and in reading theology books. The movement from 25 percent (pre-test) to 67 percent (post-test) for considering theological study in college, and the movement from 12 percent to 41 percent for reading theology books, suggests that YTM's holistic pedagogy of theological reflection is effectively fostering greater interest in and excitement for theological learning. Likewise, the data related to experiencing a call to follow in the footsteps of Christ and his ways (from half to nearly three-fourths of the youth) suggest that YTM provides space for youth to consider responding to God's call to discipleship. Given these data, it is worth exploring what YTM and other HSTPs are doing that so powerfully affects young people's habits, attitudes, and vocational trajectories.

	Pre-Test Agree %	**Post Test Agree %**
I have experienced a call to follow in the footsteps of Christ and his ways.	49%	73%
I am considering theological study in college.	25%	67%
I am considering priesthood or religious life.	48%	78%
I am considering working for the church in some capacity.	84%	91%
I read theology books.	12%	41%
	Extremely Committed	**Extremely Committed**
How committed are you to the Catholic Church?	22%	38%
	Extremely Important	**Extremely Important**
How important or unimportant is religious faith in shaping your major life decisions?	41%	57%

High School Theology Programs: A Third Way

The pedagogical approaches of the HSTPs, when placed in historical context, can be seen as a third way between two previous approaches — a schooling paradigm and a relational, experiential paradigm. The last fifty years saw a dramatic shift away from the schooling paradigm that once dominated biblical and doctrinal education, in which faith formation depended on memorizing the catechism or reciting Bible passages. Religious educators and youth ministry leaders contended that this school paradigm of formation, separated as it was from a total ecology of faith formation and from relationships, failed to foster Christian discipleship.[4]

In the 1960s, youth ministry started taking faith formation outside of the classroom, providing space for young people to encounter Jesus Christ and experience a sense of belonging. These efforts often isolated youth from the multi-generational church community, but youth ministry practitioners argued that experiences of communion with Christ and a small community would place youth on a trajectory of lifelong Christian discipleship. Youth ministry leaders developed skills for evangelizing youth with the good news of Jesus Christ, using retreats, service and mission trips, and worship expe-

4. See especially John H. Westerhoff III, *Will Our Children Have Faith*? Revised ed. (Toronto: Morehouse Publishing, 2000). In the first edition of this book, published in 1976, Westerhoff strongly criticized the schooling paradigm.

riences to help young people encounter God. As the pedagogical pendulum swung, the intellectual content of Christianity became secondary to fostering personal experiences and communicating moral content.[5] Yet as with all pendulum swings, a loss occurred. Like the seed that falls on rocky soil and sprouts quickly only to fade in the heat of the sun (Matt. 13:5-6), many young people with initial conversion experiences felt their faith life wither without the good soil of theological reflection.

Current research suggests that the church is still failing in its responsibility to sustain young Christian disciples. The "sticky faith" research of Kara Powell and Brad Griffin at the Fuller Youth Institute suggests that 40 to 50 percent of the youth engaged in youth ministry programs drift away from their faith once they go to college or leave home.[6] Further, the National Study of Youth and Religion (the largest study ever done on the religiosity of youth and their parents) showed that youth are basically illiterate about religion.[7]

In response to these data, the Catholic bishops in the United States have initiated a push for doctrinal literacy for all adolescent religion curricula in parishes and in Catholic schools, and Protestant leaders have called for a stronger emphasis on biblical literacy. A consensus is growing across denominations that intellectual engagement of the Christian tradition, its texts, and doctrines needs renewed attention. Yet it is clearly not enough simply

5. In *OMG: A Youth Ministry Handbook,* the authors note: "In 1980, sociologist Dean Hoge and his colleagues demonstrated a dramatic shift away from theological formation in youth ministries. Hoge's team compared the top outcomes sought by youth ministry in six denominations before and after 1980 *(figure 4.1).* While youth ministry before 1980 placed a high priority on engaging young people in faith-shaping spiritual practices, after 1980 spiritual formation become nearly invisible in youth ministry's priorities. By 1991, a Carnegie Council on Adolescent Development study found that the largest religious denominations and communities in the U.S. (Protestant, Catholic, and Jewish) shared two parallel goals in religious youth work: fostering faith identity (or sense of belonging in a faith community), and providing young people with safe passage into adulthood." See Dean R. Hoge et al., "Desired Outcomes of Religious Education and Youth Ministry in Six Denominations," *Review of Religious Research* 23 (March 1982): 230-54; and K. C. Dean, "A Review of Literature on Protestant, Catholic, and Jewish Religious Youth Organizations in the U.S.," white paper (Washington, DC: Carnegie Council on Adolescent Development), 1991. See Kenda Creasy Dean et al., *OMG: A Youth Ministry Handbook* (Nashville, TN: Abingdon, 2010), p. 64.

6. Kara Powell and Brad M. Griffin, "Sticky Faith Cliff Notes 15-Minute Podcast," Sticky Faith by the Fuller Youth Institute. Cited at http://stickyfaith.org/podcasts/player/sticky-faith-cliff-notes on October 3, 2013.

7. Christian Smith and Melinda Lundquist Denton, *Soul Searching: The Religious and Spiritual Lives of American Teenagers* (Oxford: Oxford University Press, 2005), p. 262.

to swing back to the old catechetical model, forgetting the lessons of youth ministry in the last fifty years.

For twenty years the youth theology programs have offered a third way, drawing on the best of the two previous pedagogical models. Unlike in the 1950s, when religious educators used biblical and doctrinal instruction nearly exclusively for cognitive learning, or more recent youth ministry approaches that have relied on experiential teaching, the theological programs for high school youth do both. They introduce youth to the texts and resources of the Christian tradition, involve them in practices of service, justice, community, worship, and vocational discernment, and challenge them to reflect theologically on those practices.

For example, in our program at St. John's University, young people study theology together in the morning, are engaged in community service in the afternoon, and experience a variety of Christian prayer forms in the evening. At the end of each day, counselors engage youth in theological reflection to help them connect the dots, appropriate faith, and discern their call to discipleship. Such an approach can effectively sustain Christian discipleship because it helps young people integrate affective, cognitive, and behavior dimensions of Christian faith as they begin to make personal commitments to live out their lives as disciples of Christ.

Key to this approach is the retrieval of intellectual aspects of faith formation through theological instruction and reflection. Many of the High School Theology Programs offer courses taught by seminary professors, who endeavor to promote biblical and doctrinal literacy. At YTM, for example, young people experience twenty hours of classroom theological instruction by seminary professors. Most of the youth come to these programs from parishes where young people have been instructed by dedicated volunteer religion teachers who have little theological training. While students are generally appreciative of their teachers at home, they express eager enthusiasm for studying with knowledgeable, professional theologians. The six courses offered at YTM in the summer of 2013 included:

- *Hidden Treasure in the Covenants of God*
- *Prophets of Yesterday, Today, and Tomorrow: Leading People to Social Change that Reflects God's Justice and Love for All*
- *Art Journaling: Praying in Color*
- *Benedictine Monasticism*
- *Leadership in Church and Society*
- *Theology and Science: Why Believers Need Both*

In addition to their hours of classroom time, YTM participants read the Bible, biblical commentaries, and theological texts designed to connect with their interests and with the content of the whole program. In 2013, those texts were Parker Palmer's *Let Your Life Speak; The Rule of St. Benedict;* Michael J. Himes's *Doing the Truth in Love: Conversations about God;* Vincent Smiles's *The Bible and Science: Longing for God in a Science-Dominated World;* Joan Chittister's *The Cry of the Prophet: A Call to the Fullness of Life;* and Michael Casey's *Strangers to the City.*

Contrary to the stereotype that paints all high school youth as disengaged or superficial, the youth in HSTPs embrace substantive theological reading, and often express happy surprise that compelling theological readings exist at all. As Kenda Creasy Dean mentioned in the introduction to this volume, young people in HSTPs frequently mention how much they appreciate "being taken seriously" enough to be challenged with deep theological reading. A student attending Calvin Seminary's HSTP explained:

> Before we came, we had to read some books. Everyone had four books to read, and each excursion site had a specific one that helped you. I have never been more inspired or more excited than I have been reading those books.

Youth at YTM also engage in fifteen hours of theological reflection. Each evening they meet in small covenant groups for an hour or more, where they and a counselor engage in theological reflection integrating the day's theology classes, service, and prayer. The classes, readings, and small groups combine to create a stimulating intellectual environment for theological exploration — often a first for our church-going participants. Participants across programs express how good it feels to be taken seriously and challenged intellectually in the context of faith formation. Many lament that they have never been asked to think seriously about what they believe in their home contexts, and others complain that when they have posed hard questions at home, they have been met with resistance or with facile answers. The HSTPs can attribute much of their success to the fact that they take young people's minds seriously, expose them to rich resources of the tradition, give them skills for interpreting and appropriating that tradition, and offer opportunities to articulate their questions and discoveries.

Yet for all their emphasis on intellectual aspects of faith formation, the High School Theology Programs also emphasize action, involving young people in practices of service, mission, worship, pilgrimage, vocational discernment, and leadership, all in the context of a supportive community. Participants do not just learn about doctrine; they reflect on its relation to lived experience as disciples. This holistic "third way," combining instruction, practice, and theological reflection, owes much to praxis models of education. Educator and theologian Thomas Groome defines praxis learning as Christian religious education done by "a group of Christians sharing in dialogue their critical reflection on present action in light of the Christian Story and its Vision toward the end of lived Christian faith."[8] For Groome, praxis learning includes both *knowing* and *being* — *knowing* the Christian faith and *being* a Christian disciple.

A story from the Youth in Theology and Ministry program illustrates the ways in which instruction, service, worship, and theological reflection are interwoven in the YTM community. In 2013, the summer theme was Eucharist, which youth studied in a number of ways. Each morning theologians gave a plenary presentation on a theological theme related to the Eucharist (covenant, real presence, body of Christ, communion, paschal mystery, justice, reconciliation, and Sabbath). Youth also took morning theology classes. One of the classes offered was entitled "Hidden Treasure in the Covenants of God." This class met for ninety minutes each day for ten days and explored the covenants in the Old Testament and the new covenant instituted by Christ at the Last Supper, thus connecting students to the theme of Eucharist. Youth read, reflected on, and discussed scriptural and theological texts related to Eucharist.

Our engagement with Eucharist did not stop with such intellectual engagement. Two YTM counselors, Jennifer Line and Alyssa Terry, both theology majors at the College of Saint Benedict, created a session focused on paschal mystery. They started the session with personal testimonies about their experiences of the paschal mystery and then invited the youth into the following prayer experience, which had been created by one their theology professors, Sister Mary Forman, OSB. During the prayer, Jennifer and Alyssa gave each youth a small cup filled with a little wine. The meditation on the wine invited the youth to reflect on their personal suffering, the suffering of the world, and on Christ's suffering. Some youth reflected on the suffering they had recently become acquainted with through their service sites. Toward the end of the prayer, Jennifer and Alyssa asked the youth to imagine uniting their suffering with the suffering of Christ. They invited each person

8. Thomas H. Groome, *Christian Religious Education: Sharing Our Story and Vision* (San Francisco: Harper & Row, 1980), p. 184.

to come to the front of the room and pour their wine into a common carafe, which represented communion with each other and Christ. At the end of the prayer, Jennifer and Alyssa explained that this carafe of wine would be consecrated at the next day's Eucharist.

Abbot John Klassen, OSB, presided at this Eucharist for the YTM community. Young people brought the bread and the wine to the table as offerings. Abbot John received these gifts and then consecrated the wine by saying the words of Christ:

> Take this, all of you, and drink from it, for this is the chalice of my blood, the blood of the new and eternal covenant, which will be poured out for you and for many for the forgiveness of sins. Do this in memory of me.

Because the youth had already reflected on Eucharist, covenant, and suffering, these words of consecration suddenly took on new meaning. Adult counselors noticed that students' faces during the words of consecration radiated new understanding. The transformation at that moment was palpable. That night small groups spent an hour reflecting on the day. As the youth talked, they discussed the Mass, their new understanding of it, their personal experiences of suffering, and, crucially, the experiences of suffering they were seeing at their service sites. This story is just one example of how HSTPs engage young people's intellects with the doctrines and Scriptures of the Christian tradition, while interweaving these reflections into young people's service in the world, worship in community, and theological reflection on experience. This is the transformative power of praxis education at work.

Theological Grounding: Holy Mystery and Intellectual Conversion

The connection between students' reflective capacities and the lifelong nurture of faith is theological — it has everything to do with who God is, and who God calls us to become as we encounter God. In Catholic tradition, the human-divine encounter is often framed in terms of Holy Mystery. At YTM, we introduce youth to the concept and experience of Holy Mystery using Isaiah 55 as a grounding text:

> For my thoughts are not your thoughts, nor are your ways my ways, says the LORD. For as the heavens are higher than the earth, so are my ways higher than your ways and my thoughts than your thoughts (Isa. 55:8-9).

For us, Holy Mystery provides a theological foundation for a pedagogy that sustains Christian discipleship because it envisions a God who invites us to seek and know more of the divine life. Ironically, it is the mystery of God that makes faith knowable in the first place, as God invites us to participate in the divine life.

Holy Mystery: The God Who Invites Us to Know More

The term "mystery" has been applied to many of the central doctrines of Christianity such as the Trinity, paschal mystery, and incarnation. Theologically, mystery includes the common notion of "something that is hidden or something that is beyond the grasp."[9] The *Catechism of the Catholic Church* explains, "The Trinity is a mystery of faith in the strict sense, one of the 'mysteries that are hidden in God, which can never be known unless they are revealed by God.' "[10] More importantly, mystery connotes layers of meaning to be discovered about God and God's activity. Even as we can never know all of a mystery, God becomes "infinitely knowable" through a lifetime of prayer, reflection, and action.

Augustine, Aquinas, and the twentieth-century theologian Karl Rahner all write about God as Holy Mystery, reminding us that human knowledge and human articulation can never exhaust or completely grasp the totality of God or of human beings.[11] Yet the limits of human thought and language do not prevent us from exploration; mystery, properly construed, should not shut down questions but invite them. Thus Pope Paul VI said in his opening allocution at the second session in 1963, "The Church is a mystery. It is a reality imbued with the hidden presence of God. It lies, therefore, within the very nature of the Church to be always open to new and greater exploration."[12]

As a theological construct, Holy Mystery conveys revelation as ongoing. Holy Mystery calls us to discern the movement of the Holy Spirit for our time, and thus provides a theological framework for lifelong learning about God that invites exploration, leading us into the "infinitely knowable." It fur-

9. Catholic Church, *Catechism of the Catholic Church* (Vatican City: Libreria Editrice Vaticana, 2000), p. 237.

10. Catholic Church, *Catechism,* p. 237.

11. Karl Rahner, *Foundations of Christian Faith: An Introduction to the Idea of Christianity* (New York: Seabury Press, 1978). See part V for a theology of "Holy Mystery."

12. Pope Paul VI, found in Vatican Council, and Walter M. Abbott, *The Documents of Vatican II* (New York: Guild Press, 1966), p. 15.

ther grounds a dialogical pedagogy because it opens space for exploration, conversation, questioning, and appropriation. A Latina teenager from YTM noted how this open space enabled her own faith exploration:

> During faith formation (in the parish), you're getting ready to be confirmed, or faith formation you've taken all your life — you know catechism and stuff — and they . . . kind of tell you what you are supposed to believe in. We were talking about this in my class [with] Professor Bernie Evans, and he was telling us that theology differs from this. Because theology studies the Bible and studies God and asks how we can apply it for today. So it's very open-ended. Like I say, at YTM they don't tell you what to believe in. . . . They raise a lot of questions out of you. You choose what you believe . . . [you] have that freedom.

Such freedom is a sign of respect for young people's abilities. Youth appreciate being invited to pursue Holy Mystery as theologians in their own right.

Unfortunately, as this young woman suggests, congregations rarely employ Holy Mystery as a foundational theological principle. In the Catholic church, the emphasis on doctrinal literacy for youth often gives the impression that revelation is closed and faith formation is simply about memorizing what has already been revealed. This static perspective on literacy promotes indoctrination in its worst forms and denies a dynamic process of discipleship.

In the Catholic world, the *Baltimore Catechism* was used as the primary catechetical text from 1885 to 1960. Ask ten elderly Catholics to answer question six from this catechism ("Why did God make you?"), and you will nearly universally receive the prescribed response: "God made me to know Him, to love Him, and to serve Him in this world, and to be happy with Him forever in heaven." Ask ten Catholic youth today this question, and you will most likely receive ten different responses, many of which are superficial or decidedly at odds with Catholic teaching. This jarring reality has caused some within the Church to go back to a 1950s style of catechesis. But such retrenchment relies on an overly simplistic understanding of literacy as the ability to produce memorized answers to basic questions.

In its work in the developing world, the United Nations has developed a helpful definition of literacy that goes far beyond the concept of simple memorization and repetition:[13]

13. My thanks to Christy Lang Hearlson for bringing this definition of literacy to my

> [Literacy is] the ability to identify, understand, interpret, create, communicate and compute, using printed and written materials associated with varying contexts. Literacy involves a continuum of learning in enabling individuals to achieve their goals, to develop their knowledge and potential, and to participate fully in their community and wider society.[14]

If we follow the U.N.'s definition of literacy, being literate about the Bible or about Christianity does not mean simply knowing the contents of memorized Bible passages and catechisms. Rather, the kind of literacy we seek is a set of skills and abilities that includes interpretation and invites people into participation in Christian discipleship and community.

The idea that literacy involves a continuum of learning so that people can "participate fully in their community and wider society" provides a bridge between the theological concept of Holy Mystery and the goal of sustaining Christian discipleship. God, who is mystery, invites us into exploration, driven by authentic questions and the delight of finding rich answers that raise yet more questions. Being literate means being equipped with the necessary knowledge and skills to explore Holy Mystery. As we encourage young people to seek Holy Mystery, we teach them skills for exploration so that they can learn, understand, act upon their learning, and participate in the Christian community.

Intellectual Conversion: Asking Our Way into Discipleship

Even though raising questions is a crucial and ongoing part of seeking Holy Mystery, the High School Theology Programs do not end with questions. Rather, they seek to foster what Bernard Lonergan refers to as "intellectual conversion" that has its ultimate goal in communion with God. In *Method in Theology* (1972), Lonergan describes three different types of conversion: intellectual, moral, and religious. He explains that common to all three types of conversion is a shift away from what is inauthentic in life toward new meaning and a commitment to a distinct way of living in the world.[15] Loner-

---

attention. Her doctoral work suggests its potential fruitfulness for efforts in the Christian church at increasing religious and biblical literacy.

14. "The Plurality of Literacy and Its Implications for Policies and Programs," *UNESCO Education Sector Position Paper* (2004): 13.

15. Bernard J. F. Lonergan, S.J., *Method in Theology* (New York: Herder and Herder, 1972), pp. 238-42.

gan argues that Christ's love is at the center of this shift from self-absorption or self-enclosure to self-transcendence. Robert Doran (2011) explains:

> What Lonergan calls religious conversion, then, is a process that frees one from the self-enclosure that Lonergan calls radical lovelessness. God is love, our scriptures tell us, and whoever abides in love abides in God, whether one acknowledges this or not. This process, more often than not, is mediated by participation in some religious community.[16]

For Lonergan, authentic humanness occurs through an ongoing dialogical movement away from lovelessness and self-absorption toward the radical love of Jesus Christ and self-transcendence. In this conversion process, the intellect (not only the emotions or heart) must be converted, because radical lovelessness distorts the horizon of one's intellectual interest and concerns, significantly limiting the range of questions one is even interested in asking. Doran adds,

> Intellectual conversion in its basic form will open that horizon of questions. It will transform one's cognitional life so that questions regarding meaning and truth are pursued for their own sake, and not for utilitarian and narrowly pragmatic purposes.[17]

Doran emphasizes that for Lonergan, intellectual conversion demands raising and answering questions. If young people are to experience intellectual conversion, they must be encouraged to ask questions — an insight shared by every High School Theology Program. A female participant from Leadership Now, the youth theology program at Lancaster Theological Seminary, remarked on how affirming it was to ask her own questions:

> Well, they make us feel very welcomed . . . [we] can ask any questions we want. They want our opinions on it too. So they are not just trying to teach us, "this is the right way," and "that is right." They want to know how we look at it from our point of view too. . . . Sometimes when you're in your teens, I feel like you're in between [being] the kid and adult, and you're

16. Robert Doran, "What Does Bernard Lonergan Mean by 'Conversion?'" (lecture delivered at University of St. Michael's College, University of Toronto, Toronto, ON, July 15, 2011), p. 7.

17. Doran, "What Does Bernard," p. 8.

> not really sure where you fit, and some people still treat you like a kid, but here we're [treated] like full-on adults.

Her comments point to what happens when teachers respect high school youth and give them freedom to think carefully about Christian faith.

Lonergan's emphasis on questions finds further support in transformational learning theory. Peter Block argues that transformational learning happens when teachers ask students real questions rather than providing the answers. Block notes that certain kinds of questions have greater impact:

> Conversations that evoke accountability and commitment can best be produced through deciding to value questions more than answers, by choosing to put as much thought into questions as we have traditionally given to answers. . . . Questions that have the power to make a difference are ones that engage people in an intimate way, confront them with their freedom, and invite them to co-create a future possibility.[18]

Just as the HSTPs let young people ask their own questions, they also consistently *ask* deep questions in order to foster intellectual conversion. One young man who attended the Perkins Youth School of Theology at Southern Methodist University remarked on the power of being questioned:

> Well, the main thing they did in class is that they gave us a case study. They gave us a situation in the church and asked us how our theology looked behind it and how we would face the situation ourselves. I went through the entire [case study] and said what I thought should be done. My response was challenged by my instructor. He wondered why I did that. He never said that I was wrong, but he gave me a different standpoint and asked how I felt about this, and I would say [whether] I agreed or disagreed. He asked me why and I gave him my reasons. It wasn't more of an argument, not even a debate, but more of a dialogue. I've never seen that before. I've never been able to contest a teacher's point before, so the moment I did that I felt so, like, enriched. It was the most awesome feeling ever. Back where I live it's the teacher who's right, so make sure you agree with the teacher or you'll be wrong. Here, it's [that] the teacher has an opinion and you do too, so try to contest with them.

18. Peter Block, *Community: The Structure of Belonging* (San Francisco: Berrett-Koehler, 2008), pp. 103-5.

> Try to dialogue, try to debate why. They will listen to you. They will seriously give you consideration.

As this young man tells it, the professor who asked hard questions created a dialogue that enriched students and gave them permission to entertain new possibilities.

Listening to and asking questions have become the hallmark of the High School Theology Programs' approach to theological reflection. While all HSTPs take young people's questions seriously, some base their entire curriculum on a series of questions. The Compass program, for instance, sponsored by Gordon-Conwell Seminary, is based on the following six questions:

- Why do bad things happen to good people?
- How can a two thousand year-old book be relevant in the twenty-first century?
- In a highly pluralistic world, can we really say that Jesus is the only way?
- Does the church really matter . . . really?
- How is one to live "in" the world but not "of" the world?
- Given the complexities of life, how do we know the will of God for our lives?

Yet unlike a catechism that envisions only one correct answer to each of these questions, Compass engages young people in exploratory conversations about these questions, even as leaders unpack various ways Christian tradition has answered them.

Gordon-Conwell and others have developed pedagogies of questions in order to help young people more deeply engage Christian tradition. High School Theology Programs encourage young people to root their responses to such questions in biblical and doctrinal teaching, while also making space for teenagers to develop their own questions in an unfolding process of intellectual conversion. Unlike the *Baltimore Catechism* that provided both the question and the answer, potentially stifling questions of great personal interest, the pedagogy of questions common in HSTPs opens up new horizons of thinking and believing. A pedagogy of real questions ultimately raises excitement for learning about God, because young people engage directly with the Holy Mystery of God. Furthermore, by immersing young people in an ordered process of discovery, these programs equip teenagers with tools that allow them to continue this reflective process when they return home. The HSTPs have seen that pedagogies of theological reflection — undertaken in supportive Christian communities where people are willing to risk asking and entertaining hard questions — create a foundation for theological literacy, and equip students to pursue Holy Mystery for life.

Implications for Forming Christian Leaders

For the last twenty years, the High School Theology Programs have experimented with pedagogies that foster excitement for theological learning and encourage young people to consider vocations in church ministry. Much evidence suggests that emphasizing theological reflection on both historic Christian tradition and present Christian action contributes to long-term discipleship. The experiment on holistic theological education at YTM and other HSTPs offers a number of implications for the church, for seminaries and schools of theology, and for anyone concerned with preparing leaders for the future church.

Congregations

Since the long-term vitality of Christianity is dependent on fostering and sustaining Christian disciples, congregations may find inspiration from how the HSTPs help young people engage faith intellectually. First, churches might embrace Holy Mystery as a theological framework that invites youth to meet God and grow in faith, prompting churches to open space for dialogue as youth and adults alike pursue answers to fresh questions. Second, Holy Mystery releases churches from indoctrination, providing both the questions and answers, on the one hand — just as it releases churches from feeling like they must manipulate youth by provoking an emotional or spiritual "conversion" experience for them. Instead congregations can combine action and reflection, offering teenagers experiences of service, worship, and learning in the midst of a practicing faith community, and work intentionally to connect these experiences to the tradition of faith. In so doing, they create meaningful opportunities for theological reflection with both young people and adults. Third, congregations can help youth engage the Christian tradition intellectually by giving them opportunity to talk with pastors and trained theologians, by helping them find theological resources they may not know exist, by opening space for their questions, and by taking their ideas seriously.

Seminaries

Seminaries, too, may find the HSTPs' approach to teaching theology helpful. For one thing, intellectual conversion is one of the primary tasks of theological education. Nurturing intellectual communities that provoke and support shifts toward new meanings, and that evoke commitment to a way of life that embodies these new meanings, is the crucial work of the theological educator (and anyone concerned with the church's intellectual, as well as moral and religious, leadership).

Furthermore, seminaries might take note of pedagogical models in the High School Theology Programs that seem to assist in such intellectual conversions. Most HSTPs rely on seminarians and seminary professors as adult leaders, and in the process train them to become holistic educators in their own right. Seminaries and theological schools that use the HSTPs as laboratories for training leaders and teachers will find that these programs tend to expand their pedagogical comfort zones, as they become familiar with action-reflection models of learning that foster and sustain Christian discipleship. Seminaries might consider how their own curriculum forms future church leaders by their pedagogical approaches to teaching theology: Do we teach theological reflection and foster theological literacy by immersing seminary students in holistic educational environments that integrate worship, service, and learning? Or do we teach theology with "talking heads"? Since people tend to teach as they were taught, seminaries that adopt praxis-oriented holistic pedagogies have potential to change the church, and in so doing, improve the durability of faith in the pews.

We hear much about how young people are leaving the church. But a great many of the youth who attend the High School Theology Programs want to "stay a little bit longer." They have experienced a Christian community committed to Christ's mission. In that supportive context, holistic pedagogies of theological reflection have integrated prayer, community, service, justice, and vocational discernment into the intellectual communities that form the backbone of the HSTPs. Like the disciples on the mount of Transfiguration, youth in these theology programs want to stay connected to the glory of Christ. But like Jesus' disciples, they are called to travel down the mountaintop to join in God's Holy Mystery as it is revealed in ministries that involve youth in healing, teaching, and preaching. Now, after twenty years of experimentation, the HSTPs are still discovering the long-term benefits of holistic theological reflection, as young people continue their journey as disciples of Jesus Christ — and their affinity for theological inquiry — years after their summer in a High School Theology Program. These programs have concocted a powerfully combustible mix of theological instruction, action in the world, and theological reflection on texts, traditions, and experience — fuel for faith over the long haul.

CHAPTER NINE

The Formative Power of Awe

Pedagogies of Worship and Wonder

Fred Edie

Students in the Lilly High School Theology Programs worship together — a lot. It is not always pretty; as one thoughtful alumna and present staff member of Emory's Youth Theology Initiative explains, worship planning was always "very fraught":

> There was lots of conflict. But it was really important conflict to work through, because it gets to issues of theological — I mean you do theological reflection — you think about ethics, you think about race, you think about class, and do we use gender inclusive language or not? And all of it comes out in worship, whether it's in worship planning or in who is speaking in worship, like, what does worship look like?

Her conclusion was one echoed by many HSTP students, staff, and alumni: "Worship is, I think, the most important pedagogical space at YTI."

This is true also of the program I know best — Duke's Youth Academy for Christian Formation (DYA) — where worship occurs daily and orients its curriculum.[1] Perhaps this is because the vast majority of High School Theology Program students are publicly, avowedly Christian, and worship is a zone of great passion, often planned and led by young people themselves.

1. This "worship as curriculum" approach is shared with other programs, including those at St. Meinrad, Notre Dame, Lutheran Theological at Gettysburg, Hellenic, and others. Of these, a number (including DYA) approach vocational discernment from the perspective of the sacrament of baptism out of their conviction that baptism is a source of Christian identity and vocation.

Like a bunch of conferencing Methodist preachers, when the call to worship comes and with it the hymned interrogative — "And are we yet alive?" — HSTP students respond in a hundred different ways with a joyous, and even deafening, doxological "YES!" In my own experience, it is impossible to worship with these students and not be filled with wonder and hope.

At the same time, all is not perfect in Youth Doxology Land, even at the High School Theology Programs. One night during communal worship at DYA, a guest preacher called students to the altar to be saved by Jesus. (He either missed the memo about our students or did not believe it.) For five excruciating minutes nobody moved from his or her seat despite the preacher's exhortations. And why should they? Our students were not there to meet Jesus for the first time; they were there to learn how to follow him more faithfully. The tension finally broke when Nelson trooped forward from the back of the chapel. In a prayer, our preacher praised Nelson and God and himself while vaguely threatening the rest of us. Confused, I approached Nelson afterwards, saying lamely, "Welcome to the Body of Christ, Nelson." He replied, "Thanks, dude, but you know I'm already Christian. I felt bad for the guy, and we were all dying in there, so I took one for the team."

Nelson and other young people are alert to youth ministry's efforts to repeatedly cast them in a repetitious liturgical version of the film *Groundhog Day*. They resent being infantilized by adults who do not trust their capacity to be faithful or who fail to recognize their desire to grow in grace. This friction also indirectly raises the question of what constitutes authentic Christian worship, especially where youth are concerned, and how worship feeds into the vocational discernment that lies at the heart of the HSTPs. The common assumption of many congregations is that they must attract Nelson and his Christian peers with "worship lite," a caffeinated mix of beach balls and boom boxes all designed to orchestrate a certain religious experience, rather than invite them to feast on the deep and lasting nourishment of Word and Sacrament. The truth is that even devoted youth — the Nelsons of the church — often feel alienated or marginalized by the consumerist liturgical fare that is too readily served on Sunday mornings to teenagers. To these youth, "worship lite" feels cheesy, and Word and Sacrament can sound like old-people speak for "dull." Habituated to the Big Buzz, even devoted youth — like their less devoted peers — often fail to comprehend the subtle transformational mysteries of grace unplugged (if, in fact, that is even being offered).

I believe the church is poised to reclaim worship of the triune God as a critical zone of formation for young Christian leaders. If, as I will claim later, we lead from who we are, then the church must look to Christian worship's capacity to shape faithful imaginations as the deep wellspring from which faithful leadership (and all discipleship) flows. In the early church, of course, worship was the only formal context for catechesis available. Yet today, reclaiming worship's power to shape the imaginations of young Christian leaders presents a complex challenge. On the one hand, young people like Nelson with callings to Christian leadership are especially in need of the "continuing conversion" that worship can catalyze.[2] On the other hand, this transformative encounter with the Holy is short-circuited when worship seems superficial and abstract, too disconnected from worshippers' own lives to inspire their participation. In order for worship to enact its potential to inspire the "continual conversion" of young people like Nelson (and indeed, of the entire church), we must help youth become "fluent" in worship — which means providing settings, like the High School Theology Programs, where worship is spoken.

The liturgical literacy I imagine has several marks. Youth should recognize authentic worship when they see it, and, equally important, when they see it being distorted. They should learn how to plan worship, participate in it or, when called upon, lead it artfully; and they should be equipped to use their imaginative capacities to taste and see the goodness of God's self-giving love through it. Fostering such liturgical literacy first requires repeated opportunities for youth to participate in the breadth and depth of the church's historic worshipping traditions. It also calls for intentionally cultivating a faithful imagination that can function at several levels in relation to worship. Finally, it entails inviting young people's improvisations upon the church's traditions so that they can call those traditions their own.

Such an approach to faith formation requires both practice and reflection, but it does more than help young people more clearly understand, or more confidently participate in, worship. To assert the formative power of worship is to say that, in the act or performance of worship, young people *actually* experience God meeting them, and can name ways in which they have been identified as God's own. In worship, God joins youth to God's saving work in the world, and truly empowers them for that vocation. Sometimes youth recognize this divine encounter spontaneously, as did seventeen-year-old Amanda from Gordon-Conwell's Compass program:

2. I'm borrowing the phrase from the Rite of Christian Initiation of Adults (RCIA) *Rite of Calling the Candidates to Continuing Conversion, #446-449*. Cf. *RCIA: Rite of Christian Initiation of Adults* (Collegeville, MN: Liturgical, 1990), p. 263.

> We climbed White Face Mountain, which is 4,786 feet high, and when we reached 4,786, we all just started screaming, um, you know, "Glory, glory, glory!" . . . We sang almost all the way up the mountain and down, because we were not only just so worn out and had to take our minds off [how tired we were] — but also because of what was around us, God's creation. We just couldn't help it, just bursting into song.

More often, however, youth in the High School Theology Programs told us about encountering God through the liturgical practices of their communities, especially when those practices were framed in a new way. At St. John's Youth in Theology and Ministry Program, sixteen-year-old Justin recalled:

> Last year one of the biggest things for me was the morning worship and all the songs we would sing, and how [singing] can be used as a prayer, and just [be] a way to praise God too. And that's what I really found. I think I'm closest to God when I'm singing and doing those worship songs. That's my favorite way of prayer.

Seventeen-year-old Rachel, from Candler's Youth Theology Initiative, remembered a recent worship service that involved her body in new ways as a time of divine encounter: "The most recent [time I experienced God at YTI] was yesterday. Yesterday was my exploratory course on . . . bodies and disability, and [worship] was very different . . . because we got to experience God through our senses, like sight, smell, touch. It was a very humbling experience."

As these youth attest, when Christian worship invites grateful praise of God, confession of sin, passing the peace, baptismal washing from pretense, and Eucharistic communion, it both envisions and actually *practices* a Christian ethic. Liturgy is performed, but it is not pretend. Instead, worship embodies a way of life that Christians must lead. When we invite young people into faithful performances of worship, we invite them to encounter the triune God, and to participate in a way of life that reflects this encounter.

My account here reflects on the experiences of teenagers like Amanda, Justin, and Rachel by making three interrelated moves. First, I review wisdom from Scripture and the church of antiquity, as well as share contemporary theological insight, to affirm worship's power to form and transform followers of Jesus. I also take soundings from Christian tradition to provide a set of norms (or at least rules of thumb) for discerning authentic Christian worship as it forms young people. Second, I suggest some reasons worship is formative and transformative, and I argue that it engages and operates on different levels of what I will describe as "faithful imagination." Finally, I attempt to show how, through imaginatively engaged worship performances, young Christians may find both their identity and vocation in Christ deepened, including vocations for leadership in the church.

The Transformational Nature of Authentic Worship and Formation

Whatever else Christians are called to do, worship is always first among them. If we confess that God has created the entire cosmos out of a surplus of love, that Jesus Christ is redeeming and bringing new life to this same cosmos that was formerly subjected to sin and death, and that the Holy Spirit inspires and empowers creation's journey to the fullness of God's reign — if we confess all this, then worship is always the church's primary calling. What more fitting response could there be than praise and gratitude for God's good work? As the Westminster Shorter Catechism famously proclaims, humanity's chief end is to "glorify *God* and enjoy [God] *forever.*" In this "work of the people" (the meaning of the word *liturgy* in the original Greek), worshippers join the ongoing prayer of Jesus and all the saints in unceasing praise.

Christian worship is first and foremost directed toward God; it is inspired by God and is offered to God. It is not first about human beings, not about re-charging our spiritual batteries, not about discovering identity and living into vocations, not even about cultivating faithful leadership for the next generation. It is for the glorification of God for God's own sake. *And yet,* the Christian triune God is always paying it forward. God receives our offerings of praise (though they amount to a pittance in relation to who God is and the gifts God provides) then serendipitously returns them to God's people as the sustaining food of faithfulness. Even though worship is for God, worshippers may receive from it the vision and power to live into Christ's new creation. Worship does not just symbolize transformation; through worship, God forms and transforms us into new creations who do what we were made to do: glorify God.

The idea that liturgical action could actually form or transform worshippers, rather than simply mimic or recall such a transformation, is a conviction as old as the faith itself. Paul, for example, notes in his letter to the Romans that persons are not baptized "because" Jesus was baptized, nor were they baptized in mere "imitation" of Jesus. Instead they are baptized *into* Jesus; specifically, according to Paul, into Jesus' death and resurrection hope (Rom. 6). Similarly, Augustine, the fourth-century bishop of Hippo, contemplates the transforming grace of Holy Communion (or "Eucharist," as he calls it) by imaginatively inverting the logic of eating. While normally we would expect the food we eat to become part of our own bodies, for Augustine, to partake of Eucharist is to be incorporated ever more deeply into *Christ's* body.[3] To borrow from Tertullian, bishop of Carthage in the early third century, worship is the setting where Christians are "made."[4] Historian Thomas Finn affirms this connection by noting that, for the earliest Christians, theology was the result of "symbols deeply lived."[5] God's gifts of transforming grace flowed through human participation in ritual symbols (word, table, font, chrism, fire, patterns of time) to "make" God's people.

To simplify massively, the church's task of "faith making" in worship changed course dramatically in the second millennium. The emphasis shifted from bodily, affective, and experiential faith to ideational faith. Now the path to salvation required getting your Christian facts straight. Indeed, despite its etymological root, the meaning of orthodoxy also shifted from "right worship" to "right belief." As a result, the context for making faith moved from the sanctuary to the school. By knowing the truth, it was thought, people could then go live it (an assumption that rather quickly proved unreliable).[6] Noting Augustine's insight that human beings are disposed to worship what they love, contemporary philosopher James K. A. Smith observes young people enrolled in Christian schools and colleges who are nevertheless engaged in "cultural liturgies" of conspicuous consumption at the mall, or a melding of rituals drawn from entertainment media, military power, and the sports industry.[7] Smith contends that these cultural liturgies shape young

3. Augustine of Hippo, Sermons 227, 228b, 229a, and 272 (http://david.heitzman.net/sermons227-229a.html, accessed October 7, 2013). The biblical text for Augustine's reflection is John 6, including v. 51, "I am the living bread that came down from heaven. Whoever eats of this bread will live forever; and the bread that I will give for the life of the world is my flesh."

4. Quoted in Maxwell E. Johnson, *The Rites of Christian Initiation: Their Evolution and Interpretation* (Collegeville, MN: Liturgical, 2007), p. xix.

5. Thomas M. Finn, *Early Christian Baptism and the Catechumenate: West and East Syria* (Collegeville, MN: Liturgical, 1992), p. 5.

6. According to James K. A. Smith, the foundations of Christian schooling in America lie in the determination to transmit a Christian worldview to students. See James K. A. Smith, *Desiring the Kingdom: Worship, Worldview, and Cultural Formation* (Grand Rapids: Baker Academic, 2009), pp. 17-18.

7. Smith, *Desiring*, pp. 19-27.

peoples' desires just as powerfully as Christian liturgy once did, forming young people's identities around what they love.

Likewise, Katherine Turpin has exposed consumerism as the dominant but inadequate faith system of Western young people today.[8] Turpin notes that young people worship at the cathedrals of shopping malls and engage in liturgies and therapies of consumption. Like Smith, Turpin rejects the idea that young people simply need to be trained to think "better." The problem, she argues, is that a young person may become cognitively aware of the evils of rampant consumerism but not have the desire to change. Turpin thus calls for a "conversion" of imagination, desire, and will, which take place as young people engage with communities that offer countercultural practices of work, fellowship, and worship.

Just how do we distinguish "authentic" Christian worship from false, damaging, or impoverished worship? At the risk of setting off another century of internecine strife, I plunge in. In the midst of its doxology, worship should proclaim and perform the truth about God so far as we know it from the witness of Scripture and tradition of the church (including liturgical tradition). By implication, worship should also proclaim and perform the truth about human beings, including the struggles and insights arising out of our efforts to live faithfully before God.[9] Christian worship should not be directed toward a god fashioned out of our navel fuzz, but to the living triune God. The God of Christian Scripture is a storied God whom we know through the saving history of covenant with Israel; through the life, death, and resurrection of Jesus reconciling us to God's covenantal intent; and through the Spirit's continuing redemption in the church and world.

As Gordon Lathrop suggests, worship is therefore most likely to enact the truth of God's revelation and the truth about humanity through structured "juxtapositions" of one liturgical "holy thing" to another.[10] For

8. Katherine Turpin, *Branded: Adolescents Converting from Consumer Faith* (Cleveland, OH: Pilgrim, 2006).

9. Don Saliers puts it this way: "Christian liturgy transforms and empowers when the vulnerability of human pathos is met by the ethos of God's vulnerability in word and sacrament." Saliers defines pathos as "the human suffering of the world. Human emotions and passions, despite vast differences, provide access to what is counted real," and the divine ethos as "the characteristic manner in which liturgy is a self-giving of God to us, the encounter whereby grace and glory find human form." *Worship as Theology: Foretaste of Glory Divine* (Nashville, TN: Abingdon, 1994), p. 22.

10. Gordon W. Lathrop, *Holy Things: A Liturgical Theology* (Minneapolis, MN: Fortress, 1998), p. 24.

example, Lathrop suggests that the juxtaposition of Word with Table is pivotal to liturgical authenticity. Placed in creative tension, these holy things mutually interpret one another. Further, in their juxtaposition with one another, holy things are also juxtaposed to the life of the assembly of faith. Through this structured tension, holy things and the community of the faithful are "broken open," enabling new revelatory insight to pour forth. For Lathrop, juxtaposition preserves an essential hermeneutical (and pedagogical) humility. Juxtapositions create paradoxical truth. They ensure that we praise the God we worship as incarnate while also acknowledging God's transcendence. They remind us that we are at once sinfully rebellious yet are being made holy by God. They enable us to sense God's reign as at once here now and yet not complete. Additional normative juxtapositions in worship include placing doxology alongside lament and beseeching, placing (baptismal) bathing beside teaching, and so on. Without these juxtapositions, Christian worship risks either claiming too much or professing too little about God.

Worship and Faithful Imagination

The deeply transformative and theologically significant effects of worship flow in part from the ways in which liturgical participation both instills and requires practices of faithful imagination.[11] Faithful imagination is more than a knack for innovation or creative flair; it serves as an interpretive matrix in which communal and personal memory shape desire or passion, bending toward hope for the future. Something like Spinoza's *conatus,* imagination funds the human drive not only to *be* but also to *be well,* to flourish.[12]

Christians engage a faithful imagination at different levels and for different tasks. On one level, worship can train worshippers' *embodied* imaginations by working through and forming dispositions. This way of imagining is

11. Pieces of this section are excerpted from Fred Edie, "Liturgy and Faith Formation: Reimagining a Partnership for the Sake of Youth" in *Liturgy* 29 (2014): 33-44.

12. *Conatus* is a seventeenth-century metaphysical category used to describe a being's will to live, or innate inclination to continue to exist and enhance itself. Spinoza understood *conatus* as a "striving" to persevere. For an expanded definition, see *Stanford Encyclopedia of Philosophy,* http://plato.stanford.edu/entries/spinoza-psychological/ (accessed October 8, 2013). The view of *conatus* discussed here in relationship to imagination is developed in Thomas H. Groome, *Sharing Faith: A Comprehensive Approach to Religious Education and Pastoral Ministry: The Way of Shared Praxis* (Eugene, OR: Wipf and Stock, 1999), pp. 28-29.

transacted and ultimately inscribed in and through habitual gestures of the body and affections of the heart. On another level, worship invites *reflective* imagination. Through ritual-symbolic-linguistic expansion and associative linking, Christian young people discover that worship contains previously unfathomable gifts that respond to their previously unfathomable wounds, blessings, and hopes. Of course, like all human capacities, imagination is subject to sinful distortion. Hence imagination, too, must find its proper *telos* in the Word made flesh, and worship is a critical zone for doing that. Thus, at a third level, worship helps shape a *critical* faithful imagination, as young people worship in ways that operate as creative responses to critical reflection about worship itself. In short, imagination is not simply key to assist young persons in discerning what makes their worship Christian; it also enables them to conceive how their present circumstances, and perhaps their worship, are not yet all that God intends. Besides prompting youth to see what is not yet, faithful imagination fuels young peoples' dreams to join with God in building God's kingdom.

Embodied Imagination: "It's Awesome, Dude"

Faithful imagining is first of all bodily and affective before it is reflective or critical. The philosopher Paul Connerton contends that persons and societies carry their most important truths at the bodily level.[13] Oddly, we human beings often experience the bodily dimensions of ourselves as tribal regions about which we know little, if we notice them at all, and over which we exert scant control. Hence, without reflection, we may not notice how worship is working in these regions, disposing us to see, feel, and act in certain ways — an obliviousness that often leads us to underestimate worship's formative potential. Nevertheless, like Nathaniel Hawthorne's contemplative who spends a lifetime gazing at the Great Stone Face, through their worship Christians may find themselves growing in resemblance to that which they admire. Repeated thoughts, feelings, and behaviors strengthen synaptic connections between neurons in the brain, automating them in the process. Habits free the conscious mind for other tasks. Yet these habits also come to characterize persons. The ways in which youth typically greet or ignore others, respond to opportunities or

13. Paul Connerton, *How Societies Remember* (Cambridge: Cambridge University Press, 1989).

crises, assume bodily postures, or even feel about themselves internally all become functions of habit. Such habits provide youth with a reliable (if not always positive) sense of who they are. The repetitions of worship, therefore, and the habits they instill are integral to forming young Christians who experience themselves as God's beloved, and who are capable of loving God and neighbor as a result.

Such formation of dispositions occurs not only through repeated bodily practice, but also through stories retold, recalled, and lived. Pastoral theologian David Hogue has suggested that liturgy's formative capacity is related to its own and to the storied nature of human beings.[14] Drawing upon neuroscience, Hogue suggests that persons naturally store their memories in narrative form. He notes that these stories of the past become associated in our memories with emotions evoked in the midst of those experiences. Christian worship operates in the realm of regularly rehearsed declarative memories (God's story of salvation) and, equally important, repeatedly evoked emotions appropriate to this story (gratitude, compassion, and hope, for example). Worship thus may become an occasion for healing people's memories of wounding stories through the graced reimagination and reinterpretation of them in the liturgy.[15]

Experiencing worship as lived story, then, can lead to healing and hope, and even inspire a sense of awe. Awe is more than a feeling or emotion. To be awed is to be moved to one's depths by the profundity of personal encounter with the God of the universe, but also to experience God's offer of relationship with the divine.[16] Emotional memory can make our declarative memories seem as if the events they capture are happening again in the present. For example, recalling one's near drowning as a child can feel as if one is drowning all over again, just as remembering one's first day at a new school or reliving one's first kiss can cause the heart to race. Similarly, singing the story of Jesus' resurrection ("Jesus Christ is risen *today* . . .") activates the emotional memory system, conveying power as we experience this stupendous event happening again in the here and now of the assembly's worship, where we are witnesses! In this understanding, teenagers' full-on declaration — "It's awesome, dude!" — is more than adolescent slang; for Hogue, this performed anamnesis is the means by which

14. David A. Hogue, *Remembering the Future, Imagining the Past: Story, Ritual, and the Human Brain* (Eugene, OR: Wipf and Stock, 2003), see especially chapter 2.

15. Hogue, *Remembering the Future,* see chapters 3 and 4.

16. See Anabel Proffitt, "The Importance of Wonder in Educational Ministry," *Religious Education* 93, no. 1 (Winter 1998): 102-13.

worshippers' stories of brokenness may be "re-written" in relation to the story of salvation. Critically, according to Hogue, when this re-narration occurs at the level of bodily practice, it transforms emotional resonances of memory even more than it shapes conscious or self-reflective awareness. Performed, bodily anamnesis is a *dispositional* imagining; it forms dispositions and affections.

Reflective Imagination: An Invitation to Wonder

Faithful imagination begins bodily and affectively, but it does not end there. Faithful imagination consists also of reflective, mindful attention that evokes young people's poetic and artistic sensibilities in response to the stories and symbols of Christian faith. Reflective imagination employs a form of reason that cultivates deepened awareness of God's graced self-revelation through worship. Yet because it remains imagination, this faithful, reflective attentiveness does not intend to rope, brand, and corral Holy Mystery. Instead, it invites young people who learn to employ a reflective imagination to connect more profoundly with the elements of worship themselves, to recognize the relationship of these elements to one another, and to discern the connections between worship and worshippers' lives.

At the Duke Youth Academy, the formation of the reflective imagination resembles catechesis. This form of catechesis is anything but mind-numbing memorization of faith facts. Its aim is deepened delight and praise. It proceeds by way of invitation to "wonder" at the ritual symbols of Christian worship.[17] It assumes that these symbols bear a great surplus of meaning and that their polyvalence may "speak" more expansively of the life of God and to young people's lives — if they acquire the eyes to see. In addition to wondering about meanings, those engaged in imaginative reflection upon holy things may work through associations as well. Youth are invited to associate ritual symbols with the biblical stories of salvation and with the emerging stories of their own lives. Indeed, reflecting on the layers of meaning within these symbols reveals something of the depths of God, and further opens worshippers to wonder and awe.

At one time, such imaginative catechesis was a constitutive practice

17. I take my cues here from Jerome W. Berryman, *Godly Play: An Imaginative Approach to Christian Education* (San Francisco: HarperSanFrancisco, 1991) and from Kieran Egan, *Imagination in Teaching and Learning* (Chicago: University of Chicago Press, 1992).

for forming persons in Christian faith. Rich expansions and improvisations on symbols are everywhere in the Bible and the early tradition. Paul associates Jesus with Israel's Passover Lamb. Matthew portrays him as the new Moses. Everywhere in Scripture older images are recast and re-associated to speak something new. For example, 1 Peter 3:20-21 claims that the story of Noah's ark "prefigures" baptism into Christ. This process of expansion and association continues in figural readings of the Scriptures. With breathtaking artistic genius, Ephrem (a fourth-century Syriac bishop) reflects that from whatever angle he gazes upon the prismatic oil of chrism, the multifaceted Christ "looks out at me from it."[18] Indeed, reflection upon these ritual symbols was not only catechetically effective; it was theologically generative, giving rise to new understandings of God and the Christian life.

We live in a different world at present, in which standardized tests celebrate teenagers' linear reason at the expense of other intelligences, and churches and denominations become known for wrangling over points of doctrinal orthodoxy rather than for the richness of their stories and symbols. We ought not be surprised when youth perceive ritual symbols as flat or even dead — water is clear; fire is hot; bread is flour mixed with water heated by fire; wine is flavored water that gives you a buzz — and then come to regard such symbols as pointless. They have never been invited to "speak" the Christian liturgical language at its depths.[19]

Critical Imagination: How Might It Be Otherwise?

Faithful imagination also moves toward a critical moment in which we discern whether our offerings to God are faithful — a critical insight that can then move us toward action and activism. Earlier I described ways in which worship may be assessed for authenticity, including attention to juxtaposition. We are called by our baptism to discern such authenticity, for the baptismal waters scrub away both pretense and unworthiness with equal effect. As Paul suggests to the Galatians, baptism constitutes

18. Thomas M. Finn, *Early Christian Baptism and the Catechumenate: West and East Syria* (Collegeville, MN: Liturgical, 1992), p. 155. For the full range of Ephrem's insights into chrism, see all of hymn seven.

19. See Brent Strawn's chapter in this volume for more on inviting young people to learn to speak the language of faith. In his case, he is concerned with the capacity of the Old Testament and the Bible as a whole to form human persons in a way of life.

Christians into a new form of community wherein old markers of status are relativized if not erased. In place of slave or free comes a shared, unified identity in Christ. Does our worship enact baptismal unity or reassert former status hierarchies? Does our holy meal express the paradox of hospitality — all are welcome yet all remain beggars at Christ's table — or are some left hungry?

Ultimately, these questions also invite a wider imaginative critique of the liturgies undertaken by Christians beyond the sanctuary. Where exactly is our community involved in the baptismal work of erasing hierarchies of power and in reconciling, unifying, justice-seeking ministry? Where are we meeting the hungers (actual and metaphorical) of the world? In this way, not only is imagination key to detecting authenticity in worship; it evokes visions of how things may be otherwise, in worship and in the world. Faithful imagination is a key that helps young people begin to see as God sees, and therefore to get involved in what God is doing.

Pedagogies of Worship and Awe: Keys to Cultivating Faithful Imagination

If, as the introduction to this book suggests, imagination is key to the formation of future church leaders (and to creating a kind of church that young people want to lead in the first place), then the ability to shape a faithful imagination is "Job One" for catechists, church leaders, and theological educators alike. The High School Theology Programs are energetic laboratories for faithful imagination, and worship has unrivaled pedagogical power for forming the Christian imagination. To be clear, HSTPs do not emphasize worship *in order to* provide youth with an effective pedagogical exercise; we worship together, as all Christians worship together, in order to come into the presence of God, to remember who we are and to respond to Christ's call to serve him in the world. Yet in the process of worshipping God together, we find our imaginations changing. We see one another a little more as Christ sees us. We desire a little more honestly what Christ desires. So what *are* the aspects of worship that, as we perform them, can become pedagogical opportunities as well, especially as they help young people begin to imagine themselves as people called to Christian discipleship and leadership? I will conclude with a few of the ways the Duke Youth Academy, and some other HSTPs, have turned to worship as a resource for shaping young people's faithful imaginations.

Forming Embodied Imagination

Across the board, High School Theology Programs make worship a place where bodies, as well as minds and emotions, are welcome. Most programs start by simply reminding students of this fact, teaching varieties of gestures for worship that may or may not feel familiar. Students at the Duke Youth Academy, for example, learn to raise hands in praise, extend them in supplication, process into a worship space, perform simple dance steps, chant Psalms, genuflect, bow, pass the peace (we use a "hug and release" method), sing the Prayer of Great Thanksgiving, and receive the elements of Holy Communion. They repeat these gestures daily in worship for two weeks. Adult staff then build on these gestures in their teaching. For example, one artist, a theologically trained biblical storyteller, instructs students in how to embody and inhabit the Scriptures they read in the assembly. Visual artists show how to contemplate iconic images, and musicians teach multiple musical forms.

We are not alone in emphasizing gesture in worship, of course. Students attending St. Meinrad's One Bread One Cup program are trained as lay Eucharistic ministers in their tradition. In addition to the theological dimensions of becoming a Eucharistic minister, students also learn the gestures of this ministry — where and how to stand, bow, genuflect, or kneel, when to tender what to the celebrant, and how to offer the host hospitably and with expectant joy to communicants.

One of the ways the Youth Hope Builders Academy forms embodied worshipful imaginations is through dance. I witnessed a group composed of current students and alumni from YHBA perform a dance that evoked the "ring shout," a practice dating back to antebellum slavery. Costumed in flowing gingham dresses and kerchiefs, the girls (all African American) moved in circles, clapping and stamping their feet, then lifting their arms in praise. The ring shout was a uniquely African American practice of worship, fueling their resistance and resilience in the face of slavery. The girls executed the dance flawlessly and with great artistry, and the congregation was powerfully moved by their performance. I do not doubt that this dance and the saving memories it bears are now inscribed in these young dancers' bodies. They carry these stories of slavery, resistance, and the hope of God's deliverance in their flesh and blood.

In my more despairing moments, I sometimes question whether DYA makes any lasting difference in forming the Christian lives of students. At annual reunions, however, I am always awed to witness the community enter bodily into Holy Communion. The prescribed bidding is offered: "Lift up your hearts!" Even after an interim of months or years, the assembly's response is immediate and sung with great relish: "We lift them up to the Lord!" The liturgy continues. Students look around and smile, perhaps like me, "re-membering" the power of these gestures. They have learned Holy Communion "by heart," and in their performance of it they witness to its power to elevate their own hearts.

Forming Reflective Imagination

As Brent Strawn notes in chapter 13 of this volume, no one is born speaking a language. Yet young people must learn the Christian liturgical language if it is to be meaningful. Anyone who has taken a high school foreign language class knows that dogmatic, authoritarian, or rationalistic pedagogies do not result in language acquisition. On the contrary, Christian tradition prompts us to recover the insight of artists and their ways of imaginative expansion and association if young people are to be moved and empowered in worship. We might follow St. Ephrem's lead regarding chrism, for example, as he links it to healings, royal anointings, and the gift of Spirit power, then further spins out its connotative resonance by considering its composition (olives) and by connecting the leaves of the olive tree to Jesus' triumphal entry into Jerusalem, and its limbs to his crucifixion. All this Ephrem gets from riffing on chrism!

Alternately, a few minutes of guided brainstorming around the significance of water easily yields a dozen or more ways water impacts human life. Young people may use this list to discover how the baptismal waters suggest a wide range of possible meanings, including water as primal source of all life and water as threat to life's existence, plus power, transport, transformation, and mixing together (as in community). These soundings provide young people the resources to imagine Christian baptism as a wondrously consequential event in their lives, and one with continuing consequence. The same exercise may be employed with bread, wine, fire, and other symbols of the liturgy — or with the gestures of worship, mentioned above. A bowed head, for example, might signal either holy fear or humiliation, depending on the context, while a broken loaf can mean wounding or sharing.

In addition to exploring symbols and gestures, DYA instructors also explore biblical stories and literature with youth, as well as liturgical figurative speech, including metaphor. Obviously, the point of metaphor in reference to God is not to name God with flattening (and domesticating) certitude. Perceiving and using metaphor makes possible the linking and interlacing of biblical stories with personal stories. Anne Wimberly, director of Youth Hope-Builders Academy, advocates a pedagogy of the African American church that links stories on three levels: personal stories to biblical stories to stories of African American Christian exemplars.[20] The point is to develop students' capacities to imagine, by sharing stories of struggles and hopes, that they are living in continuity with the stories of their forebears and, ultimately, with the Story of the God who hears and responds to the cries of oppressed peoples.

Forming Imagination in Relation to Critical Reflection

Like dispositional and reflective imagining, critical reflection can also be cultivated and formed. At DYA, as at many of the High School Theology Programs, young people work with mentors to take responsibility for planning, leading (to the extent that various faith traditions permit), and reflecting upon worship. This is a higher order pedagogical task requiring the imaginative connection of a number of variables. At DYA, the opportunity to help lead worship is the point where students' still squeaky new theologies of liturgy collide with their aesthetical preferences and the habitually embodied worshipping practices they have brought with them from home. It is never dull and sometimes explosive! Although students must operate within certain traditioned parameters (we use a Word and Table pattern under the umbrella of the Baptismal Covenant, plus a lectionary of sorts, as well as daily theological themes keyed to the lectionary), they nevertheless find themselves contending over the content and performance of worship, as well as how these factors most faithfully enact the truth of their lives before God within the DYA community. Is worship marking Christ's passion really the time for Elrod to solo "Shine Jesus Shine" on his tuba, even if he did truck it all the way from Tuscaloosa? Does Jenna's desire to blow bubbles from behind the altar appropriately signify God's forgiveness for sin and our reconciliation to God and neighbor? These scenarios — actual ones — may fall a bit on the wacky side, but they illustrate well the complexities of interpretation and imagination required for faithful worship to take flesh.

20. See Anne S. Wimberly, *Soul Stories: African American Christian Education* (Nashville, TN: Abingdon, 2011).

Participants in other HSTPs echo these sentiments about the complexity of the task. As the high school theology alumna quoted at the beginning of this chapter suggests, conflict is common as students who take responsibility for worship find their assumptions about worship clashing with the worship expectations, not to mention cultural and theological expectations, held by their new friends. Teenagers must use what they are learning in order to get something done together. They seek the best words, the most resonant gestures, and the proper aesthetic key. Using the tradition, they nevertheless seek to reimagine and improvise upon it, so that it speaks to their reality. They brainstorm, and they argue. With gentle prompting from mentors, they involve themselves in a process of critical imagination toward deepened faithfulness of expression.

Liturgy planned must then be performed. Students dance, sing, read, tell, dramatize, pray, play, share, and symbolize to the glory of the Holy Trinity. Sometimes lacking professional polish, student leaders more than offset their inexperience with passion. They have become invested in this work and are seeking to offer their very best to God. Other worshipping members of the community participate in these offerings equally as wholeheartedly because they sense that these expressions evoke the truth about their lives in this community.

Afterward, worship leaders reflect upon the entire experience. What went well or poorly? What was difficult or easy? Where did they sense the worship perform the truth about God and the truth about themselves? What new insights came through the process? Where were they surprised? Where did they encounter Holy Mystery? Here is a small sampling, from DYA and other HSTPs, of their reactions:

- "I couldn't believe I was offering the (communion) cup to the Dean. It was, like, upside down."
- "Worship made us a community."
- "Our group felt like planning worship was probably what church is really like. There was drama and there was beauty."
- "I felt close to God [in] reading Scripture (in worship)."
- "I've become hungry for Eucharist."
- "That day that we did the meal (a cookout shared with members of an HIV residential home), it felt like we had communion twice."

As a result of these programs, students glimpse the depths of Christian worship, and are better able to articulate its plurality of meanings and intent.

They become more fluent speakers and interpreters of Christian language. They also more clearly understand the worshipping traditions of the church, and improvise on them, bending these traditions toward their own contexts and cultural idioms. Further, they have expanded their repertoire of means to enter God's presence beyond the use of subwoofers and laser lights; they are more susceptible to wonder and, therefore, more willing to participate in the Spirit's graced transformative work. They learn to evaluate worship's authenticity beyond personal preference. Finally, they see in worship very real (not pretend) patterns of Christian living.

Christian Worship, Identity, Leadership

It is obvious from the students' reflections above that when young people perform and reflect upon Christian worship, it does more than help them "act more like Christians." Worship becomes generative for their Christian *identity,* their sense of inner coherence, their claim to belong to a people — to God's people. Erik Erikson has taught us that identity formation is a primary developmental task for adolescents. Emergent capacities for self-reflection cause youth to wonder about themselves. They ask, "Who am I in light of who I and others say I am?" Christian worship provides a rich context for asking and answering that question. One HSTP alumnus commented that he now recognizes how his baptism made him "another dad" to the children in his home congregation. Indeed, a significant number of HSTP alumni return home to serve as Sunday school teachers, confirmation mentors, and directors of children's choirs or dance groups.

Yet forming a Christian identity is not just about deeper self-appraisal and self-construction — that is, my ability to make sense of how to answer the question, "Who am I?" Christian identity is deeply tied to the uniquely performative nature of worship and the knowing that resides in the bodies that perform it. This makes identity less a function of who we say we are and more the result of whom or what we worship. Hence worship itself, as much as what worshippers can say about it or how they make sense of their lives in relation to it, remains key to Christians' identity formation.[21] Speaking theologically, identity comes to young Christians as a gift from God through their ongoing practices of worshipping that very same God.

21. See E. Byron Anderson, *Worship and Christian Identity: Practicing Ourselves* (Collegeville, MN: Liturgical, 2003).

What, finally, does worship-formed identity have to do with forming Christian leaders? I offer a story shared with me by Alaina Kleinbeck, Duke Youth Academy's program director, in the effort to answer this question. DYA is intentionally ecumenical, drawing students ranging from the starchiest of Episcopalians to the happiest of Pentecostals. At a worship service early in the 2012 program, sixteen-year-old Aaron noticed Peter — an exuberant charismatic who was moving in response to the preacher and the music — "behaving disrespectfully" (in Aaron's words).[22] Aaron crossed the chapel aisle in the middle of the service and told Peter to chill. Peter was confused, embarrassed, and offended. He was worshipping as he'd always worshipped.

A week later, at the close of a day in which DYA focused on the call to reconciliation, Aaron responded to the communal confession of sin in worship and the pastoral gesture of pardon by crossing the aisle once more to seek out Peter. This time, however, he confessed his sin for judging Peter previously and for embarrassing him. Aaron begged Peter's forgiveness (which was granted), and sought to be reconciled with him through the exchange of Christ's peace (long hug, eventual release).

Aaron's gesture illustrates the power of Christian worship to shape faithful imaginations, and young people's identities as Christian leaders. God not only transforms us through water, word, and song in worship; God also transforms us through each other. In relationship to others, we are a more fully doxological community, more certain of our identity in Christ, and more clear about our vocation as disciples. Over nearly two weeks of living intentionally in community and practicing daily worship, as well as daily reflection upon worship, Aaron came to know and appreciate Peter and to recognize his own liturgical parochialism. After a day with special emphasis on Christ's reconciling work, Aaron sensed himself caught up in God's present work of reconciliation within the liturgy itself. Awed, Aaron did not so much decide as he felt himself moved by the power of the Spirit to confess his sin to Peter and to seek reconciliation. That he did not choose to seek forgiveness over Facebook or privately during the daily snack break suggests that, in Aaron's deepening faithful imagination, worship was the obvious context for this gesture. It offered Aaron a real, not a pretend, way of being in the world, a source of concentrated Spirit power that called forth his best self — which, not coincidentally, was the self God was calling him to be in the first place: a reconciled child of God, his true vocation.

22. The names of youth have been changed.

CHAPTER TEN

Prepare Me for a Worthy Adventure

Pedagogies of Pilgrimage in Adolescent Formation

David Horn

Everyone knew his name in school. You had to know Devin because he seemed to be everywhere: star football player, good student, homecoming king. He was popular, and he knew it. I was surprised that he showed up at our four-week summer Compass program. I had heard through the grapevine that the only reason he applied was because of some heavy-handed pressure from his parents, but this happened to be a year when we needed all the candidates we could get, so we admitted him. For the first several days of the program, Devin's body language made it quite clear that he had absolutely no interest in anything we were doing. But then something changed.

Fast-forward ten years: Devin is about to commit the rest of his life to serving the poorest of the poor in Jakarta, Indonesia. He recently came home for his wedding after serving two years at a remote missions agency in North Africa. In Devin's words, the four-week journey he took with us in our Compass program was "the turning point of my life and the springboard into a future that I hope will glorify God in everything and will be completely motivated by the love of Christ." What happened to initiate this dramatic change? Devin had undergone pilgrimage.

Explicitly or implicitly, every High School Theology Program invites youth on pilgrimage, a journey that dislodges them from "home" — physically, theologically, existentially — and sends them forth on a shared journey toward God. Youth leave home for a week or more to go to camp with a group of strangers, or they journey together across geographical, cultural, and linguistic boundaries. In their journeys, the physical displacement of moving from *here* to *there* instigates a spiritual displacement as young people find themselves moving from who they were before the experience to a new arrangement of faith and identity.

As a pilgrimage, Compass intentionally disrupts established patterns of thought and habits of life by immersing teenagers in not one, but three disorienting experiences: a week in the wilderness, followed by a week of studying theology together on campus, followed by a week of cross-cultural mission work outside the United States. Afterward, these young pilgrims return to their home congregations to conduct a three-year ministry project with a dedicated mentor. As with all pilgrimages, Compass thrusts young people into liminal space — an experience of dangling in between the familiar and the unknown — with a community of equals.[1] Because Compass is explicitly organized around this spiritual practice of liminal space, the program illustrates how the theme of pilgrimage can be translated theologically and pedagogically for youth.

In this chapter, I will show that pilgrimage in various forms is a potent source of Christian formation for young people — and has potential to inform how we do theological education — if undertaken in a theologically reflective community and for the sake of a larger, lifelong pilgrimage. I will first explore the theological significance of pilgrimage, and then describe the way our High School Theology Program at Gordon-Conwell Seminary utilizes the practice of pilgrimage pedagogically. Finally, I will mention a few ways in which the practice of pilgrimage might inform congregational ministry and theological education.

"From Here to There": Pilgrimage as a Practice of Christian Formation

The idea of pilgrimage is a well-traveled theme in Christian spirituality. Whether on the road to Emmaus, the road to Damascas, or the desert road where Philip meets the Ethiopian eunuch, the biblical witness often presents the road as a place of unexpected divine encounters. In Scripture, getting from *here* to *there* is an experience brimming with theological meaning. Paul suggests that Adam's unintended, unhappy journey from the Garden to the briar patch is imprinted on every human being's life journey. Abram and Sarai uprooted their life in Haran and journey to a new place, receiving new

1. See Victor and Edith Turner, *Image and Pilgrimage in Christian Culture* (New York: Columbia University Press, 1978), p. 6.

names and identities along the way. Jacob dreamed of angels and wrestled with a divine stranger while exiled. Ruth and Naomi learned covenant faithfulness as traveling refugees. The Hebrew people received God's discipline and provision as they wandered, becoming a covenant people in transit. Jesus' pilgrimage with the Twelve led to his death and resurrection and laid the path to our own redemption. The disciples' journey from cringing fear to Spirit-filled courage set in motion a church called by Christ to go into the world in his name. When God's people step out on the road, we expect something to happen.

This expectation became deeply embedded in the practices, literature, and culture of the church, and indeed of Western culture, in which we witness characters journey spiritually and physically. Saucy medieval characters set off together one April in Chaucer's *Canterbury Tales,* and we know they will have adventures. Christian makes his way toward the heavenly city in *Pilgrim's Progress,* learning to trust God on the way. Frodo travels from the Shire to Mordor and discovers the power of small acts of faithfulness. Harry Angstrom journeys through the cultural landscape of middle class suburbia in John Updike's *Rabbit, Run* coming to terms with his own fears. We follow these characters as they go from here to there in their lives. We sense destiny drawing their steps, and we know their journey may lead to inner change. This is pilgrimage: the intentional "going from here to there" in life, whether externally or internally, from where we are now to where we hope to go.

Even when these scriptural or literary travelers wander in ignorance of what lies around the next bend, we know they are heading somewhere, geographically and spiritually. They travel purposefully toward a destination, even when it lies far off on a hazy horizon. As theologian Doris Donnelly writes,

> To be a pilgrim is to assume a new and risky identity, surrendering all that clutters one's life so that God takes center stage. To be a pilgrim is to live within the Paschal Mystery of holding on and letting go, over and over again. The investment is total, severe, and uncompromising.[2]

Pilgrims are attuned to the inward as well as the outward journey, opening themselves to the possibility of transformation as they move toward a sacred

2. Doris Donnelly, "Pilgrims and Tourists: Conflicting Metaphors for the Christian Journey to God," *Spirituality Today* 44 (Spring 1992): 20, http://www.spiritualitytoday.org/spir2day/92441donnelly.html (accessed October 22, 2013).

destination, surrounded by a community of fellow pilgrims. Existentially and physically, pilgrimage is costly — an "interiorization of the *via crucis,* the way of the cross," says Donnelly — and, as Devin discovered, it is filled with "unplanned, unbidden, and for the most part unwelcome" change and conversion along the way.[3] Yet pilgrims willingly incur these costs in order to gain greater spiritual riches. If the mystic traveler Thomas Merton is right, when we are "jerked clean out of the habitual, half-tied vision of things," we gain new insights into the ordinary courses of our lives.[4]

Capturing this potential for conversion and transformation, the High School Theology Programs invite young people to leave their habitual patterns and set out together in the deep, well-traveled ruts of Christian pilgrimage. For example, the Beyond Belief program at Lutheran School of Theology helps high school youth move "beyond belief" to faith in action through an urban immersion week of service in Chicago. Queen's University's Future Quest program offers a two-week summer program that begins with classes and service field trips in their community and ends with an eco-spirituality canoe trip at the Frontenac Provincial Park. Tabor College's Ministry Quest program focuses on vocational calling through a program that spans the entire year, starting with a five-day retreat called "Charting Your Course," and ending with a retreat called "Setting Your Sail." The Youth Theology Institute at Candler School of Theology sends their youth on what they call "pilgrimages" to different religious communities, exploring ways in which these diverse religious traditions work for social justice. At the Duke Youth Academy, youth travel around Durham on "Pilgrimages of Pain and Hope," in which they listen to stories about the city and wrestle with issues of class, race, gender, and oppression. Varied as these programs are, they all insist that a shared physical journey with young people can evoke a journey of the soul, especially when understood in light of Christ's own journey to the cross.

Translating Pilgrimage: A Snapshot of the Compass Program

The motif of pilgrimage defines the Compass program. The central goal of our program is to stop youth in their tracks and invite them to step out of the normal patterns of their lives and enter into a constructed pilgrimage so

3. Donnelly, "Pilgrims": 20.

4. Richard R. Niebuhr, "Pilgrims and Pioneers," *Parabola* 9, no. 3 (August 1984): 12.

that they can more fully understand the larger pilgrimage of the Christian life when they return home. Compass emphasizes the practice of intentional, reflective pilgrimage because young people are all on a journey, whether they know it or not. They travel well-worn paths from their schools to their churches to their sports fields. Their schedules are crammed full of activities as they float from one event to the next with little opportunity for thoughtful transition. Plugged in to their media devices, they face constant distraction. On any given day they are confronted with far more information than they can absorb, and they struggle to pick out a vocational path. Given this cultural menu, young people can be entertained and distracted to death, losing sight of their own goals and passions and failing to notice either the God who is calling them or the fellow travelers God puts beside them.

With this picture of a typical young sojourner in mind, the Compass program invites about thirty young people every summer to remove themselves from the normal distractions of their day-to-day journeys in order to undertake pilgrimage. We call our program Real Ministry Immersion (RMI): *real* because we seek authenticity, *ministry* because we focus on vocational calling, and *immersion* because participants enter totally into several learning environments. The core of the RMI program is made up of three interconnected pilgrimages, or "Expeditions": the Wilderness Expedition, the classroom Theological Expedition, and the cross-cultural Service Expedition, which run in sequence with minimal transition. The three experiences of wilderness, classroom, and cross-cultural service provide diverse pedagogical opportunities for us to engage our students in pilgrimage. Teaching in each of these settings is designed to be both catechetical and dialogical. A fourth "Expedition" at home follows this intense three-week experience.

The Wilderness Expedition

The first Expedition requires youth to face challenges in the Adirondack Mountains for ten days. They rappel down a mountain, bushwhack through uncharted woods, deal with harsh weather, experience a one-day "solo," and endure a final eight-mile run, all while striving to relate meaningfully to a community of equally uncomfortable tent dwellers. Throughout, they commit to "challenge by choice," and the arduous wilderness journey comes to represent the challenges of Christian life.

This first pilgrimage is not merely geographical and physical. Students also grapple with specific spiritual disciplines: daily journaling, prayer, Bible reading, and small-group reflection. These "habits of the heart" are often new to young people and are not always easy, but like the external challenge of climbing a mountain, these disciplines help youth explore, record, and reflect on the spiritual and emotional pilgrimage that accompanies their physical journey.

The Classroom Expedition

The second Expedition is no less daunting than the wilderness trek. The tools of theological reflection in the classroom replace hiking boots and mosquito netting. Over eight days, our youth confront six theological and philosophical questions: (1) Why do bad things happen to good people? (2) How can a two-thousand-year-old book be relevant in the twenty-first century? (3) In a highly pluralistic world, can we really say that Jesus is the only way? (4) Does the Church really matter . . . really? (5) How is one to live "in" the world but not "of" the world? (6) And, given the complexities of life, how do we know the will of God for our lives? Adult leaders encourage youth to consider how these questions inform and shape their everyday lives, and together they imagine how their answers to these questions can direct their steps in life. Although the second Expedition takes place in a classroom, it is no less a journey than the first, as young people move from *here* to *there* intellectually and spiritually. Together they travel with other thinkers in the Christian tradition, often ending in a different place than they began.

The Cross-Cultural Expedition

Finally, the one-month program ends with a cross-cultural immersion where young people participate in a service project that addresses the needs of a community very different from their own, including places in Mexico, Costa Rica, and Nicaragua. In this Expedition, youth are fully immersed in the complexities of daily living in a context foreign to them, even as they serve. Living with host families, they must negotiate unfamiliar or uncomfortable living conditions, and they constantly encounter new language, customs, and food. Coming up against the apparent strangeness of another context, they spend considerable time discussing with one another and their adult leaders how their home cultures have shaped their perspectives.

The Expedition at Home

A fourth Expedition extends for three years after the "Real Ministry Immersion" month. Each young person returns home to his or her church with an assigned mentor from the congregation who continues to walk with this teenager as a fellow pilgrim on the journey, as well as an advocate and interpreter for this young person in the home church. Each mentor relationship is sealed with a covenant that binds these fellow pilgrims together for the next three years, both relationally and in terms of a ministry obligation that we ask of each youth. These mentors are encouraged to participate in the last days of our three-week Compass journey, and we orient them to the journey their mentee has experienced. In this way, the intense experience of a pilgrimage away from home flows directly into a pilgrimage at home.

Pilgrimage and Pedagogy

These four Expeditions — three at Compass, and one after youth return home — break young people away from their usual paths in order to walk a road that may be quite new to them, but which follows deep ruts carved by spiritual pilgrims before them. The idea that travel can provoke change is, of course, nothing new. Many schools, denominations, and churches already offer travel opportunities for young people, and the mission trip is a staple of youth ministry. Recently I was on a plane traveling to the Dominican Republic and found myself surrounded by three large clumps of matching t-shirts, each signifying a different church's good intentions for their youth. To these churches, I would reaffirm that these journeys can be powerful, but they can also be deceptive. Left unexamined, well-intended pilgrimages can easily become tourist holidays.

Doris Donnelly distinguishes between the pilgrim and the tourist, explaining that spiritual pilgrims leave home intentionally seeking to invest themselves in both the journey and the destination for the sake of inward transformation.[5] Not so for the tourist. Tourists are interested in arriving, with as little personal cost and commitment as possible, and are far more interested in themselves than in establishing meaningful relationships with their fellow travelers. To take young people on pilgrimage, and not on a tourist holiday, therefore requires intentionality, attentiveness to both the

5. Donnelly, "Pilgrims and Tourists": 20-21.

context and theological structure of the experience, and a great deal of preparation by leaders in both the sending and receiving communities.

Over the years, Compass and other High School Theology Programs have learned crucial lessons about how to help young people become pilgrims rather than tourists. At Compass, we have found certain pedagogical approaches to be effective in establishing a community of fellow pilgrims who journey together. These include teaching through an experiential learning cycle that includes theological reflection, establishing highly structured environments, creating disorienting dilemmas, delaying gratification to heighten longing, cultivating interdependent community, and assisting young pilgrims in their return home.

Outward and Inward Journeys: Teaching through Experience

In each of our Expeditions, we approach the theological realities embedded in our practices from an experiential perspective. Reflecting on the motives of pilgrimage, Doris Donnelly notes that sometimes it is important to pack an overnight bag and to ready our cars "in order to make an outward journey which responds to an interior quest."[6] Since many youth are already on an interior quest, we provide a way for them to embark on the outward journey that accompanies that quest. But just as the outward journey *responds* to the internal quest, we have also seen the outward journey *motivate* an internal quest, dismantling assumptions, raising new questions, and altering perspectives. The outward and inward are inextricably linked.

Although we use selected texts — theological reading is a critical part of Compass — the heart of our program involves a distinctly experiential approach to pilgrimage. This experiential approach plays out dramatically in the Wilderness Expedition as our youth backpack through a marsh, and in the Cross-Cultural Expedition as they journey to another country. But even in the Theology Expedition, we work to challenge our youth experientially through concrete, practical teaching. That being said, experiences do not just speak for themselves. Human beings interpret their experiences in a context; that is what makes experiences meaningful. Young people arrive with their own previous contexts that inform their interpretation of the pilgrimage experience, and we value those contexts. At the same time, we wish to help young people form a more distinctly Christian lens for understanding their

6. Donnelly, "Pilgrims and Tourists": 20.

lives and the world. For this reason, we surround all we do with purposeful theological reflection and provide language and categories to help them process their experiences. In effect, we set them up to interpret their experiences theologically, without providing all the answers.

Following David Kolb's Experiential Learning Model, we guide our pilgrims through a path of understanding that flows from anticipation to experience to reflection. Before an experience, we intentionally ask and anticipate questions that they might encounter on their journey. If they will be on a high ropes course that day, for example, we might reflect for the group on the theological significance of what it means to live with success or failure. Afterward, we carefully debrief the theological implications of what they have just experienced, and we develop a narrative of that experience together. Or after a day spent visiting churches of different traditions in inner city Boston, we ask youth to reflect on how those churches may differ contextually from their own, and how those differences are an expression of the Kingdom of God. This pattern of Anticipate-Experience-Reflect occurs on multiple levels — individually, in small groups, and in large group settings.

Trusting the Itinerary: Teaching through Structure

In contrast to the unreflective way in which many youth are accustomed to living, Compass intentionally places youth in structured environments that require them to reflect purposefully about how and why they got "from here to there." Despite our experiential approach, this pilgrimage is no Jack Kerouac road trip, with the wind in our faces and an open-ended horizon. While HSTPs vary in their philosophies about the educational value of structured time (some emphasize its importance, while others stress the value of permitting young people to decide how, where, and with whom they will spend their time), for one month young people at Compass follow a carefully planned "road map." Although this map is not explicitly discussed with our young pilgrims, it quickly becomes clear that every aspect of the pilgrimage is designed to have meaning.

Toward that end, each day is structured in ways that define the purposes of the day. Every moment is accounted for from the time youth get up in the morning to the time they go to bed. Each day begins with what we call "Compass Time," when young people are invited to exercise certain faith disciplines such as Bible study, prayer, and journaling. Each day's corporate activities begin and end in worship, and the day's learning events conclude in a small reflection group called "Table Talk," where youth can process the day together in an assigned small group. We view these as sacred moments that youth must pass through in their daily pilgrimage with God.

At Compass, each day is also defined by specific theological emphases. As they start the day with a time alone for reflection and journaling, youth are introduced to specific theological foci: What does it mean to be called to live a life of commitment? What is the role of wonder, or radical servanthood, or community, or holiness, in our faith? The chosen theme then recurs throughout the day, and youth have opportunities for experience of and theological reflection on that theme. For example, as youth embark on a solo day in which they will be required to live for twenty-four hours alone with a piece of canvas, their Bibles, and their own uncluttered thoughts, we ask them to consider what it means to live lives filled with simple wonder and surprise. At the end of the twenty-four hours, they debrief their experience in small groups and again reflect on the theme of wonder.

Getting Lost to Be Found: Teaching through Disorientation

Like many High School Theology Programs, the Compass experience is designed to be dissonant, even disruptive, for youth. Sometimes getting from *here to there* involves living "betwixt and between," to use Victor Turner's description of liminal space,[7] as the disorientation of the "in-betweenness" of life dislodges our unexamined assumptions. Adult educators interested in transformative education call an experience that launches a process of cognitive dismantling and reconstruction the "disorienting dilemma."[8] At Compass, practices of disorientation are grounded in the assumption that the transformed life is a disrupted life, and that change for the good requires exercising one's entire being — mind, body, will, spirit, emotions. Further, a life transformed by God is not always easy; instead, it involves the full breadth of human experience, from difficult, uncertain, and even painful moments to joyful, affirming, and celebratory ones.

Through the three Expeditions at Compass, young people confront multiple disorienting dilemmas that throw them off balance or require them to

7. Victor Turner, "Betwixt and Between: The Liminal Period in Rites de Passage," in *The Forest of Symbols* (Ithaca, NY: Cornell University Press, 1967).

8. Cf. Jack Mezirow, *Transformative Dimensions of Adult Learning* (San Francisco: Jossey-Bass, 1991). While the "disorienting dilemma" is commonly associated with adult education, its power is not lost on teenagers.

find footing on uneven ground. They feel the ground literally drop away from under their feet on a high ropes course or a slippery mountainside. They live in close proximity to other youth they had never met before Compass, hearing others' perspectives and trying to articulate their own as they grapple with thorny questions. They are startled to discover that not everyone thinks or believes as they do, and they may feel a kind of spiritual eyestrain as they peer through the new theological lenses their professors hold up. Having established a cohesive community with one another, they then travel to another country and take up residence in diverse households that operate by new rules, and that eat, speak, joke, and worship in unfamiliar ways. The Expeditions are disorienting and disruptive, often uncomfortable, and because of that, they drive learning. One young woman drew a larger lesson about life from her experience of difficulty at Compass:

> When people ask me about Compass, and I know that they really wanted to know about what happened, I tell them that Compass wasn't always easy, but it was so very good. The good things in life aren't always easy. There were times during Compass when I was tired, hungry, pushed really hard, or really wanted my family, but those times helped to strengthen me. After going through Compass I know that I can push myself and that through God I can succeed. . . . So yes, Compass was not always easy, but it was wonderful and most definitely worth it.

One particularly provocative practice of disruption used at Compass and several other HSTPs is a "technology Sabbath." Given the dominance of texting, Facebook, Twitter, smartphones, computer games, and other technologies in young people's lives, living without them is deeply disorienting for most youth, and panic-inducing for some. Four whole weeks without a text to a friend? Four weeks without checking status updates or watching what is trending? How will they ever catch up when they return home? While the technology Sabbath is meant to maximize face time in community, it has the effect of heightening awareness of the way certain technologies distract and cause distance even as they purport to inform and connect people. Young people return home with a different, more nuanced and critical relationship to their phones and computers. They lose an old path in order to find a new one.

We ground these disorienting practices in larger biblical and theological themes. The incarnation embodies the notion that struggle and even suffering are at the center of the salvation story. Furthermore, the virtue of perseverance persists throughout the biblical account, from Genesis to Revelation. Whole epistles were written to encourage churches experiencing persecution. James, for example, encourages his readers: "Consider it pure joy whenever you face trials of many kinds because you know that the testing of your faith develops perseverance. Let perseverance finish its work so that you may be mature and complete, not lacking anything" (James 1:2-4, NIV).

So rather than suggesting that faith helps the believer to avoid life's ambiguities and struggles, we assume that a life of faith is lived in the midst of life's uncertainties and incongruities. If the human condition always involves confusion, unfulfilled dreams, and disappointment, and Scripture acknowledges the same, young people should not be surprised that struggle is part of the life of faith. Purposefully situating moments of disruption in controlled settings with concurrent opportunities for theological reflection stimulates spiritual reflection and becomes the occasion for spiritual transformation. Again and again, participants say that practices of intentional disorientation — getting lost on purpose — are the aspects of our program most likely to set them on a new path. One young man from the streets of Boston declared after returning from a sweaty, bug-ridden expedition in the Adirondacks: "I will never do that again. But I wouldn't trade that experience for the world."

Longing for the Far Country: Teaching through Delayed Gratification

Pilgrimage literature plays on a sense of longing: longing for glory, gold, adventure, meaning, freedom, the heavenly city, or even home. C. S. Lewis, whose work so often reflects a sense of longing, uses the German word *Sehnsucht* to describe what he understands as a primitive impulse lodged deep within the human heart, a yearning or craving that can hardly be put into words, but that nevertheless motivates everything we say and do. Using pilgrimage language, Lewis speaks of *Sehnsucht* as a "desire for our own far-off country."[9] Unfortunately, in a contemporary culture of instant gratification, many young people have lost touch with a sense of longing, instead trying to satisfy deep personal and spiritual cravings with material goods and instant experiences.

But young people yearn for more. Pay close attention to the conversations of young people, and you will see their longings rise to the surface.

9. C. S. Lewis, Preface to *The Pilgrim's Regress: An Allegorical Apology for Christianity Reason and Romanticism* (London: Geoffrey Bles, 1956), p. 10.

At Compass, we work to help our young pilgrims understand and reclaim a place for deep longing. We create space characterized by restraint, and sometimes by deprivation, as in the case of the technology Sabbath. We put youth in situations in which something is withheld, in which what they crave is not immediately accessible. They want — but do not immediately find — comfort in a rain-soaked forest, facile answers to difficult questions, or easy communication with someone who speaks another language. These situations lead to frustration, but they also lead to growth. In the middle of the Adirondack Mountains, one participant reflected:

> The thing is to *be here now.* So you don't get caught up with what is going on at home. [The Compass leaders] want you to be here with God and with your peers. So they take away all of our, like, any sense of time that we have. They take away our watches. . . . So you go with the flow. . . . It also helps you trust God more because you don't really know what you're doing.

Placed in a situation of deprivation and delayed gratification, this young woman found herself with an opportunity to alter what she yearned for, from something immediate to something far deeper and ultimately more fulfilling.

This "living in the now" is deeply eschatological. Placing youth in situations where things are not easily or immediately resolved, in which they dangle "betwixt and between," causes youth to rethink what they crave. They learn to live with anticipation, to have a sense of expectation, to distinguish hope from entitlement. By heightening their sense of expectation, we point youth toward God's Kingdom — a kingdom that calls us to live in the now, even as we long for and journey toward a far-off country.

Traveling Together: Teaching in Community

Pilgrimage is deeply communal. Few pilgrims travel alone, and even those who do rely on the hospitality of those they meet along the way. At Compass, we seek to build authentic community both as an end in itself and as a reflection of the theological reality that we are brothers and sisters in Christ. When we compare the depth of students' relationships at the end of Compass with the relationships cobbled together at the beginning of the program, we always stand back in awe. What a difference thirty days of living together in community makes! Youth arrive every summer as complete strangers to one another. You can see it in their eyes. Most of their focus is peripheral as they mentally compare themselves with those around them. By the end of the three-week program, they are deeply committed and vulnerable brothers and sisters in Christ. They have moved from being strangers to fellow pilgrims. How does this happen?

We have learned that the best way to nurture deep relationships in community is to foster interdependence. A colleague who directs another wilderness program describes the cultural safety net around affluent Western people as like "living between two mattresses." There are certainly many wonderful things that can be said about living in a well-padded, highly institutionalized, and affluent society. But one of the unintended casualties is a distorted view of dependency. We — at least those of us in middle to upper-middle class society — have become under-dependent on one another. Our well-padded life styles allow us the illusion of independence and rob us of a sense of needing one another. It is difficult to remain a Christian community if we are robbed of authentic dependency on one another — and, by extension, on Christ.

Compass is designed to intentionally develop healthy dependency — or interdependence — among our youth. In fact, we have found interdependence key to developing authentic community.[10] Each of our Expeditions challenges young people to depend upon one another as if their lives depended upon it. In many ways, their lives really do depend on it, whether when rappelling down a mountain or trusting each other as practice for trusting in Christ. In the Wilderness Expedition especially, small groups are put in situations of physical interdependence. To climb over the mountain may require that the strongest of the group repack his or her bag to add some weight from the backpack of the weakest, teaching both the stronger and the weaker about the nature of Christian community. In the Teaching Expedition, the more informed student must learn to make a theological point in a way that builds up, rather than belittles, his or her less informed classmates, since honest conversations bloom best without competition. The Cross-Cultural Expedition has for the past two years involved designing and creating pieces of public art as gifts for the people of a small village in Nicaragua. To make something long lasting and beautiful has required

10. Victor Turner speaks of the forming of community within liminal space as *communitas* and describes it as a community much like I am describing here, as shared fellowship, spontaneity, and warmth fostered by a common pilgrimage that breeds a sense of equality and harmony. See Victor and Edith Turner, *Image and Pilgrimage.*

small groups to depend upon each member's particular creative gifts, and the cooperation of the whole, to create a common project. Through such concrete experiences of interdependence, community becomes more than an abstract concept for Compass participants. They first embody community out of necessity — and then out of love.

The pilgrim communities that cohere at Compass persist after the Expeditions end. Indeed, for several years at Compass, the "problem" of persistent community kept rearing its head. Thirty or forty Compass alumni, some traveling great distances, would spontaneously show up at the end of our current program and want to participate. We groused that their presence intruded upon the final days of the current cohort's experience — that is, until we realized what their presence meant. Their arrival signaled that we had been developing a community of faith unlike any that many of these young people had ever experienced. Many of them discovered for the first time that they were not alone in their faith journeys. When we realized this truth, we embraced our "problem" and welcomed alumni, whose yearly visits have since become a legacy of Compass. They continually remind us of the fact that when pilgrimage is undertaken in an interdependent community that shares struggles and celebrations, the relationships that result are long lasting.

Coming Full Circle: Teaching toward the Return Home

Every pilgrimage has a destination — but this is a less simple statement than it seems. On the one hand, every pilgrimage is circular: our young people's journeys begin and end in their families, schools, and home churches. Sharon Daloz Parks cautions that the current religious culture tends to have "overvalued the journey at the expense of home."[11] Parks reminds us that, in contrast to immigrants who leave their homeland behind, pilgrims return home; their pilgrimages are not designed to be ends in themselves. Compass uses pilgrimage to prepare youth to return to families and churches with stories about the blessings of the journey.

Yet for some, going home is the hardest part of their pilgrimage. Some

11. Sharon Daloz Parks, "Home and Pilgrimage: Deep Rhythms in the Adolescent Soul," in *Growing Up Postmodern: Imitating Christ in the Age of 'Whatever,'* Princeton Theological Seminary Institute for Youth Ministry (Princeton, NJ: Princeton Theological Seminary, 1999), p. 55.

return to church communities and families who will never understand or help sustain the pilgrimage of faith young people have just experienced. For others, the challenges are subtler. They return home to familiar territory where they pick up their lives where they left off, complete with all their former distractions: technologies and schedules, old relationships, tired habits. For some, unfortunately, the Compass journey soon becomes an afterthought.

Indeed, the Compass journey is in some ways designed so that our youth never do go home again. Our hope is that in their return, they are far more theologically reflective than before, more intentional about their use of time and technology, more willing to be transformed by disruption and disorientation, more open to the true and hope-filled longings of their heart, and more dependent upon the Christian community around them. Our hope is that they become lifelong pilgrims. Our hope is that in Compass, they will have received gifts for the longer pilgrimage, so that as they move "from here to there" in their lives after the program, they will do so in ways far more theologically rich than they did before their pilgrimage with us.

Specifically, we believe we give participants three gifts for the lifelong journey of faith. First, we give young people certain "habits of the heart" to sustain them along the way. We realize that one month is not enough time to set these habits in stone, but for many, a daily ritual involving the disciplines of prayer, journaling, silence, individual and corporate inductive Bible study, theological study and reflection, and new perspectives on worship and community sets them on a road that makes returning to these practices more likely throughout their lives. We trust that the new patterns of thought shaped by theological reflection in the midst of the real live experiences of Compass will serve as a basis for deeper reflection as they journey onward.

A second gift youth receive at Compass is a profound memory of God's faithfulness that both informs and sustains their faith in the future. A powerful little story in the fourth chapter of Joshua illustrates the importance of memory as a pedagogical tool. After God divides the waters of the Jordan River so the people of God may enter into the Promised Land, God commands the people to deposit twelve large stones in the river. The stones are "to serve as a sign" among the Israelites, "a memorial to the people of Israel forever" of God's faithfulness. Faith is built upon memories of God's faithfulness encountered on the journey. For most alumni of High School Theology Programs, their experience in these programs becomes a faith-building memory, a "memorial" on which youth can look back as a source of strength for the future.

The Compass program gives youth a third gift in sending them off with a mentor and a task. Emphasizing that God calls them to follow and serve in their home communities, we match them with adults who will serve as resources and fellow pilgrims over the next three years. This relationship and the task that youth focus on with their mentor cannot be underestimated; without them, even the powerful experiences of the Expeditions can simply devolve into tourist holidays with a religious flavor. By expecting youth to return home as confident servant leaders who can engage in theological and personal reflection with their mentor, we help them to continue as pilgrims who seek God, rather than as tourists who simply recall a fun trip.

Lessons for Forming Disciples

What might all this mean for those charged with forming young people into disciples who see themselves as part of God's pilgrim people? What might it mean for theological education? First, and most simply, we should not underestimate the potential of a physical journey to launch the inner journey of faith. Richard Niebuhr says that we acquire ourselves not in abiding only, but also in moving.[12] In an era in which "going away to seminary" is becoming a rarer phenomenon and in which more people are training for ministry in home contexts, we must still consider ways in which people can engage in pilgrimage of body, mind, and heart. Something about the act of travel, of being displaced and "homeless," even briefly, provides tremendous opportunities for growth and personal transformation. This "ruptured" time, says Fredrick Ruf in his book, *Bewildered Travel,* is nothing short of sacred.[13]

Such ruptured time can serve as a testing ground for young people and seminarians alike, as they reexamine their assumptions about life and God and discern anew their life plans and sense of self. Such testing makes a difference in vocation. In Auburn Theological Seminary's study of best seminarians, a time of "testing" proved to be a necessary crucible for many seminarians' call to ministry.[14] Yet we seldom leave sufficient room for such testing. Many of the youth we work with at Compass have been made to

12. Niebuhr, "Pilgrims and Pioneers": 8-10.

13. Frederick J. Ruf, *Bewildered Travel: The Sacred Quest for Confusion* (Charlottesville: University of Virginia Press, 2007), p. 74.

14. Barbara Wheeler et al., "Pathways to Seminary: Where the Best Students Come From," *In Trust* (Autumn 2013): 7-8, http://www.intrust.org/Portals/39/docs/IT_Autumn2013-Wheeler.pdf (accessed November 28, 2013).

assume that failure is not part of a good pilgrimage, and that human effort should only lead to success. When youth experience the "betwixt and between" of challenging pilgrimages within a supportive community, they find safe places to test their assumptions, their courage, and their sense of call.

Providing such safe places for testing is also becoming an increasingly important role for theological institutions, as fewer seminarians arrive well formed in faith practices or knowledgeable about their own faith traditions. What might happen if more theological educators imagined and treated their students as pilgrims, remembering the ambiguity and disorientation such an identity brings with it, and providing challenge, support, and community as the necessary context of pilgrimage? More specifically, what might happen if theological schools expected all students to undertake concrete experiences of pilgrimage during their studies, as a way to help them counter the lure of immediate gratification, or to grapple with the realities of disorientation and disruption in ministry? Such pilgrimages might take the form of border-crossing immersion experiences, semesters spent at other theological institutions, a year away from classes doing full-time ministry, or service and mission expeditions with other students — all accompanied by theological reflection. These pilgrimages could make a difference not only for students but also for theological institutions if schools were receptive to the lessons their student-pilgrims learned, affirming students' journeys and providing a forum for them to share their experiences.

Such affirmation of pilgrimage matters deeply not only for seminarians, but also for young people. Our experience at Compass is proof positive that youth think deeply and passionately about theology, yet these youth are seldom treated in their home congregations as capable pilgrims on a spiritual journey. The church actually has an advantage over programs like Compass, since pilgrimages become much more meaningful when they are publicly honored and shared by the broader faith community. Congregations have the capacity to publically confirm youth as pilgrims setting out on a journey and affirm them afterward in the presence of the congregation. Doing so not only shows young people that adults care about the changes going on in their lives, but that the church considers those changes sacred. As young people embark on journeys of faith, the church can celebrate with them, reminding young people and the whole church that to be God's people is to be a pilgrim people, traveling onward in hope, seeking the far country together.

CHAPTER ELEVEN

Let Me Try

Experiential Learning in the Theological Formation of Young People

Judy Steers

Lorrie was seventeen years old when she came to Huron University College's Ask & Imagine program. She was a bright, outgoing young woman who was enthusiastically involved in the life of her home congregation. Given her "bring it on" attitude toward any new challenge, the mentor team for our High School Theology Program was not surprised that Lorrie wanted to take part in Urban Plunge, an opportunity for students to encounter the realities of youth homelessness. First, students spend time learning about homeless people and street youth. Then, on the day of the Urban Plunge, pairs of Ask & Imagine students are dropped off in downtown Toronto in the early morning with one piece of identification and two dollars in their pocket. They spend the day living as if they were homeless youth arriving in the city: they are to find out where to get a meal, locate a safe place to stay, figure out how to get a job, acquire basic health care, and find longer-term accommodation. Lorrie's Urban Plunge experience turned her world upside down.

Lorrie and her partner arrived at the central train station during the morning rush hour on a warm summer day. They felt confident and energized. Leaving the busy station, they met street youth and soon discovered that many services were readily available. Lorrie and her partner learned the locations of a number of downtown churches with lunch programs and headed to one. Arriving hot and tired after walking through the city streets, Lorrie noticed teens from a church youth group behind the counters, serving the meal. As she went through the food line, Lorrie tried to start a conversation.

"Hi," she said across the counter to a girl about her own age. "Is your youth group volunteering at this church today?"

"Yes," the girl quickly replied.

"Cool," continued Lorrie, "What church are you guys from? Is it near Toronto? I'm from near Niagara Falls."

The girl vaguely replied that her church was "somewhere outside the city." Lorrie was suddenly aware that the girl was avoiding both eye contact and conversation. Later, Lorrie reflected:

> I realized that this girl was looking at me the way I have always looked at people in need — with pity, or condescension, and she was keeping her distance from me. I suddenly realized that, in her eyes, I was one of "those people." She was giving me food, but the girl didn't want to know me, and she was suspicious of me. I was almost going to say, "Oh, I'm not really a homeless person. I'm doing a street awareness project," and then fortunately, before I opened my mouth, I realized that I would be so hypocritical if I said that. It would be like I was saying, "You think I'm one of them? I'm not really one of them." For that day, I was the person that I had always kept at arm's length and looked down on. I can never look at people the same way again. That moment changed everything.

This moment was not scripted. The leadership team could not have anticipated this outcome for Lorrie; they could only construct a context for an experience and let it unfold. Yet for Lorrie, this was the most life-changing moment in the whole two-week program.

Leaders of youth programs of all kinds hope to offer opportunities, like the Urban Plunge experience, that will fan young people's interest into life-changing insight. But for every Lorrie who has a life-changing "Aha!" moment, there are also youth who come away from experiential learning activities asking, "What was the point of that?" This raises the question: If we want youth to be changed by their experiences with us, to know what they believe, and to integrate these beliefs into their daily life, how then should we teach? What pedagogical elements must come together to fan a spark of interest into a fire of vocation?

This chapter will argue that effective experiential learning includes four key elements — *encounter, reflection, agency,* and *community* — and will show how these four elements work together in the context of the High School Theology Programs. Specifically, I will elaborate on how these elements contribute to learning in the context of three recurrent practices throughout many HSTPs: service, leadership, and artistic creation, with Ask & Imagine's own use of these practices as a reference point. In serving, leading, and creating, youth at Ask & Imagine engage in an experiential learning process that sparks their interest in Christian discipleship and fans the flames of faith and vocation in ways that a church longing for young leadership would do well to notice.

The God of Encounter: Thinking Theologically about Experiential Learning

At a parish consultation about children's and youth ministry in which we dug through various motivations parents have for bringing their children to participate in these ministries, one mother commented, "I just want my daughter to know the stories." I sensed there was more behind her remark; taking a guess, I think what this mother meant was: *I want my daughter to have an encounter with a powerful and potentially life-changing narrative about God, and I want that to happen in the context of a faith community. I want her life to be connected to the lives of people around her. I want her to know she is named and called by God to participate in the work of God's people in the world.* She wanted her daughter to "know" the stories, but in a way that exceeded cognition. I think she wanted her daughter to encounter stories, make meaning, reflect with others, and respond to those stories.

This is a faithful desire; after all, the God whom we worship is a God who seeks to encounter us in community and in sacred and everyday stories. Pentecost is about encountering God in the community, being ignited by divine passion for the world. On Pentecost, those who have encountered God in Jesus' ministry are given agency through the Spirit to act and transform the world. When we engage in experiential education, helping youth to encounter God and others and giving them agency to act within a supportive community, we live out the power of Pentecost. We also reflect Jesus' own pattern of ministry. Jesus taught his own disciples experientially. The disciples had repeated *encounters* with the grand narrative of God's grace and with the small narratives of Jesus' parables and the lives of people he met. The disciples *reflected* together on Jesus' questions, on their own mistakes, and on their life together. Jesus gave them *agency,* calling them to follow him and sending them out in his name, and he called them together into a *community.* These followers of the tradition of Jesus were experiential learners. When we engage in experiential education, we follow in their footsteps.

From the ancient catechumenate to the contemporary youth group, the Christian church has long experimented with this way of learning. Borrowing from the educational practices of the Greek *paideia,* Christians in the ancient world engaged in "mystagogical catechesis," learning the practices of faith by participating in them. Sacramental theology enacted God's gracious invitation to physically partake in Christ's life, death, and resurrection. From monastic apprenticeships to the YMCA/YWCAs of the mid-nineteenth century, Christian formation of young people has long included active learning. Today, field education is a crucial component of seminary education. In short, while experiential learning is generally associated with modern progressive educators like Maria Montessori, John Dewey, and David Kolb, the early church — taking cues from the incarnation — beat them to it by nearly two thousand years.

Despite this history, experiential education is still often neglected or misunderstood in today's churches. In a telling moment in a third-year seminary class I was teaching, one soon-to-be graduate commented, "I don't know why I need all these learning theories and teaching methods — that's what I have a Sunday school coordinator for." Another student commented, "I don't want to use experiential teaching methods; if I want people in my congregation to learn something, I just tell them. That's what sermons are for." (It was hard not to bang my head on the desk!) As these comments suggest, seminary education does not always equip future church leaders to practice robust action-reflection models of education with their congregations.

The High School Theology Programs, by contrast, have embraced experiential learning and honed compelling experiential curricula over the past twenty years. "Let me try!" is the cry of young people driven to engage with the world, yearning to convert ideas into actual experiences — and educators in the HSTPs have listened. Both the young people who participate in these programs and the adults who work with them want experiential learning to be more than simply praxis-based to-do lists or rote skill acquisition. They hope learners will be transformed. Like a spark catching fire, learners' imaginations will then be ignited by the Holy Spirit, taking on new attitudes, values, and creative ways of being in the world. Experiential educators want learners to integrate their theology and faith practices into their daily lives and so become agents of positive change in the world. At its best, experiential learning is transformational learning — it creates a fundamental change in learners and their worldviews. The "doing" becomes part of the being, as it reorients learners' sense of self and world.

Kindling the Fire of Vocation: Four Elements of Experiential Learning

Setting off Sparks: Compelling Encounters

Educators in the High School Theology Programs have found that they can fan young people's vocational fire through experiential education that includes the four elements of *encounter, reflection, agency,* and *community.* They begin by constructing a particular kind of learning experience that capitalizes on the interaction between a young person and his or her environment.[1] Pedagogically speaking, experience involves the interaction between both the objective conditions surrounding the learner (the educator's actions, the materials the learner interacts with, and the social set-up of the learning situation), and the learner's internal conditions (his or her personal needs, attitudes, desires, capacities, and purposes).[2] But experiential educators do not focus on *all* such interaction of external and internal conditions (what John Dewey called ongoing, "inchoate" experience); rather, they pay attention to those experiences that convey a sense of completion and wholeness and lead to change in the learner.[3] When we grasp that sense of completion and wholeness, Dewey says, we realize we have had "an experience."

In the HSTPs, educators seek to provide opportunities for learners to have an experience, which often takes the form of an encounter with otherness.[4] Young people encounter new environments, contexts, and people.

1. This is John Dewey's understanding of experience; see John Dewey, *Experience and Education* (New York: Macmillan, 1938), pp. 26-27.

2. "John Dewey's Philosophy of Experience and Education," International Center for Educators' Learning Styles, http://www.icels-educators-for-learning.ca/index.php?option=com_content&view=article&id=53&Itemid=68 on (accessed October 8, 2013).

3. Dewey writes, "We have *an* experience when the material experienced runs its course to fulfillment. Then and only then is it integrated within and demarcated in the general stream of experience from other experiences. A piece of work is finished in a way that is satisfactory; a problem receives its solution; a game is played through; a situation, whether that of eating a meal, playing a game of chess, carrying on a conversation, writing a book, or taking part in a political campaign, is so rounded out that its close is a consummation and not a cessation. Such an experience is a whole and carries with it its own individualizing quality and self-sufficiency. It is *an* experience." John Dewey, *Art as Experience* (New York: Hudson, 1934), pp. 36-37.

4. At Ask & Imagine, the program I direct, we use the word *encounter* to express not a casual meeting, but as related to its original meaning, which suggested confrontation. Experiential learning as "encounter" happens as we come across a person, environment, or context that runs against our perceptions of how the world is, how we function within

They hear stories of who people are, what has shaped their lives, and the blessings and wounds of their existence. In hearing such stories in context, young people suddenly see their own story and context through new eyes. Such encounters, when faced with courage and humility, have the potential to remake a learner's understanding of her relationship with God and God's relationship to the world.

Fueling the Fire: Reflection

Youth ministry practitioners have long noted that young people often prefer to "do stuff" rather than simply to listen or discuss, and a great many youth programs and curricula emphasize learning activities and projects. Yet while experiential education always involves activity, experiential educators do not simply ask young people to "do stuff." Instead, they engage them in active, ongoing reflection on their activity. David Kolb, who popularized Dewey's work in his model of experiential learning and his theory of learning styles, describes how learning happens cyclically through a continuous spiral of concrete experience, observation and reflection, formation of abstract concepts and generalizations, and finally testing through active experimentation, which leads to further experiences. He calls this process the "learning spiral."[5]

From the perspective of experiential education, it is not enough to do a one-off service project, to ask a young person to lead an element of worship or create an art project, and then claim the young person has learned something. Extracting what is meaningful, making connections to other ideas and experiences, and planning further work are all necessary in order to turn activities into learning moments. In the High School Theology Programs, such reflection is personal, communal, and theological, with the aim of transforming young people's views of themselves, others, and God.

Fanning the Flame: Agency in Response

In experiential education, the learner has agency — freedom to respond honestly and creatively to encounters. While educators may have objectives in

---

it, and how we understand God. It is a confrontation, not in a negative sense, but in a sense that it disrupts and broadens my worldview.

5. David A. Kolb, *Experiential Learning* (Upper Saddle River, NJ: Prentice Hall, 1984).

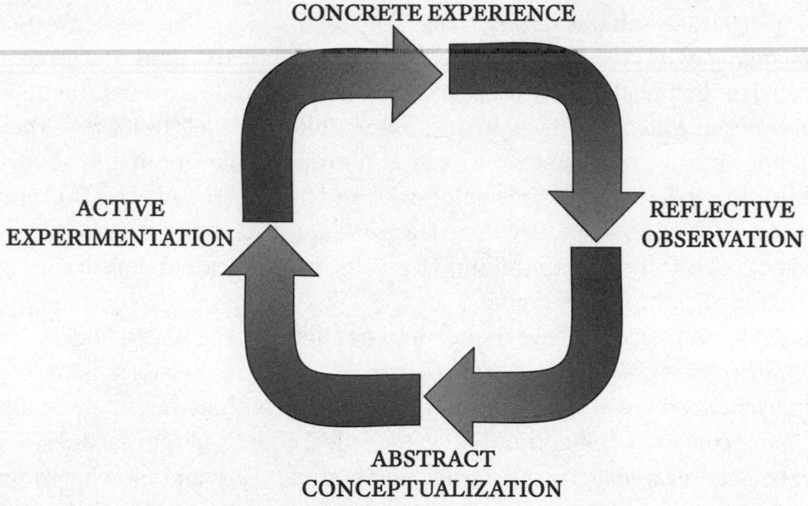

Figure 11.1 Kolb's Experiential Learning Cycle

mind for a given lesson, they do not set a single agenda for what will happen in the learning process. This means that teachers relinquish some (though not all) control of learning outcomes, which can be threatening, especially in religious contexts. In one educational consultation at a church, in which we engaged in a process of open inquiry called "wondering," one parent asked in an alarmed tone: "But what if the children think wrong thoughts? What if they think the wrong things about the story and don't get the right answer?"[6] Giving learners agency can be scary, but without some freedom there is no agency, and consequently no investment on the part of the learner.

Theologically, we might respond that the willingness to reconsider accepted beliefs about God has led in the past to important revolutions of thought and action. In my own tradition, for example, I look at the radical young students in the early sixteenth century who, inspired by "crazy" ideas and stories of church reform that they were hearing from the continent, planted the seeds of the English Reformation; as adults, these students be-

6. "Wonder" is a primary aim of Montessori educational approaches; "wondering" has been adapted for Christian education as the primary process of inquiry in Jerome Berryman's "Godly Play" curriculum, a Montessori-based interactive learning program aimed at helping children engage with Scripture and liturgy and respond creatively to it. See Jerome W. Berryman, *Teaching Godly Play: How to Mentor the Spiritual Development of Children* (Denver, CO: Morehouse, 2009).

came key leaders in this reformation. They read Scripture in the context of a changing world around them and were inspired by the same stories that Christians had read for hundreds of years, but they reinterpreted them for the times in which they lived. Our students follow in their footsteps. They read Scripture and engage the world in their particular moment in time, while reconsidering accepted orthodoxies and finding ways to love God and neighbor that ring true today. A pedagogical approach that gives such freedom to the learner risks untraditional results, but it stands as part of a great tradition of faithful questioning.

Yet even as learners have tremendous freedom in experiential education, their learning is not unguided. Experiential education is not laissez-faire. The experiential educator does not set learners loose with no parameters, but seeks to construct and appropriately fence learning experiences, finessing the balance between structure, order, and boundaries, while allowing room for spontaneity, freedom, and invigorating (as opposed to overwhelming) chaos. Dewey regarded the main task of the teacher as providing learners with quality experiences that both build on prior knowledge and spur growth and creativity for subsequent experiences[7] — surely demanding work for any teacher.

Tending the Fire: Community

While individuals are certainly capable of learning from their own experience, experiential education emphasizes a learning community, in which learners work together, observe others' actions, discuss plans, carry projects to completion, and — in an environment of safety and mutuality — offer encouragement, ideas, and criticism. For both educational and theological reasons, the HSTPs have invested themselves heavily in seeking how to best cultivate effective learning communities. Educationally, communities that offer both challenge *and* support give young people opportunities to explore what they believe, who they are, and how they want to live in the world. The encounter with new people, places, and stories is heightened when learners process their perspectives on it with others and listen to others' perspectives. Theologically, supportive and challenging communities represent *diakonia* — fellowship — in the beloved community of God. In forming such communities, the HSTPs respond to Christ's call to love one another. They also

7. Dewey, *Experience and Education,* p. 27.

recognize that, beyond the theological imperatives, a community of safety, interdependence, inclusion, and mutuality is foundational to encouraging people to take risks with new ideas and ways of being.

Experiential Education in Practice: Service, Leadership, and Creativity

Learning through Serving

One of the most basic expressions of Christian faith is the desire to give — to give generously of oneself for another, and to recognize the presence of Christ in the one being fed, clothed, visited, and sustained. Catholic theologian Jean-Luc Marion goes so far as to point out that love, understood through Jesus Christ, insists on giving, not on being — that the true calling of the human being is to be a divine gift, not a self-sufficient individual.[8] In a Christian context, service might be defined as intentional acts of living for others, or *actions that embody self-giving love.* One of the hallmarks of youth ministry and secular youth leadership programs is the engagement of young people in service ministries, such as a building project with Habitat for Humanity, or raising money or supplies for a project, or serving meals at a local drop-in center. These experiences capitalize on young people's desire for active learning; in them, teenagers powerfully encounter new stories and new ways to think about God's self-giving love.

Although service is a component of discipleship, it can quickly go wrong. As we saw in Lorrie's face-to-face encounter in the church meal program, the notion of service can polarize people into the privileged who serve and the disenfranchised who are served. This is not to say that advocacy or meeting human needs are unimportant, but our models of Christian service risk disconnecting good works from the realities of the people whom we serve. In some cases, our service (actions directed toward others) springs from ulterior motives or an alternative agenda such as *conversion of the other* ("our youth drop in centre is an opportunity for us to lead teenagers to Christ" or "we put Christian literature in the gift boxes that we send overseas"), *attracting membership* ("if kids come to the after school program then their parents might join the church"), *gaining a privilege* ("doing this will look

8. Cf. Jean-Luc Marion, *God without Being* (Chicago: University of Chicago Press, 2012).

good on a college application" or "if we volunteer at the soup kitchen every week, we get to go on the spring trip"), or perhaps even *reassuring ourselves of our own salvation.*

This last motive is a particular theological tangle, since we are not called to not serve others as a "symbol of Christ," implying that serving them will get us to heaven or earn us favor with God. This may seem obvious, but it is an idea that insidiously creeps into our language and therefore our mindset. As Lorrie's realization demonstrates, experiential learning helps young people reflect on others' real situations as they come to terms with the fact that Christian service is a not an egocentric task. Instead, one's relationship with Jesus must embody the love of Christ *in* the world (in our actions) and *for* the world (demonstrated in the radical ways Jesus lived his relationships with others in the Gospels). How can we engage in service in a way that truly honors others and responds to their real needs?

To engage in service well, we must deeply cherish the integrity of the other. Jean Vanier, philosopher, theologian, and founder of L'Arche (communities where people with developmental disabilities live together with caring friends), reflects in his writing on the importance of valuing the uniqueness and belovedness of the other:

> The message of Jesus has often been mangled. Yet Jesus came to lead us all into a society that is a *body,* where each part, weak or strong, able or disabled, finds its place and is free. This vision of humanity, which is a vision of goodness and compassion for each person, comes from a God of Love.[9]

We do not have to be the saviors of the world, Vanier argues, but simply human beings, "enfolded in weakness and in hope, called together to change our world one heart at a time."[10]

This kind of cherishing, if it is to avoid condescension and other pitfalls, requires significant *reflection* in which we help young people stop and ask, "Why are we doing what we are doing? Is the way we are doing it really of service? Is what we are doing really reflecting Christ?" We must examine the theological imperative to action, beyond simply saying, "It's good to do good" or "Christ calls us to serve others." Thoughtful experiential educators help young people ask questions like: "Who is actually being served by this action?" "How is the grace and presence of God revealed in this situation?"

9. Jean Vanier, *Becoming Human* (Mahwah, NJ: Paulist Press, 2008), p. 133.
10. Jean Vanier, *Community and Growth* (Mahwah, NJ: Paulist Press, 1989), p. 163.

"What are the broader social and cultural realities that give rise to this need?" "How does this experience challenge our life and theology?"

Such questions can profoundly disrupt learners' preconceived notions about themselves and the world — and educators should welcome such disruptions. Like the Pentecost moment when the Holy Spirit descended noisily on the disciples, moments of holy disruption open learners to God and ignite their theological and moral imaginations.[11] In the Urban Plunge encounter, Lorrie discovered that she had previously taken a paternalistic approach to service. She had viewed herself as a capable person — bright, affluent, benevolent, and kind — and thought that the essence of service was helping those "less fortunate." When she reflected on what it felt like to be a "less fortunate" person, she saw how dehumanizing her own approach had been.

In the High School Theology Programs, youth learn about giving in myriad ways, from engaging in primary acts of service to one another (at Ask & Imagine, teenagers prepare and serve one another daily meals), to visiting and learning about social outreach organizations, to volunteering with service programs. At Ask & Imagine, youth go out into the community to visit service organizations, outreach programs for people with HIV/AIDS, meal programs, homeless shelters, chaplaincies at community housing projects, advocacy and support programs for people with addictions, and farms in the Canadian Foodgrains Bank. (Lorrie's Urban Plunge experience was one of the options on this day.)

These "Faith-in-Action" days are intentionally structured, not as a day simply to "do good things," but as an opportunity to engage with people who have made intentional, faith-driven life choices to come alongside others in service. This approach to service learning, in which our presence and listening is itself a form of self-giving love whether we "do good things" or not, has led to a number of lasting results. For example, seven years ago a young man named Brian chose to go to the local HIV/AIDS coalition for his Faith in Action day. He met people there whose lives had been touched by AIDS and were, as a result, now serving those affected by the disease. Since then, Brian has participated in an International HIV/AIDS conference, joined a theatrical group that does HIV/AIDS awareness and education in schools, and continues to be part of HIV/AIDS education and advocacy initiatives around the world. Brian credits that one visit with igniting this passion.

11. Holy disruption is explored further in Andy Brubacher Kaethler's chapter in this volume.

Second, these experiences help young people recognize that true service entails vulnerability of all involved. A case in point: on one day of visits, eighteen-year-old Jocelyn listened to Dean describe his choice to live at L'Arche. As Dean spoke about the death of one of the residents and the impact this disabled man had had on his life, he began to cry. Reflecting on the conversation later, Jocelyn said,

> That was so huge for me. Dean is a person who really knows what he is about and what's important. I want to live in a way that moves me so much that I am unashamed to cry in front of strangers when talking about my life and what I do. I want to be that vulnerable and strong at the same time.

Dean's vulnerability in turn enabled Jocelyn to share honestly with her learning community, reflecting on the encounter and projecting a vision of herself into the future.

Finally, through encounter and reflection, youth often gain deeper understandings of — and confidence for working within — complex systems of poverty, hunger, prejudice, social injustice, and other problems. These layered understandings of social issues mean that, once youth leave the program, they are less likely to offer facile answers to complicated problems and more likely to seek out conversation and form nuanced responses. They are also more likely to take leadership in responding to issues they care about — the topic to which we now turn.

Learning through Leading

The leadership development aspect of Ask & Imagine did not elicit much excitement in Shannon, a shy introvert. Shannon never saw herself as a leader. She associated leadership with being an out-there, up-front, loud, and lively person. In her understanding, leaders were not shy or afraid to speak in groups. Shannon was in for a surprise. Over the two-week experience, she discovered that leaders could be people just like her who brought their quiet energy and commitment to ideas about which they were passionate. "Leadership," she said after the program, "was about having the confidence to just be myself and initiate, and not try to just imitate other leaders that I saw in other contexts."

As Shannon's story suggests, a second major area of experiential learning occurs in participants' opportunities for leadership — opportunities that often change their expectations about what leadership is. All HSTPs immerse young people in multi-layered opportunities for Christian leadership. Based on her experience directing Tomorrow's Present, a program originally hosted by St. Francis' Seminary (and now sponsored by Cardinal Stritch University), Lisa Calderone-Stewart discerned that giving teenagers *agency* as leaders and teachers provided them with transformative learning experiences that fueled their vocational discernment. She explains,

> By teaching, we learn. When young people are challenged to become teachers, they are motivated to learn more so they can teach better. They begin to care about their audiences, and they want to offer their best. They see themselves as leaders. They develop ownership for passing on their messages. . . . That was the idea behind Tomorrow's Present. Basically, we trained teenagers to teach workshops, and we watched how they learned. Here's what we observed: Not only did the youth learn, but we adults learned as well. In fact, the young people improved the workshops tremendously. And many of the youth reported that these workshop practices and presentations were among the most significant experiences of their lives. They were transformational.[12]

Because these leadership experiences were so powerful, Calderone-Stewart called her approach Transformational Ministry and grounded it in David Kolb's learning cycle. Through leading and teaching, many youth in Tomorrow's Present claimed a self-identity as Christian leaders and could foresee themselves seeking further leadership roles in faith communities in the future. Those youth who learned to teach through subject areas such as interfaith dialogue, hope building, or peace-making were often drawn to deeper study and engagement with those practices in their schools or congregations, in their post-secondary studies, or in volunteer commitments.

Using Calderone-Stewart's models, at Ask & Imagine we teach youth strategies for planning and teaching, and intentionally seek to dismantle young people's tendency to associate leadership with telling others what to do, being the boss, or leading the charge. Being a Christian leader is not about being bossy or domineering, but about being someone who, like Jesus, builds communities and enacts transformation by entering into relationship, giving oneself with passion and love, acting with courage, and giving others freedom

12. Lisa Marie Calderone-Stewart, *Changing Lives: Transformational Ministry and Today's Teens* (Dayton, OH: Pflaum, 2004), pp. 15-16.

to respond. Over time, our mentor team developed our own definition of leadership, drawing on the work of Margaret Wheatley and Harrison Owen: *leadership is a relationship that unleashes potential.*[13] Leadership is a matrix of relationships in which individuals and groups unleash potential in themselves, in people around them, and in situations or stories. In this definition, the dualism of leader and follower breaks down, and youth find themselves empowered. When youth have the opportunity to experience and reflect on leadership, they realize the potency of their own agency, and their discipleship moves from simply copying other Christians to actively listening, interpreting, creating, speaking, and discovering their own prophetic voice. This is especially true when the leadership opportunity is "for real," giving young people real agency instead of simply enacting scripts written by adults.

Learning through Creating

A final practice of experiential education that recurs throughout High School Theology Programs involves creative production. Imagine this: Five young people are standing in a circle in a classroom with two young adult mentors. They are slapping their knees and clapping their hands in a steady four-four rhythm. Their eyes sparkle with excitement. As they hold the rhythm steady for one another, they take turns punching out a thirty-two-bar rap. The theme of the rap has nothing to do with traditional rap themes of relationships, rights, sexuality, angst, or anger. Instead, these young people are riffing on ecclesiology:[14]

. . . I've got a tutorial
'bout the church as corporeal
living sleeping eating breathing
not just some memorial . . .

. . . We need room for skeptical honest interpretation
For formation of a movement towards nurturing creation . . .

13. Cf. Margaret Wheatley, *Leadership and the New Science* (San Francisco: Berrett-Koehler, 1999), and Harrison Owen, *The Spirit of Leadership: Liberating the Leader in Each of Us* (San Francisco: Berrett-Koehler, 1999).

14. To watch this performance, see: "Roots among the Rocks — Rap Video," YouTube video, 8:26, posted by "HuronUC" on November 14, 2012, http://www.youtube.com/watch?v=zMwXs6CNWhs.

. . . we intend to be
intentional community
so we can be
hearts and hands
working for the good of all humanity . . .

This rap was part of an experimental project called Roots among the Rocks, in which the Faculty of Theology at Huron University College sought to engage arts, performance, music, theater, and theology. Roots among the Rocks emerged when, upon the tenth anniversary of Ask & Imagine, the Faculty of Theology wondered how they might find other ways to connect youth with theology, and specifically, what might happen if they invited young people into deep theological discourse and reflection on real life stories, and then commissioned them to create a theatrical piece out of that engagement.

The project brought a group of young people from Anglican, Lutheran, United Church, and Mennonite backgrounds together into intentional community for a month. They explored theology, Scripture, and church history with members of the Faculty of Theology. They also gathered source material in over seventy-five interviews with people ages eight to ninety-two, asking questions like:

- If you are in church, why have you stayed?
- If you have left church, why did you leave?
- What is an experience that changed the way you understand God?

The youth then set out to make a creative work that would express their own perspective on what they heard and learned. The point was not for them to perform a predetermined script or report back the project's key message, but to engage in a creative process. They were given space to *encounter* stories, *reflect* on them together, and exercise *agency* in sharing what they had learned in *community*. The result was a project that participants deeply owned, and that changed and challenged them and their audiences.

The one-act play they created was performed in the style of theater known as Collective Creation or Devised Theater, which has been instrumental in creating performance pieces based on non-fiction stories that arise from local communities.[15] It journeyed through the themes of worship pat-

15. One well-known play that was written in the Devised Theater/Collective Creation genre is *The Laramie Project*.

terns, identity crises, resilience and grace, confession and absolution, and finding home. Characters in the play told their stories around a kitchen table while friends whispered in church pews, getting distracted while praying and then baring their souls to the audience. With candor, humor, and grace, the work dealt with the subjects of cancer, sexuality, drug addiction, clergy burnout, suicide, challenges of rural life and ministry, and aging, as well as with existential and theological problems. It raised more questions than answers, and no topic was off the table.

The rap cited above came out of a workshop with a musician after a lecture on church history and ecclesiology. The company of youth was asked to write their own answer to the question, "What is church?" in the form of a rap verse. Learning to rap was a stretch for a couple of youth who were classically trained vocalists. But their poetry was honest and hard-hitting on many issues that were causing church division. They wrote, for example,

The common cup is not a commodity —
You don't need to hold property.
There ain't no million-dollar-fee.
Jesus said:
"Ev'rybody come and get a piece o' me."

. . . I find it a pity that it is ruined by hypocrisy
Can't you see this pettiness is making a mockery
Of the things we believe?
You know you're causin' a hindrance.
Don't mean to upheave,
But you're perpetuating ignorance.
I may be naïve,
But I don't understand intolerance . . .

Clearly, these young people had reflected deeply on what they had learned, and, given agency, they spoke prophetically to their audience.

The audiences of Roots among the Rocks described it as inspiring and challenging, repeatedly saying that it offered them a fresh vision of church. At the premiere, one clergy person commented: "That was *not* what I expected — it was the most profound piece of theology that I have heard or read in years. I will be thinking about this for a long time!" Many audience members said they found encouragement and vision. One young theater student in a large urban center approached the director bluntly:

> I do a lot of theater, and I've grown up in the church too. And this play was not what I expected it to be. To be honest, most church drama really blows, you know? It's hokey, like it is trying to make a specific point and it hits you over the head repeatedly. With this play, that didn't happen. I didn't expect to be amazed and moved, but I totally was.

Numerous people who saw the play were surprised in another way. Some said, "We thought this was supposed to be youth ministry." That is, they expected a play that taught the gospel to teenagers, rather than an event that gave youth a prophetic voice in expressing their understanding of the gospel. They were amazed that young people had listened to the stories of young and old and then retold those stories to the church in a provocative and inspiring way. They were surprised that youth had exercised agency, and they were moved by the results.

This example suggests that the arts provide a second language through which theological reflection can happen, as young artists gain access to new tools to express meaning. At Ask & Imagine, young people's artistic offerings have included poetry about conformity, a video connecting cliff jumping with baptism, a painting about pain, and raps about ecclesiology. As they have workshopped their pieces, listened to feedback, and returned to the drawing board, they have discovered that creativity flourishes under the sun of sustained reflection in the context of a supportive and honest community.

This is experiential education at its best: it brings learners into encounters with new material, with others' stories, and with real-world problems. It allows for and encourages reflection on those encounters in the context of a peer learning community, and it calls them to claim agency in responding to what they have learned — in our case, within a community of faith that asks for their active interpretation of centuries-old texts and traditions. This process helps learners open themselves to feedback that provides still more encounters, starting the "learning spiral" over again at a higher level. When they are given freedom and responsibility to create in community, youth are opened in new ways to the powerful and prophetic work of the Holy Spirit, who speaks through them to the church.

When a Fire Breaks Out

Compelling encounters send out sparks. It often only takes one story or a single compelling encounter with another's narrative to catch a young person's interest. Look carefully, and you will see sparks flash around Lorrie's Urban Plunge encounter, Brian's visit to the HIV/AIDS program, and Jocelyn's experience of Dean's tears. But a spark, an ember, goes out by itself. If you have ever had to light a reluctant campfire, you will recall the tipping point when the flame caught hold, just before the tiny roar of confident flames, after you gave it just enough space, the right fuel, sufficient air, enough shelter, and gentle encouragement. Without such coaxing, the spark dies. In a lecture to High School Theology Program directors in Indianapolis in 2003, theology professor Susan Thistlethwaite cautioned us, "It is incredibly easy to kill a vocation." Put more positively, it takes deliberate care to fan the sparks of young people's interest into the fire of lifelong discipleship and Christian vocation.

The task of educators is to provide young people with the flint and tinder of compelling encounters and the solid ground of an ancient story. We help a fire catch by encouraging reflection and active response in the context of a supportive and honest community. When educators and other caring adults fan the flames, we should not be surprised when the Holy Spirit lights a fire that, like a crucible, distills the very essence of the gospel from the lives of young people and the contexts in which they live. We do not provide encounters and opportunities for reflection and response just so that young people will adopt our ideologies or think only the "right thoughts." In the process of experiential education, we honor what young people contribute — spurring them on to serve, to lead, and to express themselves prophetically to the church and the wider world.

PART FOUR

More Than Teenagers

Vocational Discernment in the Lives of Program Staff, Faculty, and Theological Institutions

From that time on my life was to be linked to theirs, their interests would be mine: I had received a call, a vocation, a direction in life.

DOROTHY DAY, *The Long Loneliness* (1952)

CHAPTER TWELVE

Becoming Christ's Hands and Feet in the World

The Vocational Formation of Staff

Elizabeth W. Corrie

Erik Christensen currently serves as the pastor of a small urban congregation in Chicago affiliated with the ELCA.[1] Now in the seventh year of his first call, he has helped a church of twelve active members grow into a vibrant community of over one hundred worshippers engaging the community together. After having spent several years post-college working with troubled and homeless youth who had little if any connection to a faith community, Erik wondered, "What theological resources can the Church offer young people living with their backs to the wall?" This question, according to Erik, "propelled me from a career in social services to a vocation in the Church." He chose Candler School of Theology because it housed the Youth Theological Initiative (YTI). Erik recalls: "YTI . . . captured my attention and signaled to me that Candler understood young people as theological subjects, and not just objects to be moved through a parish Christian Education program."

Carlton Mackey is a professional artist and filmmaker who teaches undergraduate students at Emory University. As the Chair of the Ethics and the

1. The following profiles come out of a study conducted from 2010-2013 on the impact of working at the Youth Theological Initiative on former staff members. From December 2010 through July 2011, 156 of 220 total former staff members were contacted and invited to complete an online survey. Of these, 79 completed the survey. In addition to the survey, eleven former staff members were interviewed during the summer of 2011, and in July 2013, twelve former staff members offered reflections during panel discussions at the YTI twentieth anniversary celebration. These profiles are only a sample of the dozens of stories and comments that have informed this essay. All quotations come from unpublished manuscripts and interview transcripts related to this study.

Arts Initiative for the Center for Ethics and Assistant Director of the D. Abbott Turner Program in Ethics and Servant Leadership, Carlton teaches leadership skills, directs a summer internship program, and organizes film screenings, dramatic readings, and art exhibitions that provoke reflection and dialogue about the connection between ethics and art. Working at YTI as a mentor, chaplain, and assistant director during seminary, Carlton had a clear sense of calling if not a clear idea about vocation: "I just knew that I was supposed to be here and that I was supposed to take it seriously and that it was going to be life changing. . . . I was called and compelled to be here." He credits YTI as being a transformative component of his vocational formation. He now articulates his vocation as an artist called "to use my art as a way of challenging my own assumptions about the world and other people's . . . and helping them see more clearly what can be." At the same time, he is called to be an educator, "someone who's constantly learning," but "able to connect with people and able to transfer knowledge in such a way that people want to receive it."

Kim Jackson is the Episcopal Chaplain to the Atlanta University Center, the consortium of historically black colleges in Atlanta.[2] Coming to Candler straight from her undergraduate studies, she was only twenty-two when she began working for YTI. She recalls walking into staff training the first day wearing khakis and a long-sleeved button down shirt "feeling uncomfortable, incapable, and inadequate." However, when she saw the director "in cargo shorts and a t-shirt," she began to shed the first layer of discomfort. "Then," she remembers,

> within the first few hours of training the director unknowingly began to chip away at my feelings of inadequacy. She said to all of us gathered, "We hired you to be you. You are exactly the person that we need here. So, be you." . . . and I believed her. . . . There was something about the sincerity in her voice, and the wisdom in her eyes that made me feel less inadequate and more prepared.

YTI staff members who "helped me grow more comfortable in my own skin (and thus become a better leader)" were particularly important to expanding Kim's vision of Christian leadership. These colleagues included three African American women who served as models of "smart, independent, black

2. The consortium includes Morehouse College, Spellman College, Morris Brown College, and Clark Atlanta University.

female leadership," showing her that "having a leadership role in a church was possible," that "black lesbians can break down barriers through activism," and that sharing leadership with others was important, which "stood in direct contrast to other models that I had experienced within the black community." As a young Black woman who was just beginning to discover that she was a lesbian when she came to YTI, Kim acknowledges that it may take a lifetime to work through the internalized homophobia, racism, and sexism left by "years of deprivation" of good role models. Yet she notes that "it was that first summer of YTI that set me on a course towards loving myself more fully and imagining a future in which I, a smart, black, independent lesbian, could effectively lead others."

The "Staff Effect"

As programs like YTI enter their third decade, it is clear that teenagers are not the only people whose vocations as Christian leaders are shaped by the High School Theology Programs. A strong case could be made that these programs' young staff members — who are overwhelmingly college students or seminarians — experience their own leadership as Christians to be even more powerfully shaped than the high school participants they supervise. Despite the wide theological spectrum of the HSTPs, the young adults working in these programs discern their own vocations using the same pedagogical practices they teach teenagers — which often has immediate consequences for staff members' own vocational identities.

The staff-shaping effect was so obvious at YTI that we began to conduct research on this dimension of the program specifically, which is the context in which Erik, Carlton, and Kim shared their stories. But while this chapter emerges primarily from the YTI research, the "staff effect" is well known among High School Theology Program directors, who point to countless Eriks, Carltons, and Kims, and to ministries launched thanks to young adults' staff experiences in these programs. On one level, this is hardly surprising. Every youth minister knows that leaders tend to receive the formation they want for their youth; every teacher knows that we teach best that which we most need to learn.

Yet the young adults who overwhelmingly staff the HSTPs, for whom developmental location, cultural timing, and educational immediacy all give urgency to the task of vocational discernment, have a particular readiness for the questions and practices of Christian leadership as they mentor high school students. Erik, Carlton, and Kim — and hundreds of young adults like them — consider their varied vocational trajectories to have been decisively formed by their experience as YTI staff members. They give us three glimpses in the ways in which programs dedicated to the vocational formation of high school students have a critical "spillover" effect that sharpens the vocational discernment of young adult staff as well.

The Pastor: Community-Shaping as Leadership

Inspired by his work with youth outside the church, Erik's vocational path was refined and shaped during the three summers he worked at YTI as a mentor. Erik views the High School Theology Programs as "a really useful lab for raising up a new generation of Christians because that old way of doing church . . . is passing out of the world." Erik turns to his experience at YTI regularly as a senior pastor. He realized in his early days at St. Luke's that many young adults in the community hadn't had much religious education, at least not since they were confirmed in junior high or high school. "Certainly nothing as probing and rigorous as YTI," Erik explains:

> These young adults were college graduates, professionals with advanced educations and highly developed vocabularies for describing the world through the lenses of law, medicine, social policy, engineering, and so on. But when asked to describe how their faith informed their thinking and action on issues that made a real difference in their everyday lives — community violence, racial tensions in the neighborhood or workplace, marriage equality, etc. — they struggled to find words they'd never been taught.

So, Erik did what he had learned as a staff member at YTI: he formed small groups and met with them on a regular basis to read books, share life stories, and begin to develop a theological language with which to interpret the events of the day. "We began to study our worlds with the tools of Christian Scripture and tradition," Erik recalls, "and to explore how those resources are informed by reason, experience, and the knowledge gained through other disciplines. We became 'scholars' [YTI's term for teenage participants in the program] whose lives were the curriculum for our course of study." One of the major features of Erik's ministry is now the cultivation and support of small groups engaged in theological reflection of personal and social issues. This is a model he learned and practiced at YTI.

As a leader of a church and within his denomination, Erik draws heavily on the lessons he learned at YTI. Erik remembers planning worship at YTI — where teenage scholars and staff came from Catholic and Protestant, high and low church, conservative and liberal, mainline and non-denominational worshiping traditions — for showing him "how hard, and how worthwhile, it is to craft multicultural worship that is honest." Learning how to lead and build an ecumenical community with youth prepared Erik to be the kind of liturgical leader who can draw deeply from his own Lutheran heritage while bringing together an eclectic mix of parishioners to form one united congregation.

What makes Erik a particularly exciting leader for the church is his understanding of the importance of Christians coming together to do public theology. Public theology is a core commitment at YTI, and it assumes that Christians have something meaningful to contribute to conversations in the public sphere and are called to participate in the transformation of the world. When the decline in membership and financial resources shut down his denomination's office for addressing public issues, Erik mobilized new voices to speak on issues of justice:

> YTI taught [church leaders] how to help lay people, how to help people who don't imagine themselves becoming pastors but want to be public Christians, do collective discernment on faith and public life. That's how [creating] social statements will get done . . . it'll get done over Facebook and it'll get done in networked ways as opposed to top down. It's not going to be the panel of twelve deciding what we think about genetics. [We are] going to be a much better, informed public church where pastors and lay people know how to have conversations about the connection between science and faith and politics and faith and health and faith.

The Teacher: Curating Learning as Leadership

Carlton learned to teach at YTI. Because YTI was a place to explore different methods of teaching within a community of teachers and learners, Carlton had opportunities to observe other teachers, practice skills, and take risks to teach creatively. Most important, he was able to imagine teaching differently.

> YTI helped me to see that the educational process — the teaching moment, the learning moment, the transforming moments that can happen

> while teaching don't have to make you feel like you're being taught something — can be engaging. You can stand up. You can do exercise; you can breathe . . . the type of stuff where you lead the class and you go and you do something in the field that highlights some of the stuff you're talking about. You're talking about religious diversity; you go and you visit different places where there are different religions . . . you talk about race and class and then you go to the Open Door.[3]

This vision of engaged learning is the basis for the Ethics and Servant Leadership (EASL) program that Carlton directs. "Basically," he says, "I run EASL as someone who learned how to run a program [at] YTI." He adds, "If I had to base it just on my educational experience and . . . all the other ways that I've been educated, I wouldn't have even thought to do the type of stuff in EASL that we do."

Carlton wears multiple hats at Emory, and this enables him to infuse his teaching with the other piece of his vocation, that of artist. The Ethics and the Arts program he directs "is largely an amalgamation of things learned from YTI," not only about artistic creation, but also about the dynamics of power, oppression, and human capacity for social change. For example, while serving as the chaplain at YTI and helping young people plan and lead worship services, he "learned more about the power of ritual and art-making in the development of meaning." He considers the Ethics and the Arts program to be a vehicle to teach about ritual and meaning as well as ethics:

> It is about navigating a complex landscape of meaning and virtues and experiences in a way that I believe we are all uniquely poised to do. We are wired to engage with art. It is one of our oldest forms of expression and has been used to empower, uplift, and brainwash and destroy for all of human existence. I've committed my life to revealing its powerful nature and use it as a force of good.

In his own artistic work, Carlton recently launched a website and published a book of images, scholarly essays, and personal stories entitled *50 Shades of Black,* which seeks "to be a platform for sharing, learning, growing, and healing using personal stories and art to foster a global dialogue about sexu-

3. The Open Door is an intentional Christian community living with the homeless in Atlanta, following the Catholic Worker tradition.

ality and skin tone in the formation of identity."[4] By encouraging thoughtful engagement with art around issues of social justice, Carlton lives out his vocation as artist, teacher, and public theologian.

The Chaplain: Team-Building as Leadership

After serving as a mentor her first summer at YTI, Kim became an assistant director, responsible for hiring, training, and supervising mentors as well as overseeing the daily operation of the dormitories. Kim was co-leading a team of staff members who were mostly her age or older, whose feedback helped Kim claim a relational leadership style for her current work as a college chaplain:

> At the end of an interview with a candidate for a position that I am hoping to fill, the candidate said, "Thank you, Kim. You made this interview feel conversational and normal. I feel like I got a real sense of your supervisory style without me even having to ask." This comment reminded me of something similar that a staff member for YTI once wrote in an evaluation. The person said something to the effect of, "I appreciate your willingness to take the risk of becoming friends with the people that you supervise." My willingness to be in relationship with my staff (it's not always friendship, but I certainly seek to build community) was truly cultivated by my experience on the Leadership Team at YTI.

Kim candidly acknowledges the risks of relational leadership. ("We risk becoming blind to each other's faults and become willing to be overworked on behalf of someone in the friend group. We also risk becoming deaf to outside critique because of our loyalty to each other.") But she believes the rewards outweigh the risks, especially "when we're vigilant and honest" about those risks. "Because we are friends," Kim notes, "we trust one another deeply. That type of leadership model works well for me, and I've carried parts of it with me into my ministry."

YTI's emphasis on diversity gave Kim a model for emphasizing diverse, shared leadership in her own ministry. Kim remembers a moment when the wisdom of this leadership model became personally relevant. She was caught

4. *50 Shades of Black,* http://www.50shadesofblack.com/what-is-50-shades-of-black (accessed August 24, 2013).

off guard when a young Black male scholar, confronted with YTI mentors who were both male and female, gay and straight, refused to participate in a community activity with her because, he said, his father "didn't send me all the way over here to be with all this sinfulness." Stunned and hurt, Kim was unsure how to respond. However, one of the straight women on the Leadership Team who heard his statement immediately pulled him aside and talked with him, because "she knew that it wasn't fair to me (or to the scholar) for me to address him in that moment. The situation was too heated, too personal, and too painful. . . . I don't know what she said, but I'm clear that he could hear her so much better than he ever would have heard me."

This moment drove home for Kim the importance of YTI's shared and diverse leadership model, since "there were certain conversations that only white people could lead with other white people . . . conversations that were better served when men were talking with boys, or women with girls." Kim says: "YTI taught me that one person can't be all things to all people," a lesson she applies as a college chaplain by working hard to develop partnerships with diverse constituencies. "There is a lot that I can do to connect with the young men that I serve," Kim explains, "but I know that involving men in the ministry has been really important for filling in some of the spaces that I can't fill."

Young Adult Staff: What Kind of Leaders Do They Become?

Erik, Carlton, and Kim's experience on the staff of a High School Theology Program gave them two pedagogical advantages as future church leaders. First, it gave them a context where they could live out their theological coursework in real time, "trying on" various forms of Christian leadership temporarily but explicitly. In addition, the core pedagogical commitments of the HSTPs meant that Erik, Carlton, and Kim embodied a particular *kind* of Christian leadership. All of the programs teach staff skills that enable them to engage parishioners in theological reflection that connects the Christian faith with their lives and the world around them. Each HSTP forms staff who appreciate the transformative role of worship and ritual, and who are able to draw on the Christian tradition while creatively adapting it for a post-Christian world.

Leaders who have served on the staff of a High School Theology Program see the potential for clergy and laity to develop a prophetic voice that can contribute to conversations in the public sphere even as church institutions weaken or die. They teach creatively, engaging students' hearts, minds, and bodies in learning to become agents of change for their generation. They open up new spaces for meaningful dialogue through creative expression. They are leaders who encourage others to live fully into themselves and their vocations in order to build robust, diverse teams who can work together for a common cause. Such leaders are essential to the church, the academy, and the world.

The Practice of Leadership as Indirect Pedagogy: Becoming the Full Body of Christ

In Kim's account of her experience of practicing leadership at YTI, she suggests a critical feature of the vocational formation in High School Theology Programs:

> YTI thrust me into leadership long before I felt ready. The staff working with me and the scholars walking alongside me trusted me during times when I wasn't clear about my ability to trust myself, much less clear about any ability to lead. I'm incredibly grateful for this gift from the YTI community — there is something about YTI that enables the community to see and call forth the gifts that are buried deep within each of us. I try to take that gift with me into my ministry. I try to foster an environment and create a community for my students in which their gifts are highlighted, honed, and sent forth. Thus, the gift of my YTI experience gets carried on throughout the Church and the world.

It is no accident that Kim uses the word "community" three times in a five-sentence statement. This experience of practicing leadership in a communal context is a central factor in the vocational formation of staff in all the HSTPs, and it has implications for the kinds of leaders these programs send forth to serve in churches, schools, and society.

YTI and other High School Theology Programs have core pedagogical commitments that inform their ministries with youth — commitments to diversity, to welcoming young people as subjects rather than objects of theological education, to engaging in theological reflection that critically retrieves Christian Scripture and tradition, to fostering vocational discernment and imagination, and to finding common ground even in the midst of acknowledging the reality of structural sin that deforms our lives — all practiced within an intensive, residential community. These commitments teach the staff as powerfully as the youth themselves, in part because these commitments embody leadership approaches that reflect and reinforce the very theological texts that young people study during the HSTP experience. At YTI, for instance, these "indirect pedagogies" can be viewed theologically as the process of becoming the full Body of Christ — a process that directly reflects YTI's emphasis on the imagery drawn from 1 Corinthians 12.

Interdependence in the Body

> [4]Now there are varieties of gifts, but the same Spirit. . . . [7]To each is given the manifestation of the Spirit for the common good. . . . [17]If the whole body were an eye, where would the hearing be? If the whole body were hearing, where would the sense of smell be? [18]But as it is, God arranged the members in the body, each one of them, as he chose. (1 Corinthians 12:4-18)

The Body of Christ has become a key theological symbol at YTI. We frequently cite 1 Corinthians 12:12 and Ephesians 4:11, the Pauline passages on the Body of Christ, in our opening worship service of the YTI Summer Academy. We do so in order to introduce scholars to the concept of intentional Christian community and the opportunity it affords to set aside the normal social divisions they may experience in school or other settings, in favor of a more inclusive, interdependent, yet diverse community.

This message is even more important for our staff members, as their efficacy in working with the youth depends upon their ability to embody inclusivity and interdependence in their actions. The diversity of the young people who come to YTI means that some staff members can engage certain scholars better than others; we must rely on each staff person's ability to contribute her gifts fully to the community so that no young person "falls through the cracks." We need the athletic staff members to engage scholars while playing ultimate Frisbee; we need introverted staff members comfortable sitting in the lounge with scholars reading quietly; we need Catholic staff members to help Catholic scholars think about their tradition in conversation with Protestant scholars; we need Spanish-speaking staff members able to chat with our Latino/a scholars to give them a break from English; we need staff members with different socio-economic and ethnic backgrounds to help scholars think about the intersections of race, class, and gender; we need musicians, singers, cooks, artists, dancers, Bible scholars, theology nerds, activists, black church preachers, Taizé chanters, centering prayer meditators, morning people, night owls, and so much more.

As a result of our core commitment to gathering and engaging a diverse community of youth, staff members must learn to be parts of an interconnected, interdependent body that seeks to reflect the Body of Christ. They learn how to be themselves and to let others be themselves. They learn to articulate to others who they are, how they are shaped by their experiences and commitments, and where they fit within the ecumenical landscape of Christianity. Even if, as a "foot," a staff person wonders why she cannot be a "hand," or if, as an "ear," another staff person secretly worries that he might not be part of the Body because he is not an "eye," these members soon discover their fears are unfounded. God has placed each of them in this community, in this Body, just as God wanted. As Kim recalls, she was hired "to be you," and she learned how to do just that. Not only do staff members discover who they are as individuals within the staff team, but they also discover how they complement others, and how much they need each other in order to do this work well. They learn they are unable to say, "I don't need you" (1 Cor. 12:21).

Honoring All in the Body

> . . . the members of the body that seem to be weaker are indispensable [23]and those members of the body that we think less honorable we clothe with greater honor, and our less respectable members are treated with greater respect; [24]whereas our more respectable members do not need this. . . . [26]If one member suffers, all suffer together with it; if one member is honored, all rejoice together with it. (1 Corinthians 12:22-26)

In the church and in our society, young people are often ignored or even silenced.[5] Many young people spend much of their lives in same-age groups quarantined from adult society, whether in youth groups worshipping separately from their parents, in overcrowded schools, or, increasingly,

5. For a discussion on how this has developed, see David F. White, "The Social Construction of Adolescence," in *Awakening Youth Discipleship: Christian Resistance in a Consumer Culture,* Brian J. Mahan et al. (Eugene, OR: Cascade, 2008), pp. 3-19.

and particularly for young people of color, in prisons.[6] A core assumption at YTI is that young people *as young people* are domesticated and marginalized, because they seem to represent the parts of Christ's Body that most of us, implicitly or explicitly, think are less honorable. They appear to be the weakest parts, and yet if we honor them as we are called to do, we find they are the most necessary parts.

As a result of this core commitment, staff members must allow themselves to be taught by teenage scholars, even as they lead them. They must exercise care in how they use their power and authority in teaching, ministry, and leadership. Taking young people seriously as subjects rather than objects of Christian education means that staff members must master the art of discernment. They must discern when to get out of the way and when to treat young people as conversation partners by pushing back and expressing their own views as co-learners. They learn the importance of hearing each scholar's story in order to approach topics sensitively and meet scholars where they are. Clothing young people with honor as the most necessary parts of Christ's Body pushes those in ministry with them to be self-reflective, humble, and welcoming of the distinctive voices of young people. As adults with more education and life experience, and with numerous contexts in which their voices have weight, staff members learn to accept that in the YTI community, they do not need and should not seek to be honored above the youth. If they accept this, they quickly discover what it means to suffer and rejoice together with the young people who find their voices in their midst.

Sharing Gifts in the Body

> But strive for the greater gifts. And I will show you a still more excellent way. (1 Corinthians 12:31)

Our pedagogical commitments — our desire to become the Body of Christ by emphasizing diversity, treating young people as subjects, emphasizing critical theological reflection, fostering vocational discernment and imagination, finding common ground while naming structural sin, and

6. One educational theorist who discusses the silencing of youth in society in depth is Henry A. Giroux. See for example, Henry A. Giroux, *Youth in a Suspect Society: Democracy or Disposability?* (New York: Palgrave Macmillan, 2009).

creating intensive community — often stretch staff members. Because we want to make our community a safe space to try new things, staff members model ecclesial risk-taking, doing things and going places they might not have done before in the name of reflecting more clearly the unity of Christ's body. Because we want scholars to engage the resources of the Christian tradition, we need theologically educated staff members who are willing to share what they are learning in seminary with our teenage scholars. Because we encourage reflection and taking advantage of teachable moments, staff members must be willing to reflect on their own work and to learn from failure.

As a result, working at YTI provides staff members with opportunities to practice their skills in ministry, teaching, and administration in a context in which they can learn through observing others and receiving feedback. Significantly, the feedback loops are short and frequent.[7] Staff members co-lead small group discussions and off-campus experiential education projects. They meet regularly to compare notes on the dynamics and health of the community and give each other feedback about how their work impacts scholars. They observe Candler faculty members leading plenary sessions and take note of how these more experienced teachers navigate the challenges of teaching creatively. They work with youth to plan thoughtful worship and developing skills in public reading and preaching. They engage in pastoral care with youth and with each other. They learn to articulate their own theological perspectives and help scholars make sense of the theological texts they are reading. They witness a variety of leadership styles and try on different styles as they find their place within the Body. Most importantly, they take risks and learn through failure as much as through success. Surrounded by the different members of the Body — some apostles, some prophets, some teachers — staff see how spiritual gifts are practiced and can strive for these gifts themselves. In the process, they catch a glimpse of a more excellent way.

7. Since the social cognitive work of Albert Bandura in the 1960s, the importance of feedback loops in behavioral change has been well documented and adapted for education; for one summary of this research, see Gary P. Latham and Edward A. Locke, "Self-Regulation through Goal-Setting," *Organizational Behavior and Human Decision Processes* 50 (December 1991): 212-47, http://www.sciencedirect.com/science/article/pii/074959789190021K.

A more readable commentary exists at Thomas Goetz, "Harnessing the Power of Feedback Loops," *Wired* (June 19, 2011), http://www.wired.com/magazine/2011/06/ff_feedbackloop/ (accessed September 19, 2013).

Dealing with Conflict in the Body

> . . . to lead a life worthy of the calling to which you have been called,
> [2]with all humility and gentleness, with patience, bearing with one an-
> other in love, [3]making every effort to maintain the unity of the Spirit
> in the bond of peace. . . . [14]We must no longer be children, tossed
> to and fro and blown about by every wind of doctrine, by people's
> trickery, by their craftiness in deceitful scheming. [15]But speaking the
> truth in love, we must grow up in every way into him who is the head,
> into Christ, [16]from whom the whole body, joined and knitted together
> by every ligament with which it is equipped, as each part is working
> properly, promotes the body's growth in building itself up in love.
> (Ephesians 4:1-3, 14-16)

Our pedagogical commitment to building an authentic community that takes seriously the powers and principalities that deform the *imago Dei* in each of us places staff members in a challenging yet potentially generative position. We ask staff to help young people think critically about the ways racism, sexism, classism, ageism, ableism, homophobia, and other structural forms of injustice and sin impact our lives. We challenge our scholars to consider whether they find themselves benefitting from the dominant culture or on its margins, a relationship that changes and becomes increasingly complex as we explore the multiple layers of identity and social location.

When that critical lens is turned on our own program, we come up against the limits of seeking unity in the midst of real differences and disparities of power and privilege. We have a job to do, a responsibility for creating a safe space for each member in our community, and we have to do this knowing we must live together for an extended period of time. Conflict is inevitable. Staff members often disagree about how to engage scholars in conversations about injustice and power; we catch ourselves acting out of our deep-seated prejudices, and sometimes we hurt each other. We know that we cannot avoid conflict and that maintaining a façade of unity only serves to perpetuate the injustices we say we want to change. Whether we take it head on with thoughtfulness and care or stumble into it blindsided and unprepared, every year we engage conflict. Yet we also claim to follow Christ. We believe that we must model for young people a form of discipleship that seeks to lead a life worthy of the calling to which we have been called, a discipleship that involves "bearing with one another in love, making every effort to maintain the unity of the Spirit in the bond of peace."

As a result, staff members learn how (and how not) to engage conflict, to be allies, to advocate for themselves or others, to appreciate those who are different, and to speak the truth in love. Those who normally avoid conflict learn the harm that can come from withdrawing when the community needs them to be engaged. Those who have found themselves defaulting to an authoritarian leadership style to respond to challenges discover the transformative possibilities when they resist these temptations and find more democratic and creative ways to work through disagreements and make decisions. Others come to appreciate the role of play and friendship in building bonds of trust and respect that make hard conversations constructive. Still others learn how to discern which battles to pick and which to drop, which moments to speak prophetically and which moments to be pastoral. In all of these hard lessons, staff members gain wisdom that helps them grow out of being "tossed to and fro" and begin to "grow up in every way into him who is the head, Christ."

Becoming Christ's Hands and Feet in the World

> Christ has no body now on earth but yours; no hands but yours; no feet but yours. Yours are the eyes through which the compassion of Christ must look out on the world. Yours are the feet with which He is to go about doing good. Yours are the hands with which He is to bless His people.[8]

St. Teresa reminds us of what is at stake in our formation as Christian leaders. The world requires us to grow into our full membership in the Body of Christ so that this Body, with Christ at the head, can act in the world to bless God's people. YTI and other High School Theology Programs seek to enact ministry with youth that emphasizes community, diversity, empowerment, critical engagement with the Christian tradition, worship, prayer, service, and justice. Yet indirectly, these same practices form and transform the young adults working with teenagers as well. In short, the entire community touched by a High School Theology Program risks transformation, especially young people in the midst of discerning their vocations as Christian leaders with a vision for ministry and for Church. As one staff member commented:

8. This poem is widely attributed to St. Teresa of Avila (1515-1582), but the exact source is unknown.

> For myself, and from the scholars, I learned about what it means to be "church" and worship God as a diverse and conflicted community. Philippians 2:5 says: "In your relationships with one another, have the same mindset as Christ Jesus." Elsewhere Paul also exhorts people to agree and be of like mind. I learned that, although this may be an eschatological hope, there is immense value in the striving.

Sitting as we do, between the "already" of the Kingdom that we taste again and again in our work in these programs, and the "not yet" that painfully reminds us that we still have much to learn, we live in hope that we can indeed be many members of one Body. It is this eschatological hope that our best Christian leaders hold as they go into our churches, our schools, and the world to bless God's people.

CHAPTER THIRTEEN

Teaching in a New Key

The Pedagogical Formation of Theological Faculty

Brent A. Strawn

Not long ago I was asked to speak to a group of donors at my home institution. As a professor of Old Testament, I considered it a privilege to be asked to such a gathering. Normally such a prestigious occasion would give me pause, particularly as I fished about for just the right topic. But I had no qualms in this particular instance. I knew exactly what to talk about and confidently stepped up to the podium as the PowerPoint presentation came to life with my title: "What I Have Learned from High School Students and Linguistics Professors about Teaching the Old Testament at Candler School of Theology."

A few of the donors chuckled, but the title was no joke: teaching in various High School Theology Programs, especially Candler's Youth Theological Initiative (YTI), had transformed not only how I taught my seminary Masters students the Hebrew Scriptures, but also how I thought about my vocation as a teacher. It was not until I taught Old Testament theology to high school students that I recognized the importance of teaching theological language to young people — and that literally, what I was doing as a professor of Old Testament had life and death significance for the church.[1] This insight not only changed the way I approached our donors that morning; it changed, and continues to change, the way I teach seminarians, and has

1. This is not to imply that the future of the church depends on formal theological education. But in the absence of significant systems of theological formation in families, the church, and general culture, formal theological education, for both high school students and seminarians, becomes increasingly significant for catechesis as well.

made teaching the Old Testament to high school students a lifelong passion and priority.

A Bit of Background, an Insight, and a Problem or Two

Background

By the time I joined the faculty at Candler in 2001, YTI was already in its eighth year. Not only was it well established, but it was highly regarded as well. Several of our most senior faculty, including endowed chairs appointed by the university president, taught regularly in the program to great acclaim among the student-scholars and the YTI staff. These faculty members also spoke highly of their experience.[2] In short, teaching in YTI was a *privilege.* I was honored, then, when I was finally asked to teach in the program, an invitation that did not come for several years — further proof that this was a prestigious invitation. I quickly learned firsthand why teaching at YTI was a privilege. YTI calls the students in its program "scholars" for three reasons: (1) YTI carefully selects students with an eagerness to explore theological topics; (2) these students generally possess the maturity to engage in serious theological exploration;[3] and (3) YTI understands their scholars to be doing serious theological work.[4] I was honored to teach these young theologians.[5]

2. These Candler faculty members are not alone. See, among other things, the anecdotes in Carol E. Lytch, "Summary Report I: Strategic Advances in Theological Education: Theological Programs for High School Youth, 1999–2004," *Theological Education* 42 (2006): 1-53, esp. 26-27; and the project director's report for the program at Lutheran Theological Seminary, Gettysburg.

3. See Holly Miller, "Seminary Kids: Summer Theology Programs for Teens Come of Age," *In Trust* (Autumn 2010): 7-10, who notes that one of the success factors in these programs is that "[t]he content of the program needs to be truly challenging so it complements rather than duplicates the Christian formation that teens experience at camp and in their youth groups. . . . Young people are smart, so let's get them to think about God in serious ways" (9). In a review of his experience at YTI, Erik Christensen notes, "Candler understood young people as theological subjects, and not just objects to be moved through a parish Christian Education program" ("What I Learned from Working at YTI and with Young People about Ministry, Faith, and God," unpublished manuscript, p. 1).

4. As a side note, I wonder if it might not be better to call them "theologian-scholars" — or even more directly, "theologians" — to underscore that their theological work is never solely academic-cognitive but consistently and always also reflective-practical.

5. For more on the importance of naming, see Katherine Douglass's contribution in the present volume and Christensen, "What I Learned from Working at YTI," p. 1.

My first talk for YTI was a plenary address on vocation in which I focused on what Old Testament scholars call "prophetic call narratives." Since that first talk I have participated in YTI a number of times, offering smaller one-off electives on vocation and on the "cursing" psalms, as well as delivering longer plenary addresses, some spread over more than one day, introducing the Old Testament prophets, or the Bible and its interpretation. I have also taught on the theology of creation at the Texas Youth Academy, a High School Theology Program hosted by the Texas Annual Conference of the United Methodist Church, which is modeled on Duke Divinity School's high school theology program. These experiences, bolstered by a number of opportunities to address youth ministers directly, have led me to a crucial insight about my teaching.[6]

A Crucial Insight

Although I was the putative teacher in these different programs, it comes as no surprise that I was also learning a number of important lessons along the way. For starters, the high school students were considerably younger than the students I was accustomed to teaching — *considerably* younger, much nearer my children's ages than the age of my usual Masters students. That required some pedagogical innovation on my part: a good bit more energy, a few more jokes, and some other methods to engage and retain the listeners' attention. I made sure I included my usual array of popular culture artifacts in my teaching.[7] But I quickly realized that these changes were mostly matters of rhetorical "icing." The content I was teaching — the "cake," as it were — was largely unchanged from the material I taught on a daily basis at Candler.

This was my critical pedagogical insight: *I was teaching high school stu-*

6. For example, I have taught youth ministers at Princeton Theological Seminary's Institute for Youth Ministry on numerous occasions. Because Princeton's IYM addresses youth ministers rather than youth themselves, it is not a High School Theology Program, though its core pedagogical commitments are strikingly similar.

7. In my judgment, what is important in this practice is not the immediate contemporary currency of the artifact (that is, the *latest* song or movie) but rather its utility as a generative, not just illustrative, example. For further reflections, see Brent A. Strawn, "Contemporary (Pop-)Cultural Contexts and the Old Testament Classroom," in *Contextualizing Theological Education,* ed. Theodore Brelsford and P. Alice Rogers (Cleveland, OH: Pilgrim, 2008), pp. 126-47.

dents the very same material that I taught in my graduate-level seminary classes.[8] I didn't dilute or "dumb-down" the material; I did very little adaptation of content. On the contrary, the materials, the methods, the procedure, and the results were the same, even if the high school programs required more caffeine consumption and caloric expense.

A Cultural Problem

This insight led to a question: Why was I able to use the same material in such seemingly disparate contexts? I began to notice several factors that seemed to be narrowing the generation gap between high school juniors or seniors and first year MDiv students. First, the gap between these two student sets is narrowing in terms of *chronology.* Reflecting the national trend toward younger seminarians, in my own institution the median age of entering MDiv students has been consistently declining (presently the average age is twenty-seven years) compared to when I began teaching fifteen years ago (when the average age was thirty-two years).[9] Despite the fact that they were still, on average, at least ten years older than the youth in the High School Theology Programs, MDiv students nonetheless seemed to be "in reverse" — backing up, as it were, toward the age of high school seniors, shrinking the distance between their respective life experiences.

The generation gap also seems to be closing *culturally,* this time from the high school side of the equation. At the same time that young adults increasingly face developmental tasks once associated with adolescence, media relentlessly exposes high school students to so-called "adult content."[10]

8. I have come to see that the same is true for my adult education classes in churches or in continuing education events (like Princeton's Institute for Youth Ministry). I am happy to note that Ellen F. Davis observes something similar about her own preaching for church groups — namely, that it is basically the same as her preaching in seminary chapel settings (see Ellen F. Davis, *Wondrous Depth: Preaching the Old Testament* [Louisville, KY: Westminster John Knox, 2005]).

9. The average (mean) is less dramatic: 34 years (1998) to 32 years (2012); but the number of under 30 students has changed remarkably. In the fall of 1998 only 28% of the student body was under 30 years of age; in fall 2012, 58% was under 30. Different institutions will have different statistics based on their own populations. See G. Jeffrey MacDonald, "More Young Adults Going into Ministry," *USA Today,* August 8, 2008.

10. For an extended argument on extended adolescence becoming its own life stage, see Jeffrey Arnett, *Emerging Adulthood: The Winding Road from the Late Teens through the Twenties* (New York: Oxford University Press, 2006).

Indeed, the sights of mainstream media culture and consumerist capitalism seem resolutely leveled at both high school and young adult age groups. Marketing campaigns, focused on the key demographic of seventeen-to-thirty-five year olds, draw no distinction between high school, college, graduate school, or no school — and while these age groups have different ways of processing cultural experiences, their cultural exposure is strikingly similar. High school students and young adults watch virtually the same movies and TV shows, play the same video games, buy the same products, and listen to the same music. In this way, thanks in large part to marketing, consumerism, and global media culture, teenagers and young adults in North America are having similar cultural experiences, making it seem as though high school students are on "fast forward," moving toward the beliefs, attitudes, and values of young adult seminarians.

A third factor played a role in the similarities of these two student sets: neither high school students nor seminarians had much exposure to theological formation before coming to Candler.[11] Long gone are the days when most seminary students arrived on campus with prior undergraduate training in religion, philosophy, theology, and the Bible. Such students are now the rare exception. Practically speaking, this means that much graduate theological education must be pitched at an undergraduate level. No wonder I could teach the same content to high school youth theology participants that I taught to adult seminarians. Given the proliferation of college credit courses at the high school level, even pitching material to advanced undergraduates is not terribly different from teaching high school seniors.

Teaching the Hebrew Scriptures to HSTP participants brought me face-to-face with a growing problem that every seminary educator must address sooner or later: the students I was teaching lacked any sort of sufficient grounding, background, and theological foundations to apprehend the subject matter at hand. While previous generations might have received catechesis in their families and congregations, or gleaned rudimentary theological tools from undergraduate religion programs, I could not assume that my students had a basic familiarity with the Bible, theology, or Christianity in my teaching. I had to teach these basics, and somehow embed them in

11. The low priority that parents and congregations place on the serious religious formation of young people in North America is well documented. Naturally, this has an effect on the amount of theological familiarity students have when they enter seminary as well. Cf. Christian Smith and Melinda Lunquist Denton, *Soul Searching: The Spiritual and Religious Lives of American Teenagers* (New York: Oxford University Press, 2005), which summarizes the first findings of the ongoing National Study of Youth and Religion.

all the other goals I was trying to accomplish in my classes or my talks. This problem changed the content I taught, and the reasons I was teaching it.

A Pedagogical Problem

The insight that I was teaching the same content to YTI scholars and seminarians brought me face-to-face with the dark underbelly of the closing generation gap between these two groups of students. The problem is simply this: the students I was working with — in *both* groups, I hasten to add — lacked the tools necessary to grapple meaningfully with the subjects we were studying. This came as no great surprise in the case of the high school students; one would not expect them to be thoroughly prepared for formal theological education. Yet it is common for seminary faculties to lament a lack of biblical or theological grounding among their seminary students. My experience teaching the Hebrew Scriptures to high school juniors forced me to rethink the way I taught my seminary students. If I am not surprised by a high school student's lack of formation in theological matters, and if the generation gap between the two cohorts has been narrowed if not altogether eliminated, then why should I be surprised that seminary students are similarly un(der)formed?

This question is clearly a pedagogical one and could reflect a self-obsessed concern with how all this affects the teacher (namely, *me* as teacher). And while that concern is not altogether irrelevant, the real issue when it comes to pedagogy proper is not just the pedagogue's teaching, but the students' *learning*. The question of pedagogy becomes far more interesting and pressing when we consider it from the students' side of the lectern. If students of any age are un(der)formed in some parts of the subject matter, how does that fact impact my teaching — and how does it impact the teaching of theology more generally — as teachers try to maximize student learning?

I had begun to worry about the theological inexperience of our YTI students, somewhat inchoately, even before my first experience teaching in YTI; somehow the issue bubbled up here and there in reports from various YTI directors or from faculty colleagues who had taught in the program. Specifically, I became concerned that our curriculum at YTI — and perhaps seminary generally — might be overly dominated by a pedagogy of questioning and critique. Such a pedagogical approach is certainly not bad; quite to the contrary, it has particular merit for educating those who (like adolescents) are without voice in our culture.[12] Yet without serious formation in a faith tradition, I worried that emphasizing pedagogies of critique might actually undercut YTI scholars' connection to their faith traditions. More worrisome still, I wondered if such an approach could short-circuit theologically inexperienced teenagers' very identification with or commitment to their faith.

To be clear, pedagogies of critique do not prevent the kind of questions that arise naturally to help us obtain important information, or that critically engage a learner and her subject matter. What concerned me was the effect that questions aimed at deconstruction might have on students who lacked deep formation in a faith tradition. For example, before one can raise critical questions about the Trinity and its attestation (or lack thereof) in the pages of Scripture, one needs to have at least some sense of who the Trinity is, what theologians and churches mean by it, and some desire to explore it. By assuming our students were prepared to deal critically with their faith traditions, I worried that we were effectively eviscerating something that was not completely there to begin with. Could a pedagogy based primarily on questioning and critique end up becoming a pedagogy of total eradication? Certainly, exterminating faith should not be the goal of a High School Theology Program! Students' foundations may need to be shaken, but a foundation cannot be shaken if there is nothing to shake.

My largely speculative worries on this matter were confirmed to some degree in that first plenary address on vocation for YTI. It was clear that much of what I was assuming these students would know, given their careful selection as serious-minded young theologians, could not be assumed. Even with extra caffeine, more calorie exertion, and a steady stream of jokes, a good number of my points seemed to miss their mark. To put the situation in terms of the alphabet, I couldn't responsibly teach the letters Q-R-S, let alone T-U-V, because many of my students were still at A-B-C or C-D-E.

But of course they were! How could it be otherwise? There was no problem with sixteen-year-olds being at A-B-C or C-D-E; that was normal and to be expected. I, on the other hand, had several problems: (1) I did not expect the degree of theological under-preparedness that our young people exhibited; (2) I was teaching at L-M-N (or somewhere past A-B-C

12. Critical pedagogy is, in fact, the foundation of YTI's educational approach. Cf. Paolo Friere's *Pedagogy of the Oppressed,* 30th anniversary edition, trans. Myra Bergman Ramos (New York: Bloomsbury Academic, 2000) and Thomas Groome's "shared praxis approach" to Christian education, outlined in *Christian Religious Education: Sharing Our Story and Vision* (San Francisco: Jossey-Bass, 1999).

or C-D-E); and (3) worst of all, I was getting tricky and suggesting to these students that the order might be better N-L-M, or in terms closer to their letters at least, B-E-C-D-A. Safe to say, I was not connecting with the high school students; I had yet to establish some common ground, some common language, before things could get fancy, let alone tricky. And then I wondered about the seminarians I taught all year long: had I failed to connect with them as well?

Firsthand confirmation of my earlier concerns led me to rethink some fundamental matters when it came to my subsequent teaching at YTI — a reorientation that, not surprisingly, turned out to be just as important for successfully teaching my seminary students. I started to reconsider the categories of catechism and criticism, and their interrelationship, as well as their applicability to different student sets. Ironically, I found help for this task, not from educators, but from — surprisingly — linguistic professors. Before I discuss the categories of catechism, criticism, and their interrelation, a brief digression is in order to explain.

The Lifecycle of a "Language"

During this period, to pass time on my commute, I listened to John McWhorter's lectures on human language.[13] As a young person under the spell of fantasy writers like J. R. R. Tolkien, Ursula K. LeGuin, and Patricia A. McKillip, I had long been fascinated with the power of language — a fascination that eventually led to college and graduate work in biblical and Near Eastern languages.[14] But training in language is not the same as training in linguistics, and inadvertently McWhorter opened up a whole new way to explain the way the biblical canon functioned (or failed to function) in the lives of students who had had only a modicum of Christian formation.

On my way to teach Interpretation of the Old Testament to first-year MDiv students, I was stewing on McWhorter's lectures on the lifecycle of dying languages. Suddenly several things came together for me with regard to the general decline of the use of the Old Testament in North American Chris-

13. In many ways, that course is an oral version of his book *The Power of Babel: A Natural History of Language* (New York: Perennial, 2001). This is just one of McWhorter's many writings on linguistics, but it remains the most general introduction to the wider field of human language and linguistics.

14. For Tolkien, see *The Hobbit* and *The Lord of the Rings;* for LeGuin, her *Wizard of Earthsea* cycle; for McKillip, the *Riddle-Master of Hed* trilogy.

tianity.[15] I suddenly saw an analogy between McWhorter's thesis and the way the Old Testament tends to function for twenty-first century North American Christians. The major breakthrough came in suddenly seeing the decline of the Old Testament analogically, through the lens of the language lifecycle.

It does not take long for a language to die — it can happen in a single generation, twenty to forty years. Languages die for one simple reason: lack of living speakers. A key sign of morbidity is when only the elderly speak a language. Crucial for the ongoing life of a language, then, is the existence of plenty of young speakers: parents with young children who actively teach their children the language for regular, productive use, not just passive recognition.[16]

If one thinks of the Old Testament metaphorically as a language, then it follows that the Hebrew Scriptures (or, if you will, the entire Bible, or even Christian faith as a whole) can be spoken fluently or haltingly. Even more to the point, this language can be learned — indeed, *must* be learned — if it is not to be lost altogether. Like any human language, the theological language that Christians call the canon of Scripture can die. Once a language dies, it is almost impossible to bring it back. Indeed, linguists have only one success story of saving or revitalizing a dead language. Happily, that success story is directly related to the Old Testament since the language in question is Hebrew, the original tongue of the Hebrew Bible, what Christians call the Old Testament.[17]

The resurrection of the Hebrew language notwithstanding, in my judgment the Old Testament is very sick. It seems that in many pockets of North American Christianity, the Old Testament is dying, which means that in some cases, among some communities, or for some individuals, it simply may be too late to save it.[18] In the absence of communities that immerse

15. A fuller treatment of this theme, with further engagement with linguistics, may be found in Brent A. Strawn, *The Old Testament Is Dying: A Diagnosis and Recommended Treatment* (Grand Rapids: Baker Academic, 2014).

16. For more on language death, see McWhorter, *The Power of Babel,* pp. 253-86; David Crystal, *Language Death* (Cambridge: Cambridge University Press, 2000); and Claude Hagège, *On the Death and Life of Languages,* trans. Jody Gladding (New Haven, CT: Yale University Press, 2009 [French orig.: 2000]). In light of the above comments about young people's experience with mass media consumer culture, it is worth noting that many of the world's living languages are presently endangered precisely due to factors like globalization and urbanization.

17. See Crystal, *Language Death,* chapter 5.

18. I would define the death of the Old Testament as the point at which it ceases to function in healthy ways as sacred, authoritative, canonical literature in the lives of contemporary Christians (see Crystal, *Language Death,* chapter 1). I explore this theme in more detail in Strawn, *The Old Testament Is Dying,* esp. chapters 2 and 4.

young people in the narratives of the Old Testament, very soon there will be no fluent Old Testament "speakers." And if and when the Old Testament dies, the New Testament will not be far behind, even if it takes a bit longer. And if Christian Scripture dies as a living language that is "spoken here," one might well wonder what, if anything, will remain of Christianity, which is, among other things, one of the great book religions. But what is a book religion without a book?[19]

This prospect is not merely a speculative academic exercise. The loss of theological language among young people is a much-lamented theme in youth ministry research, and practices that foster "religious articulacy" in young people have received new attention in recent years.[20] To put the linguistics and my disciplinary specialty together and make the point more

19. I do not, of course, mean to say that Christianity is only about the book or coterminous with the study of Scripture, though I think that the centrality of the book (above all in Protestantism) is a rather important matter that simply cannot be skirted. Even so, I do not want to give the impression that Christianity is solely a matter of literature and reading or language and speech. In the case of the latter, my analogical or metaphorical use of language should be clear to the reader. I am well aware of criticisms concerning any sort of "linguistic reductionism" of Christian faith (let alone doctrine per se) and do not want to be guilty of such reductionism myself. I would highlight the embodied nature of all language (even the metaphorical variety!) and, to extend my metaphor, emphasize that the "language" of Christian faith is "spoken" not just with the vocal cords but nonverbally, with the body, in actions, and within larger communities, including the community of faith with its corporate language(s) and body (bodies) within the larger world.

20. The absence of theological language in American young people, even those raised in religious traditions, is a key finding of the National Study of Youth and Religion (cf. Christian Smith with Melinda Lundquist Denton, *Soul Searching: The Religious and Spiritual Lives of American Teenagers* [New York: Oxford University Press, 2005]). For more on relationship between faith practices that cultivate religious language and faith identity, cf. Stanley Hauerwas, *Working with Words: On Learning to Speak Christian* (Eugene, OR: Wipf and Stock, 2011); in response to the National Study of Youth and Religion, cf. Kenda Creasy Dean, *Almost Christian: What the Faith of Our Teenagers Is Telling the American Church* (New York: Oxford University Press, 2011). The importance of testimony, the arts, and social media in helping young people develop faith articulacy has been the subject of several recent dissertations, including Amanda Drury, "I Have Seen and I Testify: An Articulacy Theory of Testimony in Adolescent Spiritual Development," unpublished dissertation (Princeton, NJ: Princeton Theological Seminary, 2013) and Katherine Douglass, "The Transformative Role of the Arts in the Faith Lives of Young Adults," unpublished dissertation (Princeton, NJ: Princeton Theological Seminary, 2013). Reclaiming religious articulacy is also a key strategy of Eboo Patel's Interfaith Youth Core, which sponsors presidentially recognized efforts to foster interfaith cooperation by helping young people talk deeply and honestly about their faith traditions (see http://www.ifyc.org/; accessed October 3, 2013).

clearly: the Old Testament is doomed if there are no children, no youth, no young adults who can speak it. But perhaps there remains yet some slender hope. If linguists could successfully resuscitate the Hebrew language, perhaps it is possible to resurrect the language of the Old Testament, of the Bible generally, and of the broader language of faith. If linguists are right, if this happens, it will need to begin with children, youth, and young adults.

This slender hope, along with the urgency suggested by the data on language death, made my teaching of high school students suddenly and remarkably fraught. I saw almost immediately that the stakes were as high as possible, the matter quite literally one of life and death — for the Old Testament, and for the Christian faith. I could see with new clarity how the "language" I was teaching was under serious threat, facing imminent extinction. Both high school and seminary students were un(der)formed in the language of the Bible and the language of faith. If they did not learn the language at an early stage of their formation, full fluency (a difficult achievement, even in the best case) was almost certainly out of reach. The only things preventing that untimely demise would be (1) the cultivation of living speakers, especially young ones;[21] and (2) the cultivation of teachers who would teach these youth how to speak, then how to read, then how to produce meaningful sentences — and then how to communicate efficiently, complexly, deftly, and artistically until finally they dream in the language of Scripture.[22]

Catechism and Criticism

The problem of language death inspired me, to say the least, and reignited my passion about why I teach, why early learners are so important, and why

21. The sentiment expressed by some faculty at Catholic Theological Union at the prospects of a youth theology program — namely, "[w]e have no business teaching theology to teenagers. We are a graduate level school of theology" — is tragic at this point. Happily, that sentiment was overturned by experience with the youth such that later, faculty and staff alike spoke of being "transformed" by their work in this program. See Lytch, "Summary Report I": 26-27.

22. See n. 20 above on the embodied nature of language. I would add two clarifying remarks about the "dreaming" in question: (1) First, it is often said that one does not really know or has not fully mastered a language until one dreams in it. That may not be accurate, but the point is that the dreaming above is not a "pipe dream" or case of "imagination" but proof of deep, thorough mastery. (2) Second, ever since Freud and his discovery of the unconscious and the import of dreams in revealing it, psychoanalysts have noted the close connections between dreams and deepest desires. Once again, then, the dreaming-in-Scripture is not fantasizing but reflective of the deepest imaginable engagement with the faith.

I should say "yes" to teach in any High School Theology Program that would have me.[23] The lessons from linguistics also gelled with my earlier insight on teaching the same content to different student sets and helped explain why that was the case — namely, because both groups were developmentally early in their language learning. But linguistics also provided additional handholds on the problems posed by my students' state of un(der)formation. No one is born knowing a language. Instead, people must *learn* languages, and they typically learn them in intimate settings (with caregivers — parents, siblings, extended family), over long stretches of time, in bits and pieces, with practice and mistakes along the way. In addition, concrete strategies exist for helping children learn to speak, read, write, and compose.[24]

My foray into linguistics brought me back to my conundrum about using critical questioning pedagogies with the students of YTI — or with seminarians, for that matter. The analogical application of these strategies for teaching language to teaching the Old Testament specifically (or Christian faith, more generally) are legion, and I do not have time to unpack them here. But here is one rather important obvious observation (among many): children have to learn basic phonology before they can speak, let alone before they can analyze morphosyntax or Chomsky's theory of Universal Grammar. In terms of the High School Theology Programs, before we question or teach to question, we must help young people lay down some basic groundwork. Before we can critique, we must catechize. In linguistic terms, language learners need instruction in the fundamentals before they can write metered verse. Or, in the terms I used earlier: the foundations must be poured before they can be shaken or reshaped.

This argument is hardly novel and seems like garden variety common sense. But it was my first experiences in YTI and my concurrent thinking about linguistics that helped solidify my opinion that catechesis was as im-

23. Such urgency reaches beyond even the HSTPs. That is, if the Old Testament language is truly endangered, then almost everyone (no matter their age or life stage) is an early language learner; this raises the stakes in any teaching setting, be it ecclesial or seminary based.

24. See, among other items, Patsy M. Lightbrown and Nina Spada, *How Languages Are Learned,* 3rd ed. (Oxford: Oxford University Press, 2006); Jack C. Richards and Theodore S. Rodgers, *Approaches and Methods in Language Teaching: A Description and Analysis* (Cambridge: Cambridge University Press, 1986); Alison J. Elliot, *Child Language* (Cambridge: Cambridge University Press, 1981); and Barbara Lust, *Child Language: Acquisition and Growth* (Cambridge: Cambridge University Press, 2006). For the full analogy between language acquisition and the Old Testament, see Strawn, *The Old Testament Is Dying.*

portant as criticism — or, rather, to put it more boldly, that catechesis was, if push came to shove, far more important than criticism within the HSTPs. Ideally, catechesis and criticism proceed together in something of a feedback loop or, to shift metaphors, a complex and intricate partner dance. Without the groundwork of catechesis, questions and criticism make little sense and can do more harm than good. Criticism will not teach the language because it is not designed to provide basic instruction in the initial stages of the language that are so crucial for all subsequent learning and for higher levels of thought.

To be sure, catechesis makes some people nervous, especially when young people are in view.[25] Catechesis (in Latin, the word means "oral instruction") is sometimes confused with heavy-handed or manipulative religious formation; hence, the negative valences of "indoctrination," especially when it comes to children. But such misuse need not accompany catechesis. It is not difficult to argue that every human community, in all sorts of tasks and cultural projects (if not in every one), participates in basic oral instruction — i.e., catechesis — of a kind.[26] Indeed, to return to the linguistic analogy, this is the way we learn a culture's "language" — we study the culture's ABCs before launching into iambic pentameter. Requiring a young person to know the alphabet is definitely instructional, and in literate societies, it is necessary to participate in higher order forms of cultural reflection.[27] Rather than being coterminous with oppressive brainwashing, catechesis in this light becomes an essential building block for intelligent engagement with one's culture and, indeed, one's faith.

As categories of learning, then, catechesis and criticism must proceed together. That is partly because of those we are teaching: youth will question — it is part of who they are and where they are in life. Even the biblical

25. One notes the recent criticisms leveled against religion on the subject of child adherents in New Atheist writers like Richard Dawkins, *The God Delusion* (New York: Mariner Books, 2006), pp. 349-87.

26. Cf. the analogical arguments about the ubiquity of worship and gratitude, even in secular modes, in James K. A. Smith, *Desiring the Kingdom: Worship, Worldview, and Cultural Formation* (Grand Rapids: Baker Academic, 2009); and George Steiner, *Real Presences* (Chicago: University of Chicago Press, 1991).

27. Educational theorists often refer to this progression using the so-called "Bloom's Taxonomy," a schemata developed by educational psychologist Benjamin Bloom (*Taxonomy of Educational Objectives* [Boston: Allyn and Bacon, 1956]) that contributed to the theory of mastery learning. Bloom understood learning to occur in three domains (cognitive, affective, and psychomotor) with higher levels of learning (analyzing, evaluating, creating) depending on lower level forms of knowledge and skills (remembering, understanding, applying).

writers recognized the inquisitive nature of children, and sought to prepare the community to receive these questions. The book of Deuteronomy, for example, advises:

> When your children ask you in time to come, "What is the meaning of the decrees and statutes and ordinances that the Lord our God has commanded you?" then you shall say to your children, "We were Pharaoh's slaves in Egypt, but the Lord brought us out of Egypt with a mighty hand. The Lord displayed before our eyes great and awesome signs and wonders against Egypt, and against Pharaoh and his household. He brought us out from there in order to bring us in, to give us the land that he promised on oath to our ancestors. Then the Lord commanded us to observe all these statutes, to fear the Lord our God, for our lasting good, so as to keep us alive, as is now the case. If we diligently observe this entire commandment before the Lord our God, as he has commanded, we will be in the right." (Deut. 6:20-25)

At the same time, we are well aware of problems that surface whenever catechesis and criticism do *not* proceed together — problems, say, when a catechism is not sufficiently self-critical, or when we attempt critique without first building a catechetical scaffolding to stand on in the process of deconstruction. We know that the best catechisms — not to mention the biblical canon and the Christian faith writ large — are the result of long, protracted, centuries-long discussions, often intense and certainly critical.[28] Many catechisms reflect this history and include a critical element by adopting a question-answer structure.

In the end, these issues led me to develop a plenary session for YTI that would, I hoped, include key moments of basic Bible instruction (catechesis)

28. Cf. Berard L. Marthaler, *The Catechism Yesterday and Today: The Evolution of a Genre* (Collegeville, MN: Liturgical, 1995) on catechisms; and, for the Bible, Morton Smith, *Palestinian Parties and Politics that Shaped the Old Testament,* 2nd ed. (Philadelphia: SCM/Trinity Press International, 1988); Susan E. Gillingham, *One Bible, Many Voices: Different Approaches to Biblical Studies* (Grand Rapids: Eerdmans, 1999); and Israel Knohl, *The Divine Symphony: The Bible's Many Voices* (Philadelphia: Jewish Publication Society, 2003). Note also Walter Brueggemann, *The Creative Word: Canon as a Model for Biblical Education* (Philadelphia: Fortress, 1982) for the way the Old Testament canon conjoins fundamental material (Torah) with material that draws such material out into new and different settings, often in critical mode (the Prophets and the Writings). I thank Fred Edie for bringing this connection to my attention.

along with moments of more advanced instruction (criticism). I entitled the talk "Twelve Theses on the Bible and Its Interpretation." It was designed to take students from a fundamental starting point about the place of the Bible within Christian faith and practice, all the way into higher-order reflection on the nature of Scripture *qua* Scripture. The twelve theses are as follows:

- Thesis 1:
  Christianity is a book religion.
- Thesis 2:
  The Bible's "bookishness" means it must be read and studied.
- Thesis 3:
  For the Bible to be practiced, it must be made usable and relevant now; it must not only be read (Thesis 2), but also interpreted.
- Thesis 4:
  Interpreting the Bible is not easy and is almost always debated — sometimes hotly.
- Thesis 5:
  Many disciplines have arisen to assist in the process of interpretation.
- Thesis 6:
  Where one begins matters (Part 1): One's priorities impinge on one's interpretation and can lead to different readings.
- Thesis 7:
  Interpretation requires adjudication.
- Thesis 8:
  Interpretation involves "stuff" besides the text at hand.
- Thesis 9:
  Personal, existential, transformative (i.e., "theological") engagement with Scripture marks the kind of interpretation that matters most for the church and the world.
- Thesis 10:
  The Christian Bible is made up of two equally important parts.
- Thesis 11:
  Where one begins matters (Part 2): One's understanding of the Bible's macro-genre is definitive.
- Thesis 12:
  The genre of Holy Scripture is . . . Holy Scripture.

Space does not permit an explication of the theses here, but three points are important to understand their design. First, I intentionally called these statements "theses," not "axioms." Axioms are self-evident and require no additional proof; theses, on the other hand, are by definition contestable. By calling these twelve statements "theses," then, I am already signaling that the *catechetical* work they are doing is subject to discussion and debate, which is to say, *criticism.* Criticism is also explicitly built into the twelve theses at various points, especially in theses 3, 4, and 7 (which concern the contested nature of interpretation); thesis 5 (where I introduce some of the major methods in biblical criticism), and theses 6-8 (which treat the important role of the interpreter, additional material that impinges on interpretation, and decision-making). The twelve theses are catechetical, but not without criticism; and they are critical, but not without catechesis.

Second, this plenary session of YTI afforded me the opportunity to work up a tight sequence that, while not above criticism (by design), has nevertheless proved helpful in introducing students to the Bible in catechetical and critical ways. I never would have developed this sequence if not for YTI and the crucial (re)thinking it caused me to do about catechesis and criticism, coupled with a concern for early language learners.

The third point is that the twelve theses have proven so effective that I now regularly use them as the first unit in my introduction to Old Testament classes at Candler. I have come full circle, then: I started teaching high school students the same content I teach to seminarians; I now teach seminarians the same thing that I originally taught to high school students. This "same thing," however, is something that I was only able to develop because of my teaching in YTI. Teaching in a High School Theology Program, therefore, has fundamentally reshaped my thinking about seminary teaching. I cannot imagine ever again teaching an introduction to Old Testament class without thinking about catechesis, which is the lesson I learned from YTI.

Conclusion

Catechize. Critique. Repeat.

That is one way to summarize what I have learned from teaching in High School Theology Programs. On the one hand, there is nothing earth-shattering here. And yet, setting the task of teaching biblical material in an interdisciplinary context, especially beside linguists studying language death, invests our theological task with more urgency.

In the words of the noted literary critic George Steiner, *"Language is the main instrument of [hu]man[ity]'s refusal to accept the world as it is."*[29] Steiner's words explain why catechism and criticism are so important when it comes to learning the language of Scripture and faith, especially among seventeen- to thirty-five-year-olds. How can those new to the world — whether they are young in years, or just novices in learning — resist what needs to be resisted if they lack a language to do so? They will be at a disadvantage, if not altogether incapable of "refusing to accept the world as it is," in the face of the onslaught of messages offered to them twenty-four hours a day, 365 days a year, in all possible media, and to every sense perception.

Catechesis can help, of course, but it is hardly foolproof, especially if it is of an inflexible and short-sighted variety — the kind that strands believers from eighteen to eighty with nothing more than a third- or fourth-grade theology. If television allows young people to switch from the Disney Junior channel or the Sprout network to more "adult" content — and if the church does not — then we have already communicated to young people that faith is an infantile pursuit.[30] In my judgment, the Christian Church has a desperate need for "grown-up" Christians who can think in complex theological ways about the world and its adult content; if such complex reflection is absent, then Christians are in fact (especially without a language of resistance) simply passively ingesting, accepting, and thereby learning to speak this worldly language — natively! In different words, what the Christian Church needs are dexterous linguists, speakers fluent in faith.

According to Stanley Hauerwas, "To learn to be a Christian, to learn the discipline of the faith, is not just similar to learning another language. It *is* learning another language."[31] If so, the literature on both second language acquisition and religious literacy suggests that there are crucial windows of opportunity in this task.[32] None is more crucial than the youth of the

29. George Steiner, *After Babel: Aspects of Language and Translation,* 3rd ed. (Oxford: Oxford University Press, 1998), p. 228 (his emphasis).

30. The high school students know this too. A young woman in the Catholic Theological Union told the staff: "Whatever you do, please don't give us the Fisher-Price version of theology" (Lytch, "Summary Report I": 26).

31. Stanley Hauerwas, *Working with Words: On Learning to Speak Christianly* (Eugene, OR: Wipf and Stock, 2011), p. 87.

32. For language acquisition, see Wolfgang Klein, *Second Language Acquisition* (Cambridge: Cambridge University Press, 1986); Lydia White, *Second Language Acquisition and Universal Grammar* (Cambridge: Cambridge University Press, 2003); and Jürgen M. Meisel, *First and Second Language Acquisition: Parallels and Differences* (Cambridge: Cambridge University Press, 2011). For religious literacy, see the Pew Forum on Religion and Public Life, *U.S. Religious Knowledge Survey,* September 2010 (Washington, DC: Pew Research Center,

learner. Any faculty member who refuses to teach early language learners (of any age) — any seminary professor content with bemoaning bygone days in "graduate" theological education while delving further into ever more arcane sub-specialties — should not be surprised when the student body dwindles and the institution dries up. That is what happens when languages die. Those of us who refuse to teach the language to those who are young enough to learn it fluently have done nothing but accelerate the demise of our language of faith.

"Let those with ears to hear listen to what the Spirit is saying to the churches." [33]

2010); online at http://www.pewforum.org/uploadedFiles/Topics/Belief_and_Practices/religious-knowledge-full-report.pdf (accessed February 7, 2013); Stephen Prothero, *Religious Literacy: What Every American Needs to Know — and Doesn't* (New York: HarperOne, 2008); and Christian Smith with Melinda Lundquist Denton, *Soul Searching: The Religious and Spiritual Lives of American Teenagers* (Oxford: Oxford University Press, 2009).

33. Revelation 2:7, 11, 17, 29; 3:6, 13, 22.

CHAPTER FOURTEEN

Hitting It Out of the Park

Why Churches Needs Farm Teams

Kenda Creasy Dean

> *If you want to build a ship, don't drum up people to collect wood and don't assign tasks and work, but rather teach them to long for the endless immensity of the sea.*
>
> ANTOINE DE SAINT-EXUPÉRY, *Citadelle* (1948)

If Branch Rickey had been a theological educator, he would have been intensely interested in High School Theology Programs. We now think of Rickey as a Harrison Ford creation from the movie *42*. But W. Branch Rickey, the ardently Methodist (W. stood for "Wesley") baseball manager who in 1945 signed Jackie Robinson to the Brooklyn Dodgers, changed modern baseball. Signing Robinson may have been the most revolutionary thing Rickey did, but he also invented batting cages, pitching machines, and batting helmets, was the first to track player statistics, and — always a sucker for young talent — was the first manager in baseball history to develop a farm team. Rickey had coached college baseball at Allegheny College and Ohio Wesleyan University when his own playing career tanked, and he knew that a ball club was only as good as the depth of its young talent. So he invented the farm team system, a strategy designed to deepen the pool of young players who could step into professional-level baseball, ready to play. By aligning Minor League clubs with Major League franchises like the St. Louis Cardinals and the Brooklyn Dodgers, Rickey could corral and refine young, passionate players for his teams' futures.

The farm system allowed Rickey to create baseball dynasties. As other teams began copying Rickey's methods, it became obvious that ball clubs with farm systems did far better than clubs without them. Today, every Major League team has a farm system, a set of affiliated lower-level teams that invest in promising young players by giving them experience, practice, and highly invested teammates while grooming them to become Major League players.[1]

Farm teams do not cultivate talent; they cultivate readiness. Talent is assumed in every player who plays on a farm team; these players already know baseball and have a sense of what their particular abilities — already noticed and named by others — contribute. The point of the farm team is to groom young players with noticeable potential and an unquenchable passion for the game for the moment when their particular gifts and passions are called for by the Major League parent team. Playing for a farm team gives players already hooked on baseball access to coaches, training, and practical experience, as well as a community of similarly impassioned teammates who understand what it means to feel like baseball is a calling.

The Minor Leagues of Church Leadership

Just as Minor League baseball existed before Rickey co-opted it as a training ground for the Majors, "farm systems" for theological leadership existed long before the Lilly Endowment gathered youth ministers and professors teaching youth ministry to invent High School Theology Programs. For several generations, confirmation programs, church camps, volunteer corps, and denominational youth leadership organizations all gave spiritually curious teenagers opportunities to deepen their affinity for the church and to cultivate a readiness for Christian leadership. These programs were seldom teenagers' first introduction to faith; for the most part, teenagers who entered these programs had already been exposed to Christianity at home or in a local congregation, and consequently they already had a rudimentary faith vocabulary and, sometimes, deep theological curiosity. Often, their potential for Christian leadership had already been noticed. Done well, these youth programs served — and still serve — as greenhouses for vocational readiness. Done poorly, they served — and still serve — as colossal wasted opportunities.

1. Cf. "1942: Home Grown Champions," *This Great Game* (2014), http://www.thisgreatgame.com/1942-baseball-history.html (accessed August 8, 2014).

Take church camp, for example. Wayne Meisel, Director of the Center for Faith and Service at McCormick Theological Seminary, describes Christian camps as "the minor leagues for church membership and leadership" because these camps inspire, identify, and train young people as church leaders.[2] Thousands of young people find Christian community more palpable — and their gifts more utilized — in the course of summer camp than in their congregations or youth groups, and for these young people, camp becomes "the new church." Meisel's assessment is borne out by a 2013 Presbyterian Church (USA) survey reporting that 43 percent of PCUSA pastors say their most significant "spiritual experience" happened at a camp, retreat, or conference (compared to about one-fourth of their parishioners, who were more likely to have significant spiritual experiences in congregations). More than three out of four church leaders, both lay and ordained, identified camps as either "important" or "very important" for developing Christian young adults as leaders, even declaring their "highest priority" to be providing camp scholarships to new members (a statement that seems to reflect more hope than action, given Presbyterian camps' recent difficulties in garnering dollars and participants).[3]

Another oft-cited training ground for Christian leadership are denominational volunteer corps. Catholics are among those making use of such ministries for leadership formation; a 2013 survey of alumni from Catholic volunteer service organizations called "volunteering for a year of service in a faith-based volunteer service organization . . . a next step in a young adult's [vocational] discernment process."[4] The study found that volunteer service years both attract those already interested in ministry (77 percent considered ordained ministry or religious life prior to participating in a volunteer service year) and serve as important contexts for ongoing vocational

2. Wayne Meisel, "Where Faith Still Thrives: Summer Camps and the Future of the Church," *The Huffington Post* (May 23, 2014), http://www.huffingtonpost.com/wayne-meisel/where-faith-still-thrives_b_5379846.html (accessed August 9, 2014).

3. PCUSA Camps and Conference Ministries, "Spiritual Growth Experiences and Church Retreats," *The Presbyterian Panel* (May 2012), http://www.pcusa.org/site_media/media/uploads/research/pdfs/may_2012_panel_report_camps_and_conference_centers,pdf.pdf (accessed August 9, 2014).

4. Center for Applied Research in the Apostolate, "Special Report: Nurturing Vocations to Religious Life and Priesthood: The Impact of a Volunteer Service Year," Spring 2014 (Washington, DC: Georgetown University), p. 6, http://cara.georgetown.edu/Publications/NurturingVocations.pdf (accessed August 9, 2014). It should be noted that the Catholic use of the term "vocation" to mean specifically ordained or lay ecclesial service is more restrictive than the definition used by HSTPs.

discernment (nearly half continued to discern a call to religious vocation during volunteer service years).[5] Twice as many Catholic women and more than ten times as many Catholic men seek ordination, attend seminary, or serve in church leadership roles after a volunteer service year than those without this experience.

While youth ministries like camps and service corps have long sought to deepen young people's faith — and while the vocational influence of such programs can be profound — this formation is also sporadic. It is more often the result of a fortuitous combination of volunteer leaders than a coordinated curricular effort, suggesting that church leaders are either unaware of these ministries' genius for encouraging vocational discernment, or are uncertain why it matters. Whether these experiences are substantive, intentional, abundant, or compelling enough to create deep pools rather than puddles of young talent is unclear. Nor is it clear whether the "Major Leagues" of Christian vocational formation — congregations, denominations, and theological schools — are prepared to make room for this young talent when it appears.

High School Theology Programs build on existing youth ministry programs but add both intentionality and curricular support to the task of vocational discernment. Most youth leave the womb of a High School Theology Program thinking of themselves as leaders in their congregations and communities, and they re-enter their home congregations with high expectations for contributing there (as we saw in chapter 6, the degree to which churches welcome these contributions varies widely).

High School Theology Programs differ from farm teams in two important respects, however. First, unlike the minor leagues, High School Theology Programs do not view themselves as preparatory holding tanks for future players. High School Theology Program leaders are steadfast in their insistence that young people are the church of *right now* and not just tomorrow: every HSTP impresses on teenagers that the church re-

5. The effect continues after the service year. Controlling for gender in Catholic volunteer alumni, 7% of women have "very seriously" considered a religious vocation, compared to 2% of never married Catholic women in general. Among men, 19% of alumni have "very seriously" considered a religious vocation, compared to 3% of never married Catholic men. See Center for Applied Research in the Apostolate, "Special Report." Protestants report similar effects, though research connecting volunteer service and vocation in these programs is scarce. One exception is Life Together, an Episcopalian intentional community network in Boston, serving young people in the Episcopal Service Corps; the Rev. Arrington Chambliss, Executive Director. See http://www.lifetogethercommunity.org/contact-us (accessed July 31, 2012).

quires their leadership *immediately,* and that youth, not their managers, decide that they are ready to enter the game. Second, unlike farm teams that prepare players for baseball's established roles, High School Theology Program leaders encourage switch-hitting and experimentation; the roles their alumni will play in the church are unknown, and "hacking" the system is encouraged.

Now What?

What theological educators learn about vocational formation from this conversation depends significantly on how we choose to use the findings in this book. You could read these pages in a number of ways: as a handbook, as an indictment, or as a mirror. These vantage points are useful in different ways.

A Handbook: Field Guide for Better Pedagogy

The obvious way to use this book is as a pedagogical resource. High School Theology Programs serve as proving grounds for experiential, embodied, personally invested, and communal learning as effective means for handing on living arts like Christian discipleship, where social modeling and existential openness are as critical to learning as understanding content.

What could this mean for untangling some of the wicked problems facing theological education? What would it look like, for instance, if theological content were used — unapologetically — to evoke experiences of liminality, competence, holy struggle, and belonging because these experiences are so closely aligned with vocational transformation? Would church leaders lead differently if seminaries were cultures of mentoring, or if preparing for ministry required immersion in pilgrimages, intentional disruption, service, and the arts? How would divinity schools change if the theological curriculum openly addressed, not only students who have answered a "call," but students who are still wondering if they have one?

Of course, many theological educators already attend to these nuances. Take, for example, the growing commitment to culturally responsive pedagogies — a top priority for North American educators seeking to address increasingly diverse students. Educators committed to culturally-reponsive teaching use the liminality and struggle inherent in encountering cultural others a pedagogical opportunities, not as problems to be solved.[6] Still, institutions change habits far more slowly than individual educators. If we use this study primarily as a pedagogical resource, we will find that the High School Theology Programs mostly reinforce what we already know about education. For the most part, teachers already know the value of the pedagogies used by HSTPs. We simply fail to use them in graduate school, for both personal and institutional reasons.

Without pedagogical intentionality, educational institutions do not shape students' attention; they consume it. We confuse exposure with learning, and send our students off to spin the data we dispense into wisdom they can use. We now have nearly two decades of evidence from HSTPs affirming what postmodern educators take for granted: we are shaped by our experience as well as by the people who experience the world alongside us; our bodies, and our communities, store knowledge; authenticity begets authenticity; preparing young people to lead healthy, life-giving Christian communities requires experience in such communities; plunging teenagers into communities of leadership practices tends to cause them to think of themselves as leaders. We did not need High School Theology Programs to know these things. So the real question HSTPs awaken in educators is not "What must we do?" to make vocational formation more effective, but rather "Why aren't we doing it?"

An Indictment: Evidence of Problems in North American Youth Ministry

You could easily interpret our research on High School Theology Programs as an indictment of the goals, practices, and outcomes of North America's dominant "fellowship" models of youth ministry. High School Theology Pro-

6. By 2020, whites in the Unted States will be the statistical minority; in 2012, the U.S. Census showed more non-whites were born in the United States than whites. In March 2014, Gallup estimated 54% of Americans between the ages of 18-29 were non-Hispanic white, compared to 71% in 1995, the first year Gallup measured Hispanic ethnicity. See Jeffrey Jones, "Young Americans' Affinity for Democratic Party Has Grown," *Gallup Politics* (March 28, 2014), http://www.gallup.com/poll/168125/young-americans-affinity-democratic-party-grown.aspx (accessed August 21, 2014). On culturally responsive teaching, see Anthony Kudjo Donkor, "Higher Education and Culturally Responsive Teaching: A Way Forward," *Journal of Multiculturalism in Education* 7 (December 2011), http://www.wtamu.edu/webres/File/Journals/MCJ/Volume%207-1/Anthony%20K%20Donkor.pdf (accessed August 21, 2014). The vocational pedagogies described in this book readily align with the relational, experiential, and embodied teaching methods associated with culturally-responsive educational practices.

grams emerged from the Lilly Endowment's dissatisfaction with the kind of vocational formation taking place (or not) in North American congregations through existing youth ministry programs. This was especially true for spiritually interested teenagers, for whom ministry based primarily on teenagers' social needs left them theologically malnourished and vocationally unchallenged.

Thanks to research of the last decade, we now know that this form of youth ministry not only failed to deepen the faith of spiritually interested teenagers; it did little to deepen the faith of *anyone.* Intuitively, teenagers recognized the impotence of our good intentions, shrugging their way through confirmation, Sunday school, youth group, and other formative practices while taking advantage of youth ministry's social networks.[7] Most teenagers do not view their experience in youth ministry negatively; they are glad for the role these activities play in their lives, and grateful for the connections they make with peers and adults.[8] In a society where alienation often has tragic consequences for teenagers, this is no small matter. Nonetheless, teenagers frequently graduate from their congregational youth ministries with little to show in terms of theological formation, and are relatively untouched vocationally.

One of the comments we heard most frequently from teenagers we interviewed was their profound appreciation for "being taken seriously" in High School Theology Programs. As we saw in chapter 2, the experience of "being taken seriously" comes in many forms: being assigned challenging theological readings, being taught by "real" seminary professors, being challenged to work with people very different from themselves, being genuinely "heard" by caring adults, being given responsibilities and leadership tasks that seemed beyond their capacities, only to be encouraged and cheered when they succeeded. Many youth contrasted the HSTP's seriousness of purpose and permission to speak plainly with experiences they had had elsewhere in youth ministry, where both purpose and permission were in short supply.

If we were to view High School Theology Programs as an implicit cri-

7. See Christian Smith with Melinda Lundquist Denton, *Soul Searching: The Religious and Spiritual Lives of American Teenagers* (New York: Oxford University Press, 2005), and Christian Smith with Patricia Snell, *Souls in Transition: The Religious and Spiritual Lives of Emerging Adults* (New York: Oxford University Press, 2009).

8. Patricia Snell, "What Difference Does Youth Group Make? A Longitudinal Analysis of Religious Youth Group Participation and Religious Life Outcomes," *Journal for the Scientific Study of Religion,* 48, no. 3 (2009): 572-87.

tique of North America's dominant forms of youth ministry, we would find little resistance from most youth ministers, who recoil from being cast as purveyors of "juvenile" (i.e., immature) faith. The "juvenilization" thesis in youth ministry — namely, that youth ministry is responsible for originating a kind of shallow, immature Christianity that has spread like pinkeye through adult congregations — is wrong (research overwhelmingly suggests that teenagers learn their faith from adults, not vice versa), but the view is compelling and widespread.[9] Equating youth ministry with immaturity, in faith formation or anything else, causes even those who *want* to do ministry with teenagers to eschew the title "youth minister," especially if they want to be taken seriously by theological educators and graduate schools.

The irony is that "fellowship models" of youth ministry were instituted, not to entertain teenagers socially, but to give them leadership experience they would presumably use in their future as active adult church members. Youth groups have been standard fare in American churches since Christian Endeavor swept the United States and Canada in the late nineteenth century, but these youth "societies" were youth-directed, and intended as training grounds for church leadership skills. Young people were expected to show up and speak up, and Christian Endeavor mobilized many vocal young people as spokespersons for the social gospel movement and for leadership in Christian Endeavor itself. Even in the 1940s, when fellowship groups replaced youth societies, these groups cultivated young leaders for the ecumenical church and the broader society. Fellowship groups reflected postwar America's faith in institutions, as well as the ecumenical movement's optimism in the power of Christians gathering together, and taught young people ecclesial governance and ways to mobilize groups for social change — which they did, especially around racial equality, two decades before adults in their denominations followed suit.[10]

9. See Thomas Bergler, *The Juvenilization of American Christianity* (Grand Rapids: Eerdmans, 2012). My critique of this thesis may be found in K. C. Dean, "Pointing the Finger in the Wrong Direction: Thomas Bergler's *The Juvenilization of American Christianity*," *Theology Today* 70 (April 2013): 79-81; and, in more detail, in K. C. Dean, "Beyond Truthiness: How the 'Juvenilization Thesis' in Youth Ministry Is Both Wrong and Right," *Immerse* (Fall 2012): 11-16.

10. Cf. Sara Little, *Our Church — A Fellowship* (New York: Friendship Press, 1951) and, almost fifty years later, her 1998 lecture at Princeton Theological Seminary, "Youth Ministry: Historical Reflections Near the End of the Twentieth Century" (Princeton, NJ: Princeton Lectures on Youth, Church and Culture, 1998), http://www2.ptsem.edu/uploadedFiles/IYM/YCCL/Little-Youth.pdf (accessed July 23, 2014).

Yet the fellowship era also reflected America's emerging youth culture, which promoted age stratification and replaced community organizations and institutions as teenagers' primary source of tribal identity. As age-segregation became normative in churches as well as in the culture at large, youth spent less time with adults they admired and less time in intergenerational communities eavesdropping on the experience of other generations. Instead of entering adulthood first as *de facto* "apprentices" to elders they admired, North American teenagers increasingly began raising each other, causing journalist Patricia Hersch to conclude in 1999 that North American teenagers were, in fact, "a tribe apart."[11]

Amidst these shifts, youth groups' original purpose of being training grounds for Christian leadership shifted, too. As churches felt their credibility erode among teenagers, the field of youth ministry became more concerned with the vocation of the youth pastor than the vocation of the teenager. Youth groups became another node in peer culture, a redundant place for teenagers to hang out with friends and with caring adults. Presumably what set youth fellowship groups apart from countless competing activities and social networks was the fact that youth groups gave teenagers peers who shared their faith.[12] Where this was true, it was generally significant. The problem was that it was less often true than we thought. Just because teenagers came to church did not mean they could distinguish Christian faith from the "moralistic therapeutic deist" culture at large. In fact, by the mid-twentieth century, churches had become extremely effective vehicles for socializing young people into a bland, homogenized Christendom, from which moralistic therapeutic deism sprang.

Most youth ministers would be grateful for High School Theology Programs' critique of what youth "fellowships" have become (after all, youth ministers helped design HSTPs as a way to offer a form of vocational formation not currently available in most yourth groups). HSTPs directly challenge the bland religiosity that dominates North American culture, and explicitly counter the "juvenile" stereotype associated with adolescents. By treating teenagers as young adults, as "scholars," as leaders — and by expecting a level of maturity and reflexivity seldom expected of adolescents

11. Patricia Hersch, *A Tribe Apart* (New York: Ballantine Books, 1999).

12. The "wholesome" activities that overwhelm middle class youth continue to more or less bypass other teenagers, rich and poor alike. Wealthy teenagers do not need the social networks made possible by involvement in such activities, and poor teenagers cannot afford to miss work to belong to them — or lack other assets (transportation, parent approval, freedom from responsibility) that make extracurricular participation possible.

— HSTPs give teenagers an experience of legitimacy associated with adulthood. This is a status young people crave, in churches as elsewhere; recall the young woman we met in chapter 1, pleading at the Catholic Theological Union: "Whatever you do, please don't give us the Fisher-Price version of theology!" By focusing on spiritually interested young people, High School Theology Programs unapologetically address the mostly convinced, but they also affirm — in a boots-on-the-ground, lives-are-at-stake kind of way — these teenagers' hope that Christianity actually matters, that living one's faith makes a decisive difference in the world, and that the God of Abraham, Moses, and Mary has bigger plans than Sunday night youth group.

A Mirror: Why Do We Do What We Do?

A third way to use this study of the vocational pedagogies used by High School Theology Programs is as a mirror we can hold up to churches, denominations, and theological schools to help us think critically about our current systems of Christian leadership formation, as we ask how well those systems prepare young leaders for the twenty-first-century church. In particular, this book suggests four reflections that are worth thinking about:

1. What is seminary for?

If you happened to be a seminarian at the Renk Theological College in South Sudan, you would be studying for the salvation business in very literal ways. In South Sudan, first semester seminarians are not introduced to theology, church history, youth ministry, preaching, or pastoral care. Instead, the first four classes required of every student at Renk Theological College are biblical Greek, biblical Hebrew, agriculture, and public health.[13] The first semester curriculum at Renk is indicative of the purpose of seminary in South Sudan. Students come to seminary primarily *to save lives* — physically and existentially — which is why their seminary education begins with the growing and healing arts: the care of the soul (biblical Greek, biblical Hebrew) and the care of the community (agriculture, public health).

13. L. Gregory Jones, "Learning Curve," *The Christian Century* (May 18, 2010), http://www.christiancentury.org/article/2010-05/learning-curve (accessed August 22, 2014).

On the whole, seminaries in North America are far more directed towards saving churches than saving lives. A good deal of time is devoted to dispensing information that we want pastors to have, and to teaching students how to think in the disciplined ways that we want pastors to think. Biblical, historical, theological, philosophical, and practical studies infuse North American theological education; "saving lives" is something best left to Jesus, or so we say. Meanwhile, the assumptions governing our seminary curricula (for example, that students come to seminary to prepare to lead churches) do not always match the assumptions of students (who may be in seminary to discern whether they are called to ministry in the first place).

At the same time, some seminary leaders argue that the MDiv degree — once a standard requirement for ordination — now functions more like an MBA: beneficial, but optional.[14] Ironically, this shift is taking place at a time when the ecology of Christian formation has collapsed; many churchgoers cannot articulate the difference between following Jesus and working for Google (official slogan: "Don't be evil"). The upshot is that seminaries often now face new responsibilities in providing basic Christian education for their students whose own religious formation is quite sketchy, and who may one day have responsibility for discipling others.

In an educational climate where the life-giving arts have been siphoned off to medical schools and social work; justice has become the terrain of law schools; the art of community-building is given to engineers, educators, and social planners; and changing the world belongs to social entrepreneurs — seminary education is fishing for purpose. As we mentioned in chapter 1, one trend facing theological education in the early twenty-first century is the fact that Christian young people who want to make a difference often do not seem to think the church is the best place to do it. High School Theology Programs offer young people a way of thinking about theological education as a route to multiple vocations that represent Christ in the world — and they go a long way toward putting ministry on young people's vocational radars. Theological education becomes a way to do more than save churches; it becomes a way to join in God's work to save lives, in multiple ways.

14. L. Gregory Jones, "Pastors by Degree: Evolution of a Vocation," *The Christian Century* (December 15, 2009), http://www.christiancentury.org/article/2009-12/pastors-degree (accessed August 22, 2014).

2. Should theological education be a post-undergraduate degree?

The word "seminary" means "seedbed" — suggesting a slow, nurturing environment for a growing, living organism as it takes root. The clarion call from Auburn Theological Seminary's 2013 research on seminary students is that intentional, long-term nurturing environments matter enormously for vocational discernment, since "seminarians don't come from nowhere." Barbara Wheeler explains,

> None of the interviewees and, from what we can tell from the survey data, very few students in the total population wander into seminary out of curiosity or are snatched by us from a wholly secular culture. Almost all seminary students have been embedded in religious communities, involved in religious institutions, and exposed to religious role models for a long time, usually since birth.[15]

In other words, if the seed of Christian vocation is not planted early, it is very unlikely to spontaneously sprout at age twenty-one. Despite numerous factors that appear significant in shaping a young person's decision to attend seminary, Wheeler contends that nothing replaces the long, slow nurture of faith by families and congregations.

This should not surprise us. Go back to Joshua Bell's unexpected concert in the subway station, described in chapter 1. Here's how Gene Weingarten, writing in *The Washington Post,* described people's reactions that morning:

> There was no ethnic or demographic pattern to distinguish the people who stayed to watch Bell, or the ones who gave money, from that vast majority who hurried on past, unheeding. Whites, blacks and Asians, young and old, men and women, were represented in all three groups. But the behavior of one demographic remained absolutely consistent. *Every single*

15. Quote is from Barbara Wheeler's "Pathways to Seminary" address at a Lilly Endowment meeting for High School Theology Program directors and senior executives at program schools (Barbara G. Wheeler, "Pathways to Seminary: Where the Best Students Come From," speech, January 22, 2014). The address summarized findings of the Auburn Theological Seminary research reported by Barbara G. Wheeler, "On Our Way: A Study of Students' Paths to Seminary," unpublished report of survey data submitted to the Lilly Endowment (August 2013), http://www.auburnseminary.org/religion-and-research (accessed August 24, 2014).

> *time a child walked past, he or she tried to stop and watch. And every single time, a parent scooted the kid away.*[16] (italics mine)

Weingarten reminds us of the poet Billy Collins' joke that all babies are born with an innate knowledge of poetry, because, according to Collins, the mother's heart beats in iambic meter. But then, Collins said, "Life slowly starts to choke the poetry out of us." Weingarten wonders if maybe that is true of music, too.

Their suspicions are justified; studies show a sharp decline in creativity in children once they start school, with the most significant decline occurring between kindergarten and third grade.[17] In 1991, Harvard child psychiatrist Robert Coles' landmark research on young children and spirituality reported, with some awe, that after scores of conversations with children, even those whose parents were atheists and had never attended a religious service initiated conversations about God.[18] Coles concluded that theological thinking comes naturally to children as they try to make sense of their world — at least, it seems, until they get old enough to care what people think.

If calling is a creative practice of communities, then the church benefits by engaging younger people in vocational discernment. Maybe the "blue ocean" of theological formation is not found in developing more creative forms of graduate theological education, but in creating more opportunities for children and youth to participate in high-touch ecologies of vocational discernment, capitalizing on certain "critical periods" for vocational formation — periods of spiritual readiness (or at least openness) that seem especially conducive to entertaining the idea of a "call." Adolescence and emerging adulthood seem to be two such periods. As we saw in chapter 12, young adult staff members and mentors in High School Theology Programs seem to find the vocational practices intended for high school students significant in helping them discern their own vocational trajectories. These

16. Gene Weingarten, "Pearls before Breakfast," *The Washington Post* (April 8, 2007), http://www.washingtonpost.com/wp-dyn/content/article/2007/04/04/AR2007040401721.html (accessed August 24, 2014).

17. Cf. Kyung Hee Kim, "The Creativity Crisis: The Decrease in Creative Thinking Scores on the Torrance Tests of Creative Thinking," *Creativity Research Journal* 23 (2011): 285-95. Sir Ken Robinson's 2006 TED talk, "How Schools Kill Creativity" (the most-viewed TED talk of all time), develops this thesis in detail. See http://www.ted.com/talks/ken_robinson_says_schools_kill_creativity (accessed August 24, 2014).

18. Robert Coles, *The Spiritual Life of Children* (New York: Mariner, 1991), pp. xiii, xvii.

young staff members are able to respond to vocational formation in part because they are building on prior scaffolding supplied by earlier periods of religious formation.[19]

One possibility for seminaries to consider may be offering theological education in stages, rather than save it for graduate school. To seriously consider "staging" vocational formation will require graduate theological schools to make hard choices about deploying funds and leadership. Are we willing to divert funds into programs (like High School Theology Programs) that may or may not pay off in terms of later enrollment? Is engaging children and youth in communities of vocational practices what is needed to pique young people's desire for graduate theological education, once they are old enough to attend? Should seminaries become actively engaged in supporting congregational practices of vocational discernment with young people? Some stages of formation may require new investments for theological schools (like High School Theology Programs), but some may simply be a matter of helping congregations re-tool practices already familiar and dear to them.

Confirmation, for instance, is a kind of vocational discernment process, at least theologically speaking. Recasting confirmation as a way to help teenagers begin to discern a call to both Christian discipleship and Christian leadership starts with a congregation, which names young people's gifts, and then confirms this vocation by letting youth use those gifts for ministry. But this approach requires congregations, pastors, and youth ministers to rid ourselves of perfunctory versions of confirmation, allowing it to become an occasion for experiences of liminality, competence, deep belonging, and holy struggle, and for honing their leadership through service, witness, and stewardship.[20]

3. Is the schooling model for theological education the best model we have?

Among the most explicit aims of High School Theology Programs is to help teenagers "fall in love with theology." Mastering theology is not the objec-

19. Wheeler, "On Our Way": 7.

20. For instance, Chris Hughes' confirmation program, the Foundation for Christian Formation (http://www.fcfconfirm.net), and in more detail, Chris Hughes, *Consecration 3x3 - A Disciple Making Sequence: Profession of Faith, Confirmation, and Commissioning: Testing Our Assumptions and Improving Our Process of Adolescent Disciple Making* (Pneumanaut Publishing, 2012).

tive; *loving* theology is — making the goal of HSTPs the formation of desires as well as the formation of vocation. Many theological educators would hope for something similar among their own students, as well. We know the limits of academic theology: while seminary does an admirable job exposing future church leaders to the foundations of Christian theology and introduces them to certain habits of mind that we want Christian leaders to exhibit, it is less clear how degree programs, graded curriculum, academic calendars, and for-credit courses help students fall in love with "the study of God."

The point is not to rid ourselves of academic programs or denigrate theological scholarship. Both of these are critical for a new generation of intellectually engaged, theologically disciplined church leaders. High School Theology Programs draw significantly on these resources. But scores of theologically interested HSTP alumni challenge the assumption that schooling models of theological education are the only effective vehicles for teaching and inspiring theological leadership. HSTP alumni frequently describe discovering a "lifelong love for theology" during their High School Theology Programs that made them look for ways to continue being part of theological conversations as they entered college and beyond. Wheeler's research underscores the importance of both informal *and* formal educational experiences in young people's vocational formation. For example, the influence of religious formation in school settings, especially colleges, is a factor in encouraging young people to attend seminary — though it is less clear whether this influence stems from religious coursework or from participating in a subculture that makes room for theological conversations about vocation.

Wheeler also reminds us that early and sustained religious formation through a family and congregation remain the most important tools for vocational formation that we know. Role models in faith leadership, the presence of a faithful peer group, and participation in formative micro-cultures like church camps, religious "niche" cultures, and/or parachurch youth ministries all have measurable impacts on young people's likelihood to attend seminary. Among other things, these experiences seem to give students tools that help them frame disruptive experiences in light of a religious tradition. As Wheeler notes, "Almost all seminary students have been embedded in religious communities, involved in religious institutions, and exposed to religious role models for a long time, usually since birth."[21] Of course, there is nothing stopping formal theological education from providing analogous experiences. The problem is that for a young person to wait until seminary

21. Wheeler, "Pathways to Seminary," p. 3.

to discover religious role models, faithful peer groups, disruptive existential experiences, and so on means it is highly unlikely that he or she will go to seminary at all.

High School Theology Programs remind us that formal theological education is one way — but not the only way — to form Christian leaders. Desperation has its advantages; dwindling congregations and the loss of young leadership have forced experimentation on the part of both seminaries and denominations, even where ordination is concerned. The upshot has been an increasing number of intriguing (if embryonic) experiments around new models of leadership formation. Promising experiments are multiplying. The Anglican mission pioneer program in the United Kingdom offers a multitiered, multiple platform delivery system for theological education for lay and ordained leaders. The Center for Youth Ministry Training "flipped" the ratio of classroom and congregational experience for master's degree students in youth ministry. Post-seminary residencies in mentoring congregations, such as the Lilly Pastoral Residency Program, rely on learning communities that work with, but go beyond, traditional MDiv education. These communities tend to include networks of mutual accountability, relational authority through mentoring and coaching, apprenticeship learning and immersion experiences that work in concert with more traditional educational delivery systems. These hybrid programs challenge the compartmentalized "university approach" as the only, or best, approach to formal theological education.

4. Are "best practices stupid"?

So suggests the misleading (but marketable) title of business innovation consultant Steve Shapiro's 2011 book. Shapiro reminds us that "best practice" models are beneficial for some goals, but tend to work against innovation.[22] Given the fact that most pedagogical studies in theological education (including this one) tend to favor "best practices" approaches, caution is merited. Many of Shapiro's forty principles of innovation are useful for theological educators, but here are three that help us work within the limits of "best practices" approaches while working toward innovation in theological education:

22. Stephen M. Shapiro, *Best Practices Are Stupid: 40 Ways to Out-Innovate the Competition* (London: Portfolio, 2011).

1. *Asking for ideas is a bad idea.* In the era of crowdsourcing, asking for ideas is an excellent way to harvest the collective intelligence of the masses. The problem for innovation is simply that "the masses" tend to be very, very conventional. Despite our dissatisfaction with current conditions, most of us will still opt to perpetuate the familiar, with minor alterations, rather than leap into an entirely new paradigm. In short, Shapiro reminds us, if we need lots of ideas — and buy-in from lots of different people — then seeking input from multiple sectors is a good strategy. However, if we need *new* ideas, then innovation research is astonishingly consistent: seek the input of outliers (say, for instance, teenagers.)

2. *Best practices help solve identical problems.* Shapiro's advice here is straightforward: if you have a problem to solve that everyone else has to solve, too, in reasonably similar contexts, then best practices are the way to go. This is why collecting data on vocational pedagogy is beneficial; most formal systems of theological formation, from summer camps to divinity schools, struggle with similar issues: decreased enrollment, reduced donor bases, and insufficient numbers of young leaders to reverse the aging trends of most North American congregations. To the extent that North American churches still reflect middle class values if not a middle class demographic, best practices may well help us. On the other hand, if a problem emerges that is specific to a particular context, leadership style, or needs of a community — or if our hope is to address a new context or demographic — then our best hope lies in innovation, not in best practices.

3. *Simplification is the best innovation.* One of the most consistently successful forms of innovation is simplification.[23] Think about Apple's design strategy, or the hundreds of "life-hacking" websites that show easier and more efficient ways to make a grilled cheese or invent new uses for Ikea furniture. In a complicated world, the most influential innovation may involve taking away a variable rather than adding a new one.

Sometimes the "best practice" in theological formation, the one that yields a sense of peace and improves our sightlines to Jesus, is the practice of moving things out of the way — what Christian mystics called purgation. Purgative practices were considered the first steps toward one's true vocation, union with God. Given the "busyness bubble" that has captured North American culture — the saturation point for the number of activities, opportunities, and responsibilities we can take on, or that young people can

23. Larry Keeley et al., *Ten Types of Innovation: The Discipline of Building Breakthroughs* (Hoboken, NJ: Wiley, 2013).

— practices of purgation are enjoying a small renaissance. As I write this, for example, Marie Kondo's book *The Life-Changing Magic of Tidying Up: The Japanese Art of Decluttering and Organizing* has spent fifty-four weeks on the New York Times best-sellers list.[24] "Mindfulness" is in the news; *Time* calls mindfulness a "revolution," the *Huffington Post* heralded 2014 as a "year of mindful living," and marketers have identified "mindfulness" as one of the ten trends shaping the world.[25] Young people are among those ardently pursuing less. Interest in life/work balance, intentional food practices, economic and ecological sustainability, and other "slowing" practices run high among millennials, many of whom watched the busyness bubble bury their parents, usually metaphorically (sadly, not always).

Churches, denominations, and theological schools — captured in the busyness bubble like everyone else — are having mindfulness revolutions of their own. Renewed interest in spiritual practices like walking the labyrinth, silent retreats, and Sabbath-keeping, as well as a renaissance in simple living, sustainability, and local sourcing among young adults, all point to purgative practices that contribute to young people's vocational decisions. The teenagers in our interviews were reliably fascinated, and inspired, by practices like Sabbath-keeping, silence, and fasting and by those who undertook them.

Often, churches' first reaction to secular social trends is to create parallel ministries that capture these innovations in ways that are more explicitly Christian. Yet true innovation may involve a simpler — and likely more gracious — approach. An emergent skill of Christian leadership seems to be the ability to forge community partnerships, allowing churches to come alongside secular organizations to work for "the common good," together. In this scenario, churches act as supportive partners, making no apology for our faith while recognizing that God's work in the world is not limited to

24. Greg Mckeown, "Why We Humblebrag about Being Busy," *Harvard Business Review Magazine* (June 2014), http://blogs.hbr.org/2014/06/why-we-humblebrag-about-being-busy/ (accessed August 29, 2014); Marie Kondo, *The Life-Changing Magic of Tidying Up: The Japanese Art of Decluttering and Organizing* (Emeryville, CA: Ten Speed, 2014).

25. "10 Trends That Will Shape the World in 2014 and Beyond," *JWT Worldwide* (December 4, 2013), http://www.jwt.com/blog/consumer_insights/10-trends-that-will-shape-our-world-in-2014-and-beyond/ (accessed August 26, 2014). *The Huffington Post* also predicted 2014 as "the year of mindful living." See Carolyn Gregoire, "Why 2014 Will Be the Year of Mindful Living," *The Huffington Post* (January 2, 2014), http://www.huffingtonpost.com/2014/01/02/will-2014-be-the-year-of-_0_n_4523975.html (accessed August 26, 2014). *Time* referred to "mindfulness" as a "revolution"; see Kate Pickert, "The Mindful Revolution," *Time* (January 23, 2014), http://time.com/1556/the-mindful-revolution/ (accessed August 26, 2014).

activities we call "ministry." Christians would be hard pressed not to see the Holy Spirit at work in secular efforts like Café Momentum in Dallas, founded by a young chef who sold his four-star restaurant to teach teenagers coming out of prison how to cook; or in the P.R.E.P. program ("Patience, Responsibility, Empathy, and Partnership") that teaches compassion and responsibility to incarcerated teenagers by hiring them to train shelter dogs. Watsi was founded by a Peace Corps volunteer to crowdsource medical funding for people in developing countries; New Jersey teenager Maggie Doyne, hiking through the Himalayas on a gap year in 2006, came home and invested $5000 of her babysitting money to work with local Nepalese to build the Kopila Valley Children's Home and School, where Maggie and her staff now teach and care for more than 300 children.[26] These social innovations are not ministries, yet Christians would see in their work evidence of God's grace afoot in the world — making the church's support an important gesture of hospitality.

A Glimpse of the Future of Youth Ministry — and Theological Education

Despite the mystery surrounding the kind of workforce the next generation church requires, and the kind of theological preparation that workforce will need, perhaps we can assume some basics as we imagine vocational formation for next generation Christian leaders:

- *De-professionalization.* Professional models of church leadership that dominated North American church life throughout the twentieth century are increasingly unsustainable, nor do they capture the radical nature of discipleship. As a result, young people seeking organic forms of community tend to gravitate toward a more seamless integration of church and mission. This integration gives fresh energy to new church starts, tentmaking ministries, nonprofit work, and hybrid ministries that

26. See cafemomentum.org; https://watsi.org/; Christina Rosales, "Dallas County Juvenile Offender Program Teaches Leadership, Commitment with Shelter Dog Training," *Dallas Morning News* (August 6, 2011), http://www.dallasnews.com/news/community-news/dallas/headlines/20110806-dallas-county-juvenile-offender-program-teaches-leadership-commitment-with-shelter-dog-training.ece; Maggie Doyne, "Why the Human Family Can Do Better," *Do Lectures 2010,* https://www.youtube.com/watch?v=O-Xv9h5nBls (accessed August 27, 2014).

serve congregations and communities simultaneously, often through mutually beneficial entrepreneurial enterprises.

- *Early stage theological education.* Deep vocational formation — including formation in the Christian story itself — must remain the primary task of theological education, but this task need not be limited to seminary education. Intentional programs of vocational discernment, including confirmation programs, church camps, service corps, and programs like HSTPs can form a constellation of experiences that expand vocational formation to include early adolescence through early adulthood. These programs will have maximal impact when they offer young people tools for intellectual theological reflection while simultaneously immersing them in a community trying to imitate Christ in real time.
- *Expanded leadership skills.* As we have suggested, theological education must include new leadership skills, since next generation church leaders will move more fluidly between established Christian institutions and spontaneous communities that emerge around common needs. In the futture, Christian life will be less associated with "church activities" than with communitties of human flourishing. As a result, Christian leaders' toolkits will increasingly need skills such as:
    - » *Community development.* Churches — lacking substantial denominational support enjoyed by twentieth century churches — will increasingly partner with other community organizations with sympathetic missions to mobilize community change.
    - » *Missional entrepreneurship.* Since traditional funding models are no longer sufficient to support most churches, mission will become more local, more entrepreneurial, and more integrated into the economic lives of both global and immediate neighbors.
    - » *Hacking.* The ability to devise practical shortcuts through existing structures that make them more useful will be prized as next generation church leaders hack their way through a thicket of habits and bureaucracies that no longer speak to the North American church's cultural location.
- *Missional communities.* As youth ministry moves away from youth fellowship models, young people longing for community are finding it in missional communities. Among the important changes this signals is a movement away from creating ministries for young people to participate in, toward supporting young people in ministries that they themselves create — a significant step toward the vocational formation of spiritually motivated teenagers.

- *Life-long vocational discernment.* Vocational discernment is increasingly a life-cycle concern, not just an age-level concern, especially in the first third of life. As churches learn to recognize and leverage certain "critical periods" for vocational discernment (especially late adolescence/early adulthood), ministry and work apprenticeships will become more common as forms of ministry with young people.
- *Early leadership experience.* Early leadership experience begets adult leadership. Young people who are participants — not spectators — in Christian leadership, and who have received primary experiences of service, witness, and stewardship (accompanied by theological reflection on these experiences) are the most likely to emerge as Christian leaders.
- *Building ecologies of discernment.* Ecologies of vocational discernment attend to two layers of practices:
  - » *"Baseline" vocational practices* that cultivate safe space for vocational exploration, such as creating intentional Christian communities, developing networks of mentors, seizing "naming and commissioning" opportunities, and making space for young people who want to use those newly developed leadership skills in the context of their "back home" faith communities.
  - » *Exploratory practices* that frame vocational discernment as an adolescent adventure, especially by creating and leveraging experiences of liminality, competence, deep belonging, and holy struggle. Pedagogies that decenter teenagers and/or give them practice in theological reflection, worship, pilgrimage, service, leadership, and the arts seem especially evocative for vocational exploration.

None of these paths to vocational discernment will happen by accident, of course. High School Theology Programs offer one hedge against ecclesial uncertainty by intentionally encouraging youth to experiment with the theological tools of Christian tradition as they hammer out forms of discipleship that authentically represent Christ to their generation. HSTPs encourage youth to imagine what bearing witness to Christ in the twenty-first century requires, and they give youth a social laboratory in which to test out this witness.

While the Lilly Endowment's original vision for HSTPs was to create feeder systems — farm teams, if you will — for future clergy and church workers (by any measure, HSTPs have succeeded admirably in this regard), it is clear that these programs' alumni are also participating in a significant ecclesial shift. While HSTP participants pursue vocations of church leadership in disproportionate numbers, they also universally view other kinds of work as discipleship as well, blurring the lines between sacred and secular callings, complexifying what constitutes "ministry" in the first place. In their hands, church leadership will undoubtedly be the task of teachers, doctors, nonprofit leaders, stay-at-home parents, entrepreneurs, and engineers, as well as professional church workers — who may or may not find their pastoral niches in the established roles of the church. As theological educators lament the murky future of a changing church, High School Theology Programs view this ambiguity as an opportunity. As teenagers reinterpret Christian witness for their moment in history, they reinterpret the church itself.

Mystagogical Farm Teams

High School Theology Program directors insist that the pedagogical strategies they employ are neither new nor unique; they are merely faithful ways of helping teenagers recognize, discern, and enact their callings as Christian disciples. Using what he calls a "mystagogical" approach to teaching that "respects the experience of the person we're speaking to," St. Meinrad's program director Godfrey Mullen insists that diving into teenagers' experience head-first with them is a profoundly incarnational move — and that in fact, this kind of formation has created what amounts to farm teams of Christian leadership for centuries. Describing his teaching method as "fourth century mystagogical preaching,"[27] Mullen says:

> You can't speak the language that youth don't understand and expect them to understand what you're saying. . . . Mystagogical preaching [says]: experience Scripture and some new demand on my life. People are like, "That is a brilliant way to teach!" It is, and that's why it's endured for 1600 years. It's not because I dreamt it up one day.

Mullens is referring to the early catechumenate's practice of offering intentional instruction to newly baptized Christians. In the early church, this instruction explored the "mysteries" of faith (i.e., sacraments) that these new Christians had already experienced, but did not yet deeply understand. The

27. It should be noted that catechesis was accomplished through preaching in the early church; preaching in this sense is a form of pedagogy. See Craig Alan Satterlee, *Ambrose of Milan's Method of Mystagogical Preaching* (Collegeville, MN: Liturgical, 2002), p. 1.

order mattered: the *experience* of God's mystery preceded human instruction *about* that mystery.

High School Theology Programs approach theological formation similarly, holding up the adolescent's prior experience of God's call as a mystery of faith that should be explored more fully. Like farm team players in baseball, most young people in HSTPs already long for a way to participate in the church leadership game, and they long to be with others who share their passion for the spiritual life. They are hungry for coaches and guidance. But they are still rookie players — neophytes, in the catechetical language — baptized into faith without fully recognizing what God is up to in their lives. High School Theology Programs set out to explore this mystery in ways reminiscent of the early church, bringing together new disciples to understand the *litourgia* — the "work of the people" — as they participate in this work themselves.[28]

By focusing on teenagers' informed *participation* in the practices of Christian community — and by giving them a team to practice with, rather than merely instructing them *about* these practices — young people begin to exercise agency as people of faith.[29] Teenagers recognize that their theological agency is intensified by their experiences in High School Theology Programs. Many students we talked to openly wondered what it would be like to go back to "real life" in their churches and schools, now that they had tasted theological reflection with equally interested others, and now that they thought of themselves as potential leaders in the Christian community. They wondered whether the church as they know it has room for them, or whether God might best use their leadership elsewhere.

We will see.

28. In the latter stages of catechetical instruction, participating in the shared life of the Christian community was believed to have catechetical power. Cf. Satterlee, *Ambrose of Milan,* p. 6.

29. We could say that High School Theology Programs are to local church youth programs what studying in France is to high school French class. French class introduces a subject, and teaches its necessary grammar and rudimentary structures — scaffolding that allows limited access to a culture that would otherwise remain out of reach. But actually *going* to France gives the French language life and force; experiencing French culture firsthand makes speaking French personally and contextually relevant. Speaking French daily, like exercising a muscle, makes it stronger, more flexible, and more useful. Attending an HSTP, like going to France, builds upon local congregations' catechetical instruction by translating technical understandings of Christ's call into a robust and personal claim on teenagers' lives. Thanks to researcher Katie Douglass for making this connection.

APPENDIX A

Research Methods for the High School Youth Theology Program Seminar

KATHERINE M. DOUGLASS WITH KENDA CREASY DEAN

This research model was explicitly patterned after another Lilly-initiated project focusing on religious practices, the Valparaiso Project on the Education and Formation of People in Faith's "Seminar on Practical Theology and Christian Ministry" (2004-2005), one of several religious practices initiatives born out of the religious practices discussion launched by the collaborations leading to *Practicing Our Faith* (Dorothy Bass and Craig Dykstra, eds., [San Francisco: Jossey-Bass, 1997]) and *Practicing Theology* (Dorothy Bass and Miroslav Volf [San Francisco: Jossey-Bass, 2001]). Utilizing similar research methods and theoretical foundations in the religious practices movement, the present project focuses specifically on the practices of vocational formation employed by the High School Theology Projects, especially since 1998.

Research Team

This research was conducted by an invested team of practical theologians including thoughtful practitioners, graduate student researchers, and professors who provide a multiplicity of vantage points for gleaning subjective and objective information about youth theology programs. As both "outsiders" and "insiders," this group has contributed to this book in unique ways that offer a prism through which to view these programs rather than a single lens. This intentional "inside-outside" perspective allowed for a more nuanced interpretation of these programs' formative practices and governing theological perspectives than any one research group could have offered.

As "outsiders," graduate student researchers[1] conducted site visits and interviews, and read deeply into the written histories of these programs to compare and contrast programs, identify innovative praxis, highlight trends, and begin to analyze the unique contributions that youth theology programs make to the greater ecology of Christian formation.

As "insiders," program directors involved with this project were asked to reflect on the unique pedagogical and theological practices of their programs that foster Christian leadership. These reflections made explicit many of the implicit theologies and pedagogies that inform the practices of youth theology programs, but until this project had not been openly analyzed.

Research Methods

The research methods were devised primarily to help seminar members curate and reflect upon existing but unexplored data, including the reflections of participant-observers. After perusing this data, we identified our "hunches" about the importance of various practices in awakening young Christians to leadership, and tested the reliability of those provisional conclusions through qualitative research "soundings" that augmented existing data streams. Qualitative data were collected through multiple streams, from multiple sources, both over time and in the context of observed action. Five data streams were explicitly identified:

- *HSTP program archives* housed at the Lilly Endowment, Inc. Annual reports and case studies from all ninety-eight HSTPs that Lilly has funded since 1992 (starting with exploratory programs) were reviewed.
- *Existing published literature on youth ministry.* The graduate research team provided seminar members with an extensive, theologically annotated bibliography of "100 influential books" in youth ministry, eliminating curriculum and "how to" books and cross referencing the one hundred top selling youth ministry books on Amazon with a number

1. The team consisted of five doctoral students, supplemented by two senior MDiv students who had taken a doctoral research methods seminar at Princeton Theological Seminary. One doctoral student was an alumnus of an early HSTP that was not included in the scope of this research.

of "lists," for example: the most commonly assigned texts in youth ministry in undergraduate youth ministry classrooms,[2] Youth Cartel Mark Oestreicher's "most influential" books in youth ministry,[3] as well as lists of "most influential" youth ministry books compiled by research team members (all of whom were engaged in masters or doctoral-level research in youth ministry).

- *Detailed theological self-analyses written by all forty-eight current program directors about their programs* in 2011, submitted to the Lilly Endowment's Religion Division just prior to the current project. These self-reports served as the basis for our research team's initial discernment of common theological themes, patterns, and gaps running through these analyses.
- *Theological and pedagogical reflections generated by program directors and practical theologians on the research team,* who wrote on pedagogies deemed to have special significance for forming young leaders in their programs, including case studies illustrating how young people had been transformed as they participated in these practices.
- *Site visits.* Eight members of the graduate research team engaged in participant-observation research of fifteen programs in the summer of 2012. In addition to direct observation, these site visits included interviews with youth, mentors, and program directors. In some cases, follow-up conversations with program directors after the program also took place.

Choices and Limitations

As with every research project, our research choices have shaped this project's findings. For example, in the site visit phase we decided to interview not only youth and program directors, but also the staff mentors who helped lead these programs in various ways. This led to an unexpected facet on our research prism, as we powerfully witnessed the vocational significance these programs had for college and graduate students serving as staff, as well as for teenagers themselves. Some of the most interesting

2. Andrew S. Jack and Barrett W. McRae, "Tassel-Flipping: A Portrait of the Well-Educated Youth Ministry Graduate," *Journal of Youth Ministry* 4 (Fall 2005): 53-73.

3. Mark Oestreicher, "The Top 10 Books That Have Influenced Youth Ministry" (January 10, 2007), accessed November 7, 2013, https://www.luthersem.edu/cyf/children/childrensministrybibliography.pdf.

findings (with strong implications for seminary education) emerged from that research decision. Having made the decision to interview staff mentors in order to "cover our bases, " we came to recognize how programs that are intentionally designed to foster leadership among youth have a "spillover" effect that influences the vocational discernment of young adult program leaders as well.

Similarly, we did not plan to interview faculty teaching in these programs. This was a mistake, as we learned quickly from program directors who regaled us with stories about faculty involvement in these programs. In this book, we chose to include the personal narrative of one faculty member simply to "bookmark" this area for future research, and to note that seminary faculty often find the experience of teaching theology to high school students transformative for their own pedagogies as well.

Our research design focused on discovering how these programs define and foster Christian leadership in the lives of youth. This focus emerged from strong evidence from program alumni, as well as program reviews by Carol Lytch and the recent research of Barbara Wheeler,[4] suggesting that the HSTPs were indeed occasions for young people to grow spiritually — but they were specifically valuable in awakening youth to the possibility of their own leadership, in the present and in the future, in the church and in the world.

Timeline

While numerous studies have emerged from data collected at youth theology programs,[5] until now there has been no comprehensive study that considered the unique pedagogical contributions that youth theology programs have to offer to the broader church, and to theological education more generally. In the fall of 2011, Lilly Foundation Inc. — having invested over fifty million dollars in these programs since 1992 — approached

4. Carol Lytch, "Summary Report I: Strategic Advances in Theological Education: Theological Programs for High School Youth, 1999-2004," *Theological Education* 42 (2006); Barbara Wheeler, "On Our Way: A Study of Students' Paths to Seminary," unpublished report of survey data submitted to the Lilly Endowment (August 2013).

5. See David F. White, *Practicing Discernment with Youth: A Transformative Youth Ministry Approach* (Cleveland, OH: Pilgrim, 2005); Katherine Turpin, *Branded* (Cleveland, OH: Pilgrim, 2006); Dori Grinenko Baker and Joyce Ann Mercer, *Lives to Offer* (Cleveland, OH: Pilgrim, 2007); Fred P. Edie, *Book, Bath, Table and Time,* (Cleveland, OH: Pilgrim, 2007).

Princeton Theological Seminary to develop such a study, starting with the archival data Lilly had been collecting on these programs for nearly two decades. Project co-directors Christopher Coble (then a program director in Lilly's religion division) and Kenda Creasy Dean (Mary D. Synnott Professor of Youth, Church and Culture at Princeton Theological Seminary) met with seminar members in various capacities over the course of eighteen months, focusing on programs' practices of vocational formation. After eight graduate researchers made fifteen on-site visits in the summer of 2012, their interviews and field notes were transcribed and uploaded to NVivo, a qualitative analysis program that provides researchers with tools for content analysis.

Analysis

Analysis of data occurred in two stages. The principle investigators (Dean and Coble) and graduate student researchers began the analysis of these programs through reflection upon the interviews, site visits, theological self-reflections and written histories submitted by HSTP program directors. This analysis was then brought into conversation with the written and oral self-reflections of program directors, shared during three three-day seminars over the course of this project. This multi-dimensional analysis was then used by Dean, Coble, and project associate Christy Lang Hearlson to create a framework for reporting data. This framework gave rise to the chapters in this book.

Writing and Reporting

Coble and Dean, with co-editor Christy Lang Hearlson, invited program directors whose programs exemplified the key pedagogical practices emerging from this analysis to write about these topics. In addition to the program directors, authors of this volume also include a guest professor from a High School Theology Program; editors Dean, Hearlson, and Coble; and one researcher who had been part of the graduate research team during her PhD program. Authors were invited to not only reflect on their own programs, but where relevant, to use the analysis and findings of both the seminar conversations and the NVivo transcripts to broaden their chapters' reflections to include other HSTPs.

Editing and Reviewing

In order to bring this project full circle, the various chapters were reviewed and edited, first by the editors, and then also by an expanded team of graduate student researchers to ensure that the reporting of findings resonated with the observations and findings that emerged from site visits, and to ensure readability to those who were not already familiar with these programs.

This multi-faceted process of data collection, analysis, writing, reviewing, and editing, accomplished by a large team of collaborators rather than by an individual, capitalizes on the value that multiple perspectives offer to a research project. This dialogical process of writing is similar to other projects on religious practices, especially Dorothy Bass's "Seminar on Practical Theology and Christian Ministry" (2004-2005). The collaborative approach to writing is also resonant with the writing approach used in other practical theological and educational literature, such as Brian Mahan et al.'s *Awakening Youth Discipleship* and Mary Belenky et al.'s *Women's Ways of Knowing.*[6]

The limitation of this methodological approach is the risk that dissenting voices may not be adequately acknowledged, especially since these dissenting voices might have interpreted or highlighted various findings differently. It also must be clear that no one person has an omniscient view of these programs.

Our intention was to invite those who are closest to and most invested in these practices to reflect on them within our community of practical theologians, so that their excellent praxis might be amplified and shared for the sake of sparking a reformation in theological education.

6. See Brian Mahan, Michael Warren, and David F. White, *Awakening Youth Discipleship: Christian Resistance in a Consumer Culture* (Eugene, OR: Cascade, 2008); Mary Field Belenky et al., *Women's Ways of Knowing* (New York: Basic Books, 1997).

APPENDIX B

Members of the High School Theology Program Seminar (2011-2013)

Seminar Members

Reggie Blount serves on the faculty of Garrett-Evangelical Theological Seminary as assistant professor of formation, youth and culture. He teaches in the area of youth ministry, Christian education and congregational development. He is also pastor of Arnett Chapel A.M.E. Church in Chicago. He's spoken nationally and internationally at numerous conferences and workshops helping faith communities envision new and creative ways to minister to, with, and on behalf of young people. He is a contributor in "Making God Real for a Next Generation: Ministry with Millennials Born from 1982 to 1999" (Discipleship Resources, 2003).

Elizabeth W. Corrie is assistant professor in the practice of youth education and peacebuilding, and director of the Youth Theological Initiative at Candler School of Theology, Emory University in Atlanta. Her research interests include practical theology and conflict transformation. She serves on the advisory board of the Lilly Youth Theology Network, and speaks regularly in churches and schools on topics related to youth, contemporary culture, and the role people of faith can play in building peace.

Kenda Creasy Dean served as the HSTP seminar's co-director with Chris Coble. The Mary D. Synnott Professor of Youth, Church and Culture at Princeton Theological Seminary in Princeton, New Jersey, and coordinating pastor of Kingston United Methodist Church, she has written widely on youth and the church, including *Almost Christian: What the Faith of Our Teenagers Is*

Telling the American Church and *The Godbearing Life: The Art of Soul Tending for Youth Ministry* (with Ron Foster).

Drew Dyson served as a practical theology consultant for the HSTP seminar. A district superintendent in the Greater New Jersey Annual Conference, Drew previously served as a local church pastor, youth ministry executive for the UMC, and as the James C. Logan Chair in Evangelism at Wesley Theological Seminary. His research and teaching interests include the intersection of Wesleyan missional theology and emerging adulthood, evangelism, and practical theology.

Fred Edie is associate professor for the practice of Christian education at Duke Divinity School in Durham, North Carolina. He is also faculty advisor for Duke's Youth Academy for Christian Formation. His most recent book is titled *Book, Bath, Table and Time: Christian Worship as Source and Resource for Youth Ministry.* Edie is married to Alison and is the parent to two semi-adult children and one semi-adult standard poodle. He looks for excuses to be outside including running, cycling, hiking, and sailing.

Kristie Finley served as project manager for the HSTP seminar, and served as a research fellow in summer 2012. A graduate of Princeton Theological Seminary, she currently manages The Confirmation Project, a research initiative studying confirmation practices across denominations. Kristie's experience as a youth minister led to her current passion of resourcing parents to be the faith leaders in their families.

Christy Lang Hearlson served as associate editor for the HSTP seminar and as a research fellow. She is an ordained minister in the Presbyterian Church (USA) and is a PhD candidate at Princeton Theological Seminary in Princeton, New Jersey, as well as a visiting scholar at Andover Newton Theological School outside of Boston. She has served churches on both the west and east coasts (most recently at The Brick Presbyterian Church of New York City, where she served as associate pastor for Christian education and discipleship from 2005-2010). Her doctoral research focuses on American biblical and religious literacy and adolescents. She lives with her family in Newton, Massachusetts.

Ashley Coates Higgins was the High School Theology Program seminar's project assistant, and a research fellow in 2012. A graduate of Princeton Theological Seminary, she currently serves as director of young adult and high school ministries at First Presbyterian Church in Nashville, Tennessee.

David Horn is the director of the Ockenga Institute of Gordon-Conwell Theological Seminary in South Hamilton, Massachusetts, where he oversees multiple centers and programs that reflect the seminary's commitment to offering theological education to constituencies beyond the traditional student body. He developed and oversees the Compass Youth Initiative.

Andrew Brubacher Kaethler has directed the !Explore program and has been assistant professor of faith formation and culture at Anabaptist Mennonite Biblical Seminary in Elkhart, Indiana since 2003. Andy has been actively involved with faith formation for more than twenty years in camp, congregational, denominational, and school settings, and co-edited *Youth Ministry at a Crossroads* (with Bob Yoder).

Jeffrey Kaster has served as the director of the Youth in Theology and Ministry program at St. John's University School of Theology Seminary in Collegeville, Minnesota since 2000. He teaches courses in practical theology, Christian education, and youth ministry at St. John's University and the College of Saint Benedict. He also serves as the coordinator of the Lilly Youth Theology Network. Jeff's research and publications focus on program evaluation and assessment of adolescent Christian discipleship formation.

Jeff Keuss is professor of Christian ministry, theology and culture within the School of Theology at Seattle Pacific University in Seattle, Washington and director of the University Scholars program. He served as a consulting practical theologian for the High School Theology Program Seminar. An ordained minister in the Presbyterian Church (USA) who has served in churches both in the USA and Scotland, Jeff has published numerous books, articles, chapters, and reviews on the interdisciplinary engagement of theology, ministry, and culture and is the general editor for the journal *Literature and Theology* (Oxford University Press). His most recent book is *Blur: A New Paradigm for Understanding Youth Culture.*

Gordon S. Mikoski serves as associate professor of Christian education at Princeton Theological Seminary in Princeton, New Jersey, as well as editor of *Theology Today.* His books include *Opening the Field of Practical Theology: An Introduction* (with Kathleen Cahalan), *Straining at the Oars: Case Studies in Pastoral Leadership* (with H. Dana Fearon), *With Piety and Learning: The History of Practical Theology at Princeton Theological Seminary 1812-2012* (with Richard R. Osmer), and *Baptism and Christian Identity: Teaching in the Triune Name.* Prior to returning to academia, he served as associate pastor for education at the Grosse Pointe Memorial Church in the Detroit area.

Anabel Proffitt serves as faculty advisor to the Leadership Now program for High School Youth at Lancaster Theological Seminary in Lancaster, Pennsylvania where she is associate professor of educational ministries. Her areas of writing and research focus on the sense of wonder in educational ministry and youth ministry.

Judy Steers is the program director of Ask & Imagine, the High School Theology Program at Huron University College in London, Ontario, Canada, where she also teaches faith formation for children and youth. She is the coordinator for Youth Initiatives for the Anglican Church of Canada and is a trainer with Godly Play Canada. Judy spent several years with L'Arche Daybreak and thus community is at the foundation of her teaching, writing, consulting, and workshop leading. She uses rubber chickens, drums, good food, stones, and inspiring stories to teach about community, theology, and keeping it real. Judy is a contributing writer to *Befriending Life: Encounters with Henri Nouwen* (edited by Beth Porter) and most recently is the project coordinator for a modular learning program: *Trailblazing: On-line Theological Formation for Youth Ministry.*

Anne Streaty Wimberly is the executive director of the Youth Hope-Builders Academy (YHBA) at Interdenominational Theological Center (ITC) in Atlanta. She is professor emerita of Christian education at ITC, and has numerous publications on the church's educational ministry and on youth ministry including *Soul Stories: African American Christian Education; Keep It Real: Working with Today's Black Youth* (editor); and *Youth Ministry in the Black Church: Centered in Hope* (with Sandra L. Barnes and Karma D. Johnson).

Research Fellows

Stephen Cady serves as a minister at Asbury First United Methodist Church in Rochester, New York, and as an adjunct faculty member at Colgate Rochester Crozer Divinity School, where he teaches courses in practical theology and Christian education and formation. His doctoral research at Princeton Theological Seminary was in the area of youth and worship.

Katherine M. Douglass is an ordained minister in the PCUSA and is the co-director of The Confirmation Project, a multi-institutional, multi-denominational initiative researching the practice of confirmation in the United States. She lives in Seattle and is doing post-doctoral research at Princeton Theological Seminary.

Kristie Finley (see above)

Christy Lang Hearlson (see above)

Ashley Coates Higgins (see above)

Marcus A. Hong is currently writing a doctoral dissertation at Princeton Theological Seminary about worship, music, the Psalms, and spiritual formation. A long-time youth minister and musician, composer, and worship leader, he has published musical arrangements of several psalms in the recently released Psalter *Psalms for All Seasons* and has been working on a forthcoming collaborative worship resource for college and university campus ministries called *UWorship* (see www.ukirk.org).

Wendy Mohler-Seib is a graduate of Princeton Theological Seminary and an ordained elder in the United Methodist Church. She serves as the senior associate pastor at Chapel Hill United Methodist Church in Wichita, Kansas.

McLane Stone was a research fellow for the High School Theology Program seminar. A graduate of Princeton Theological Seminary, he currently serves as director of youth ministries at the National Presbyterian Church in Washington, DC.

Nathan T. Stucky currently lives in Princeton, New Jersey, where he is finishing his dissertation on youth and Sabbath at Princeton Theological Seminary. A lifelong Mennonite, veteran youth worker, and farmer, Nathan also offers leadership within the Princeton Theological Seminary conversation on the integration of theological education, the arts, and agrarianism.

APPENDIX C

Theological Programs for High School Youth, Lilly Endowment Inc. (active in 2014)

Note: Lilly has funded a total of forty-seven seminary-based programs since their inception[1]

Seminary-based High School Theology Programs			
	Theological School	*Program*	*Program Director*
1.	Anabaptist Mennonite Biblical Seminary	!Explore	Andrew Brubacher Kaethler
2.	Calvin Theological Seminary	Facing Your Future	Jessica Driesenga
3.	Candler School of Theology (Emory University)	Youth Theology Initiative	Elizabeth Corrie
4.	Concordia Theological Seminary (Ft. Wayne)	Christ Academy	Andrew Yeager
5.	Concordia Seminary (St. Louis)	Vocatio	Michael Redeker
6.	Duke Divinity School	Duke Youth Academy	Jeff Conklin-Miller
7.	Emmanuel Christian Seminary	Youth in Ministry	Phyllis Fox
8.	Gordon-Conwell Theological Seminary	Compass Program	David Horn
9.	Huron University College	Ask & Imagine	Judy Steers
10.	Hellenic College/Holy Cross Greek Orthodox School of Theology	CrossRoad	Ann Bezzerides
11.	Interdenominational Theological Center	Youth Hope-Builders Academy	Anne Streaty Wimberly
12.	Lancaster Theological Seminary	Leadership Now	Megan Malick
13.	Lincoln Christian College and Seminary	Worldview Eyes	Richard Knopp
14.	Lutheran School of Theology at Chicago	Youth in Mission	Kristin Johnson
15.	Lutheran Theological Seminary at Gettysburg and Philadelphia	Theological Education with Youth	Chelle Huth

1. Originally Philadelphia and Gettysburg Lutheran Seminaries sponsored two distinct programs.

16.	Multnomah University	Spring Thaw	Rob Hildebrand
17.	Perkins School of Theology (Southern Methodist University)	Faith Calls	Tonya Burton
18.	Pittsburgh Theological Seminary	Miller Summer Youth Institute	Erin Davenport
19.	Reformed Presbyterian Theological Seminary	Theological Foundations for Youth	David Whitlaw
20.	St. John's Seminary School of Theology	Youth in Theology and Ministry	Jeffrey Kaster
21.	St. Mary's Seminary and University	Youth Theological Studies	Pat LeNoir
22.	St. Meinrad Seminary and School of Theology	One Bread, One Cup	Godfrey Mullen/ Collette Kinnett
23.	Trinity Lutheran Theological Seminary	Summer Seminary Sampler	Ruth C. Fortis Laura Book
24.	Wartburg Theological Seminary	Wartburg Youth Leadership School	Nathan Frambach
College-based High School Theology Programs			
	College/University	*Program*	*Program Director*
1.	Augsburg College	Youth Theology Institute	Jeremy Myers
2.	Furman University	Summer Connections	Eric Cain
3.	Luther College	WIYLDE (Wholly Iowa Youth Leadership Discipling Event)	Mike Blair
4.	Maryville College	Horizons	Anne McKee
5.	University of Notre Dame	Notre Dame Vision	Leonard DeLorenzo
Other High School Theology (and Related) Programs			
	Sponsor	*Program*	*Program Director*
1.	Bethany Theological Seminary	Youth: Explore Your Call	Russell Haitch/ Rebekah Houff
2.	Tabor College[a]	Ministry Quest	Wendell Loewen/ Jules Glanzer
3.	Texas Annual Conference	Texas Youth Academy	Dan Conway

a. Initially funded through Lilly Endowment initiative at Mennonite Brethren Biblical Seminary in Fresno, CA and then moved to Tabor College.

Subject Index